Pascal
for
Science and Engineering

CW00746403

Pascal
for
Science and Engineering

James J McGregor and Alan H Watt
Department of Computer Science
University of Sheffield

PITMAN PUBLISHING
128 Long Acre, London WC2E 9AN

© James J. McGregor and Alan H. Watt 1983

First published in Great Britain 1983
Reprinted 1985, 1987

Printed and bound in Great Britain at
The Bath Press, Avon

Preface

A computer program is a set of instructions that tell a computer how to carry out a calculation or perform some other operation. These instructions have to be expressed in one of the many computer programming languages available.

No scientist or engineer can consider his training complete until he has obtained some familiarity with the use of computers and their application in his subject area. By far the best way of doing this is to learn a computer programming language and to obtain some practice in using it. In the past, the two programming languages FORTRAN and BASIC have been the most widely used languages in science and engineering. However, the inadequacies of these languages have long been recognized by computer scientists and the programming language Pascal is now firmly established as one of the programming languages most widely used in degree courses in Computer Science and Mathematics. Use of Pascal is now spreading to Science and Engineering courses where its use has many advantages.

The main advantage of Pascal is its readability. Well written programs are easy to understand and easy to modify. The wide variety of language constructions available make it easy to teach good programming style. The language has been designed with a view to stopping the user from making mistakes that pass unnoticed. Even with these advantages of readability and error protection, programs written in Pascal are efficient.

The primary purpose of this book is to teach you how to write computer programs in Pascal. It is intended to be a genuine introductory text for beginners. The main problem encountered by beginners, is in expressing what they want the computer to do in terms of the instructions available in the programming language being used. For this reason, we aim at teaching how to write programs in Pascal without presenting more information than is absolutely necessary about the internal operation of the computer. Unnecessary use of computing jargon is also avoided.

The complete language is covered with the exception of some string handling facilities, and advanced use of sets and pointers. We have concentrated on the aspects of the language that are most likely to find application in science and engineering.

Throughout the book, general ideas are introduced by means of examples. At first, the examples are extremely simple programs that may not seem convincingly useful. We must ask the reader to be very patient: a clear understanding of the elementary techniques introduced in these examples is essential before programs of real practical use can be written. We believe that programming is a skill learned mainly by reading and writing programs, and we urge the reader to attempt most of the exercises set in each chapter.

This book is written in two parts. The first part provides instruction in Pascal. The second part examines the computer applications that are of interest to the scientist or engineer and these application areas are used to further illustrate the use of Pascal.

Finally thanks are due to Pete Harley, Simon Kingsley and Chris Brown.

Contents

Introduction

The following very simple Pascal program will be used to illustrate a number of fundamental points. We shall explain shortly what this program tells the computer to do.

```
PROGRAM rectangle(output);

BEGIN
    writeln('Area is ', 79*43, ' square metres.');
    writeln('Perimeter is ', 2*(79+43), ' metres.')
END.
```

Notice that some of the words in the program are printed entirely in capital letters. Words like these have a special significance in Pascal programs. Printing them in capitals makes them stand out and makes a printed program easier to read. In handwritten programs, these special words are usually underlined and in some books you will find that heavy type is used to distinguish them from the rest of the program.

Unless it has special equipment, a computer cannot read characters that are simply typed on paper. A common way of getting a program into a computer is to type it at a typewriter keyboard that is somehow connected to the computer. An old-fashioned method is to type it on special apparatus that punches a different pattern of holes corresponding to each different character. These holes are punched in cards in a manner that allows the computer to read a program easily. When you find out how to get programs into your particular computer you may find that only capital letters are available, and programs may have to be typed entirely in capital letters.

Once a program has been typed into the computer, the computer can check it and attempt to obey it. The checking is usually carried out by a Pascal **compiler**. (A compiler is a program that reads and checks your program!) Your program may be compiled and obeyed automatically on the system you are using, or you may have to type commands at the keyboard telling the computer what to do at each step. Instead of obeying the program, we sometimes talk of **executing** or **running** the program.

The first line of our introductory program:

```
PROGRAM rectangle(output);
```

contains the name - "rectangle" - that we have invented for this particular program. The word "output" in brackets tells the computer to be ready to print something when the program is obeyed. The part of the program that tells the computer what to do comes between BEGIN and END. Here we always have a list of statements (only two in this case) separated by semicolons. In Pascal, a so-called statement is in fact an instruction which tells the computer to do something. The first statement obeyed in this program is

        writeln('Area is ', 79*43, ' square metres.');

This tells the computer to print the information specified between the brackets. In this case we have three items, separated from each other by commas, to be printed:

'Area is '   The characters between the
                                quotation marks are printed
                                exactly as they stand.

79*43   The value of the expression
                                is calculated and printed.
                                * is used as a multiplication
                                sign to avoid confusion with
                                the letter x.

' square metres.'   The characters between the
                                quotation marks are printed
                                exactly as they stand.

Thus when the computer obeys this statement it will print:

    Area is 3397 square metres.

Depending on the computer system you are using, the output may appear on a video screen attached to your keyboard, or it may be printed on a device known as a line-printer. The exact layout used for printing the output value, 3397, will vary from one Pascal system to another. Your system may print extra spaces before the number.

    The appearance of the characters "ln" at the end of the word "writeln" indicates that a new line is to be started **after** the output has been printed. This is explained in more detail later.

    When the computer has obeyed one statement it goes on to the next. Thus, when the computer obeys our introductory program, it will print the area and perimeter of a 79m.x43m. rectangle:

    Area is 3397 square metres.
    Perimeter is 244 metres.

    In order to make it easy for a program to be processed by a machine, the grammatical rules in Pascal are very strict. You will find, for example, that you must put commas and semicolons in just

2

the right places. If you do not, the computer will report that there is a **syntax error** in your program and will not be able to obey it. The rules for the layout of a program are less strict. We can insert as many spaces as we like between the words, symbols and numbers in the program, providing that we insert at least one space between words. We are also free to choose how we set the program out on separate lines, as long as we do not start a new line in the middle of a word or number. We shall make use of this freedom of layout to make our programs as readable as possible. This is very important, not only because we may wish someone else to read and understand our programs, but also because we may wish to re-read them ourselves at some later date when we want to extend or modify them.

Even if a program is grammatically or syntactically correct, and the computer attempts to obey it, something may go wrong while the program is being obeyed. For example, the result of a calculation may be a number that is too big for your computer to handle. If such an **execution error** or **run-time error** occurs, the computer will stop obeying your program and print a message explaining what has happened.

You should remember that, even if the computer successfully executes a program, this does not necessarily mean that correct answers have been produced. If, in our introductory program, we mistyped the expression for the perimeter as "2*(79-43)", telling the computer to subtract the length of our rectangle from its width, the computer would still successfully obey the program. It would print

    Area is 3397 square metres.
    Perimeter is 72 metres.

which is of course wrong. Detection of such **logical errors** is entirely the responsibility of the programmer.

Programs, once written, can be obeyed over and over again and this is one of the main advantages of a computer. We could, for instance, write a weekly payroll program which is executed 52 times a year. Our introductory example is not very useful however, because if it were obeyed again it would produce exactly the same output.

Programs are usually written in more general terms so that the calculations described in a program can be performed on different numbers or **data** on different occasions. For example, to use a structural analysis program to analyze a bridge design, the program would have to be given the dimensions and loadings for the particular bridge under consideration.

Our "rectangle" program calculates the area and perimeter for a rectangle with particular dimensions. A program that could perform the same calculations, but for different rectangles on different occasions, would be more generally useful. Making a program general in this sense is one of the main topics in Chapter 1.

1 Doing calculations

In this chapter, we cover the essential groundwork that is needed to enable you to write programs to do straightforward numerical calculations.

1.1 Getting information into a program

In our introductory program, the statement

```
writeln('Area is ', 79*43, ' square metres.');
```

caused the computer to print the area of a particular rectangle. It is much more usual when programming to give names to the values involved in a calculation. This enables us to describe a calculation in more general terms, for example:

```
writeln('Area is ', length*width, ' square metres.');
```

In describing the calculation that the computer is to carry out, we have used names to refer to the length and width of the rectangle. "Length" and "width" are going to be the names of two **variables.** It is useful to think of a variable as a named box or **memory location** in which a program can store a value:

length | 79 | width | 43 |

We say that "length" is the name of a box containing 79 and "width" is the name of a box containing 43. We shall soon see how these values get there. When the computer evaluates the expression "length*width" it multiplies the **contents** of "length" by the **contents** of "width". Of course the boxes "length" and "width" need not necessarily contain the numbers 79 and 43. They could contain any numbers that are not too big for the size of the box (more about that later).

For example:

length | 50 | width | 35 |

This is why we use the term **variable.** Now we can rewrite our program "rectangle" in such a way that each time it is executed or obeyed different numbers may be put in the boxes "length" and "width".

4

Program <u>1.1</u>

This program works out the area and perimeter of a rectangle of **any** length and width.

```
PROGRAM rectangle2(input, output);

VAR length, width : integer;

BEGIN
   read(length, width);
   writeln('Area is ', length*width, ' square metres.');
   writeln('Perimeter is ', 2*(length+width), ' metres.')
END.
```

The second line of the program simply tells the computer to set aside space for two variables, "length" and "width". More information about this appears in Section 1.3.

The statement:

```
read(length, width);
```

is the means whereby particular values are put in memory locations and associated with the names "length" and "width" each time the program is executed. When the computer obeys this statement it pauses and waits until two numbers are supplied. We shall assume, for the time being, that such numbers are supplied directly from a keyboard while the computer is obeying the program:

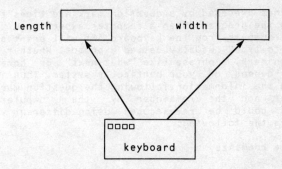

The program then continues execution and evaluates the expressions

```
length*width
```

and

```
2*(length + width)
```

using the values for "length" and "width" that are contained in the boxes with these names. These are the values that have just been supplied from the keyboard. The appearance of the word

5

"input" in the first line of the above program tells the computer
to be prepared to receive input during the execution of the
program. The values supplied as input are sometimes called the
data for the program. When numbers are typed as input for a Pascal
program, they are separated by spaces (as many as we like) and can
be spread over as many lines as we like.

1.2 Executing a program

After you have typed your program it is stored in a way peculiar
to your own computer. You have given your program a name in the
first line - let us assume that your system uses this name to
distinguish it from other programs that you may have written and
stored. To make the computer obey or execute your program you have
to type something like:

    execute rectangle2

where "execute" is the command that causes the computer to execute
your program. This is not a Pascal statement but a command that
tells the computer what to do with a Pascal program. The commands
for your computer are probably different. The result of executing
the program could be a display like:

    ? execute rectangle2

    ? 79 43

    Area is 3397 square metres.

    Perimeter is 244 metres.

The two lines preceded by a question mark are lines typed by the
person using the program. When a computer expects you to type a
command or numbers from the keyboard, it will print some sort of
"invitation to type", usually called a prompt. Whether this prompt
is a question mark, a phrase like "what next" or something else
will again depend on your particular system. Thus in the above
illustration the information following the question marks is typed
by the user and the remainder by the computer. Program
"rectangle2" could be re-executed using different values. This
might produce the following:

    ? execute roomsize

    ? 50 35

    Area is 1750 square metres.

    Perimeter is 170 metres.

Now when a program is to be controlled from a keyboard as above,
it is good programming practice to precede a read statement with a
write statement that prints a message telling or reminding the
user what to type next. If we execute a particular program months
after it has been written, or if another person (not the
programmer) executes the program, then it is vital that the
program informs the user what information is to be typed and in

6

what order.

Program 1.2

This is identical to Program 1.1 except that the program will type
a request for input when it is required.

```
PROGRAM rectangle3(input, output);

VAR length, width : integer;

BEGIN
    writeln('Type in length and width of rectangle.');
    read(length, width);
    writeln('Area is ', length*width, ' square metres.');
    writeln('Perimeter is ', 2*(length+width), ' metres.')
END.
```

This will produce a display like the following:

    ? execute roomsize2

    Type in length and width of rectangle.

    ? 74 32

    Area is 2368 square metres.

    Perimeter is 212 metres.

The appearance of the second line in the display serves to remind
you or another user, what the program does and the information it
requires. We will not always do this in examples in this book
because it takes up space and adds nothing to the instructive
value of the program; but you should always use the technique in
practice.

One further point that you should bear in mind when operating a
computer from a keyboard is that, when you are requested to type
something, the computer may be in one of several states. For
example, it may be waiting for you to type the next line of a
Pascal program; it may be waiting for a command telling it to
execute a program or to modify it in some way; it may be waiting
for data to be typed into a program that is currently being
executed. The computer must always be provided with the kind of
information it expects.

1.3 Variables and declarations

In programs 1.1 and 1.2 the line:

        VAR length, width : integer;

gives the computer three pieces of information: you require two
boxes or variables; the names of these boxes are to be "length"

and "width"; you are going to put quantities in these boxes which are integer numbers or whole numbers. This is called a variable declaration and in its simplest form comprises two parts:

(1) A list of names chosen by the programmer, and separated by commas. A name consists of a sequence of letters and numeric digits starting with a letter; except that reserved words like "begin", "end", "var" etc. must not be used. The words are of course reserved just so that there is no confusion between these words and variable names. Even if we usually type these words in capital letters when they are used correctly in a program, we still can not use the same words in lower case letters as variable names. A complete list of reserved words is given in Appendix 1. At this stage, you do not need to know what all the reserved words mean but you must not attempt to use them as variable names.

You should choose mnemonically meaningful names. For example in the above context choose the names "length" and "width" rather than "l" and "w", or worse still "p" and "q". This makes it much easier for your program to be read by other people or by yourself in the future if you wish to develop it further. Names can be of any length but you may find your particular computer system specifies a maximum length. Spaces must not be typed in the middle of a word; but this is not too inconvenient, it means you must use, for example, "nooftimes" rather than "no of times". Capital letters can be used to distinguish the separate words in such a composite name. For example, we could write the above name as "NoOfTimes".

(2) The type of quantity the box is going to contain. For the moment we are going to use only two types : "integer" and "real". A real number is a number with a fractional part.

Real numbers and integers are represented in different ways inside the computer and there are good reasons for distinguishing between them in a program. You need not worry about the reasons for the distinction. You need only remember that the computer will not allow you to put a real number into an integer variable. (It will, however, allow you to put an integer value into a real variable.) Integer variables are generally used in a program for counting things and real variables are used for holding the results of arithmetic calculations.

Now consider the following examples:

     VAR noofyears, noofmonths : integer;

means that the program is going to use two variables called "noofyears" and "noofmonths" which are going to contain integers, for example:

noofyears | 53 | noofmonths | 4 |

8

The following declaration:

```
VAR temperature : real;
```

means that the program is going to use one variable called "temperature" which is going to contain a real number, for example:

temperature | 93.75

The following declaration:

```
VAR noofyears, noofmonths : integer;
    temperature : real;
```

means the program is going to use three variables two of which are going to contain integers and one a real number. Note that the word VAR appears only once in such a declaration.

Now there is a limit to the maximum size of integer that can be put in an integer variable and, similarly, a limit to the maximum size of real number that can be put in a real variable. These limits are dependent on your particular computer system and you will find them in the documentation for your system.

Incidentally, for reasons we cannot go into at this stage, the words "real" and "integer" are not reserved words, but it would be inadvisable to try to use them as variable names.

Program 1.3

The total rainfall in millimetres and the total hours of sunshine have been measured over a period of days. This program calculates the average daily rainfall and the average daily sunshine over the period.

```
PROGRAM weather(input, output);

VAR totalrain, totalsun : real;
    days : integer;

BEGIN
   writeln('Input total rainfall, total sunshine.');
   read(totalrain, totalsun);
   writeln('Input number of days.');  read(days);
   writeln('Average daily rainfall: ', totalrain/days);
   writeln('Average daily sunshine: ', totalsun/days)
END.
```

Note that the symbol "/" means "divided by".

1.4 Write

Up to now we have been using "writeln" in various contexts where it is reasonably obvious what the effect will be. Each item in the list between the brackets of a write statement tells the computer to output something. An item enclosed in single quotation marks is copied character by character exactly as it appears in the program. If an item is not enclosed in quotation marks, then the computer prints a value, possibly after doing a calculation to obtain the value. An item in a write list might just be a single variable name in which case the value of the variable is printed.

The following table shows what output is produced by various write statements if the variables "x" and "y" contain the values shown.

x   7   y   2

statement	computer prints
writeln(x)	7
writeln(y)	2
writeln('x contains ',x)	x contains 7
writeln('y contains ',y)	y contains 2
writeln('sum of x & y is ',x+y)	sum of x & y is 9
writeln('sum of ',x,'& ',y,'is ',x+y)	sum of 7 & 2 is 9
writeln('x + y = ',x + y)	x + y = 9
writeln(x,' + ',y,' = ',x+y)	7 + 2 = 9

You should examine carefully the differences in the effects of the last four statements.

In the absence of formatting information (as discussed in Appendix 4) any values in a write statement will be printed in some standard way that has been defined by the people who designed your particular Pascal system. We shall assume throughout this book that, when formatting information is not used, integer numbers and real numbers are printed without any additional spaces before or after, and that reals are printed with two digits after the decimal point. Thus we will assume that

        writeln(2*3, ' and ', 65.734*2)

produces

6 and 131.47

This may not match the conventions used in your system. In the absence of formatting information, most systems print reals in what is called floating-point form, for example:

    1.31468E02

This is the computer's way of saying

$$1.31468 \times 10^2$$

This notation is useful mainly for representing very large or very small numbers. It is rather a clumsy notation for beginners and you can avoid it, if necessary, by providing formatting information as described Appendix 4. For the time being, all that you need to do is to add the characters ":6:2" to any item in a write list that represents a real number. This will ensure that your real numbers are printed with two digits after the decimal point and without too many extra spaces. For example:

```
writeln('Average daily sunshine: ',
          totalsun/days :6:2, ' hours')
```

If your system prints too many spaces before an integer, then for the time being we suggest that you insert ":3" after any integer value in a write list. For example:

```
writeln(2*3 :3, ' and ', 65.734*2 :6:2)
```

A detailed study of Appendix 4 can safely be left until later.

Recall that the statement "writeln" causes the computer to start a new line in the output **after** its list of items has been printed. The statement "write" behaves in exactly the same way as "writeln" except that the computer does not start a new line in the output.

For example:

statements	computer prints
write('1st line '); write('still on 1st line')	1st line still on 1st line

---

statements	computer prints
writeln('1st line'); write ('2nd line')	1st line 2nd line

"Writeln" can be used on its own (i.e. with no brackets) and this causes the computer to start a new line for subsequent output. This does not necessarily imply that a blank line is printed. For example:

statements	computer prints
write('1st line'); writeln; writeln('2nd line')	1st line 2nd line

---

statements	computer prints
writeln('1st line'); writeln; writeln('3rd line')	1st line 3rd line

There is a similar distinction between "read" and "readln". "Readln" tells the computer to find the start of a new line in the input **after** values have been read into the variables in the read list. "Readln" is occasionally used to tell the computer to ignore any other information on a line of input that appears after a value that has been read. It is more commonly used to ensure that a user at a terminal types the end-of-line key to terminate an input number. For example, the layout of the display produced by executing Program 1.3 could be improved by using the following combination of statements:

```
write('Total rainfall?');   readln(totalrain);
write('Total sunshine?');   readln(totalsun);
write('Period in days?');   readln(days);
```

This would produce a display such as:

```
Total rainfall?73.5
Total sunshine?51.4
Period in days?7
```

where the numbers are typed by the user. After each number, the end-of-line key has to be pressed by the user before the computer will obey the next statement. (On most computer terminals, the key marked 'RETURN' is used as the end-of-line key, although some systems use other keys.)

Exercises

(1) A student has taken four examination papers. Write a program which reads his four marks (integers) and prints his average mark.

(2) Write a program that converts a temperature in Fahrenheit into the equivalent temperature in Centigrade.

(3) Write a program that converts a given length in yards, feet and inches into inches.

(4) Write a program that expresses a length in yards, feet and inches as a real number of metres (to two decimal places).

(5) Write a program which reads two integers and reports their sum and product in the form of two equations.
For example, if the input is:

```
4  7
```

the output should be

```
4 + 7 = 11
4 * 7 = 28
```

(6) Write a program that accepts as input the radius of a circle and prints the diameter, circumference and area of the circle.

1.5 Assignment statements

To put a value or number into a variable we can write:

    read(x)

If the value 3 is supplied as input when the program is obeyed, this value is placed in the variable named "x":

x   `| 3 |`

The statement

    x := 3

also places 3 in the variable "x". This is known as an assignment statement because it assigns a value to the variable. The symbol ":=" should be read as "becomes equal to" and is not to be interpreted as an ordinary equals sign which is used in a totally different context as we shall see later. The left-hand side of an assignment statement must be the name of a variable to which the right-hand side is to be assigned. In the simplest cases, the right-hand side can be a constant as in the above example or another variable name:

    x := y

In this example the contents of "y" are put into "x" (the previous contents of "x" being destroyed or overwritten).

Thus, if before the statement is obeyed we have:

x   `| 2 |`   y   `| 3 |`

then after the statement is obeyed we have:

x   `| 3 |`   y   `| 3 |`

Note that the value in "y" is left unchanged. We do not **take out** the value in "y", but **copy** it into "x".

The right-hand side of an assignment statement can in fact be any arithmetic expression:

    x := y + z

If before the above statement is obeyed we have:

x   `| 3 |`   y   `| 4 |`   z   `| 5 |`

then immediately after the statement is obeyed we have:

x [9]   y [4]   z [5]

Note that a statement such as:

    x := x + y

which, when compared with an algebraic equation, may seem somewhat peculiar, is perfectly valid and means: the value of "x" becomes equal to what it was before plus the value of "y". The right-hand side of an assignment statement is always evaluated first regardless of what variable appears on the left.

Thus if we have:

x [3]   y [4]

then immediately after the above statement is obeyed we have:

x [7]   y [4]

Now consider part of a program which finds the sum and average of three numbers:

    read(x, y, z);
    writeln('Sum is ', x + y + z,
            '. Average is ', (x + y + z)/3)

This would be better written as:

    read(x, y, z);
    sum := x + y + z;
    writeln('Sum is ', sum, '. Average is ', sum/3)

In the second version the expression "x + y + z" is evaluated only once instead of twice and the second version is easier to read. As the programs you write get more complicated you should tend to organize your programs in this way. Note that in this case we could also have written:

    x := x + y + z

or

    y := x + y + z

and avoided using the extra variable "sum". However, this would detract from the readability of the program.

Program 1.4

Given the dimensions and the weight of a rectangular block of material, this program prints the volume of the block and the density of the material. A variable is used to store the volume of the block which would otherwise have to be recalculated.

```
PROGRAM density(input, output);

VAR length, width, height, weight, volume : real;

BEGIN
    write('length(cms):'); readln(length);
    write('width(cms):');  readln(width);
    write('height(cms):'); readln(height);
    write('weight(gms):'); readln(weight);
    volume := length*width*height;
    writeln('Volume is ',  volume :6:2, 'ccs.');
    writeln('Density is ', weight/volume :6:2, 'gms/cc.')
END.
```

1.6 Arithmetic expressions - order of evaluation

In arithmetic expressions above we have sometimes used round brackets. For example:

```
average := (x + y + z)/3
```

or

```
perimeter := 2*(length + width)
```

In each case we have used the brackets to clarify our intentions. We want the computer to calculate:

$$\frac{x + y + z}{3}$$

so we write:

```
(x + y + z)/3
```

This is simply a consequence of the fact that we are using a keyboard and arithmetic expressions must be typed as a sequence of characters one after another.

If we missed out the brackets:

    average := x + y + z/3

the computer would calculate:

$$x + y + \frac{z}{3}$$

which is not what we intended.

In the other example, if we removed the brackets:

    perimeter : = 2*length + width

the computer would calculate:

    (2*length) + width

You can see from this that the computer has rules for dealing with the evaluation of arithmetic expressions.

   Let us begin by listing the operators that have been informally introduced so far:

    *   multiplication
    /   division
    +   addition
    -    subtraction

The computer can perform only one of these operations at a time. To perform an operation it requires two operands, which are the quantities on either side of the operator. In the absence of brackets, multiplication and division are carried out before addition and subtraction.

Consider the expression:

    a/b + c/d*e

The computer evaluates this as follows:

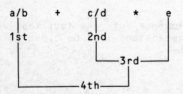

    1st result evaluated   a/b
    2nd result evaluated   c/d
    3rd result evaluated   2nd result * e
    4th result evaluated   1st result + 3rd result

Thus the computer evaluates:

$$\frac{a}{b} + \frac{c}{d} \star e$$

If instead we wanted the computer to evaluate

$$\frac{a}{b} + \frac{c}{d \star e}$$

then we would use brackets as follows:

a/b + c/(d*e)

Anything inside brackets is evaluated first. For the operators introduced so far, we can summarize this order of **priority**, as it is called, as follows:

order of priority: 1st anything inside brackets
2nd multiplication and division
3rd addition and subtraction

Adjacent operators of the same priority are applied from left to right.

Program 1.5

This program finds the roots of the simultaneous equations

$$a_1 x + b_1 y = c_1$$
$$a_2 x + b_2 y = c_2$$

Given the values of the coefficients, the program outputs the values of the roots.

```
PROGRAM simultaneous(input, output);

VAR a1,b1,c1, a2,b2,c2, x, y : real;

BEGIN
   write('Equation 1 coefficients:');  readln(a1, b1, c1);
   write('Equation 2 coefficients:');  readln(a2, b2, c2);
   x := (b1*c2 - b2*c1)/(a2*b1 - a1*b2);
   y := (a1*c2 - a2*c1)/(a1*b2 - a2*b1);
   writeln('x = ', x:6:2, ',  y = ', y:6:2)
END.
```

1.7 Special integer operators

There are two special arithmetic operators that operate only on integers:

DIV   has the same effect as normal division except that any fractional part is removed, thus producing an integer result.

MOD   supplies the remainder after dividing two integers

DIV and MOD have the same priority as "*" and "/".

Consider the following examples:

expression	value
16/5	3.2
16 DIV 5	3
16 MOD 5	1
19/5	3.8
19 DIV 5	3
19 MOD 5	4
8 DIV 3 * 3	6
7 + 5 DIV 3	8
13 - 5 MOD 3	11

The behaviour of these operators on negative operands varies from one Pascal system to another and should not be relied upon.

Program 1.6

This is a supermarket "checkout" program that prints the number and denomination of coins required to make up a given amount of change (a whole number of pennies). The program indicates the number of 50p, 20p, 10p, 5p, 2p, and 1p coins to be paid out.

```
        PROGRAM coinage(input,output);

        VAR  change, noof50s, noof20s, noof10s,
                 noof5s,  noof2s,  noof1s   : integer;

        BEGIN
           write('Change?');  readln(change);

           noof50s := change DIV 50;   change := change MOD 50;
           noof20s := change DIV 20;   change := change MOD 20;
           noof10s := change DIV 10;   change := change MOD 10;
           noof5s  := change DIV 5 ;   change := change MOD 5 ;
           noof2s  := change DIV 2 ;   change := change MOD 2 ;

           noof1s  := change;

           writeln('change due is:  no of 50s   ', noof50s);
           writeln('                no of 20s   ', noof20s);
           writeln('                no of 10s   ', noof10s);
           writeln('                no of  5s   ', noof5s);
           writeln('                no of  2s   ', noof2s);
           writeln('                no of  1s   ', noof1s)
        END.
```

We have now introduced six arithmetic operators and two of these
can be applied only to integer quantities. A complete list of
operators (some of which have not yet been introduced) is given in
Appendix 2.

1.8 More about integer and real variables

   At this point some further notes on the differences between
integer and real variables is appropriate. You have already seen
that we distinguish between variables which are going to contain
integer numbers and variables which are going to contain real
numbers. For example:

```
        VAR numberchildren, numberfamilies : integer;
            childrenperfamily : real;

        BEGIN
            .
            .
            childrenperfamily := numberchildren/numberfamilies;
            .
            :
```

Although "numberchildren" and "numberfamilies" will have integer
values, the result of applying the operator "/" is classified as a
real quantity - it may have a fractional part - and
"childrenperfamily" must therefore be declared as a real variable.
In general, you should ensure that integer variables are used for
values which can only be whole numbers and real variables are used
for values which **may** have a fractional part.

The classification of a variable as "integer" or "real" is called its **type**. In Pascal there are many types that we can use to classify variables. Up to now we have introduced only two, but others will be introduced later. The computer uses this type information to detect errors made by the programmer, and this is why it is so important to use types accurately. If a programmer says he wants to put to put oranges into a box which he specified earlier was to contain only apples, then the computer can inform the programmer that he has made a mistake. It is a way of building automatic protection into a program.

For example, if you write

```
VAR numberchildren, numberfamilies,
                childrenperfamily : integer;

BEGIN
        .
        .
        .
    childrenperfamily := numberchildren/numberfamilies;
        .
        .
        .
```

the computer will inform you that you have made a type error and the program will not be run. In this example you have asked the computer to assign a real quantity to an integer variable.

Finally you should remember that the computer stores integer numbers and real numbers in a different way. Although this is normally of little concern to the programmer, it does mean that the largest real number the computer can handle is much bigger than the largest integer number. You should look in your system documentation for information on the size of integers and real numbers that can be handled. The largest positive integer may only be 32767 on a small computer or more than 2000000000 on others. The largest real number that can be handled will usually have at least 40 digits, but only the first 7 to 15 digits will be accurate (7 on some small computers, 15 or more on large ones). This is because only the first few significant digits of a real number are represented internally in the memory.

1.9 Standard functions

A number of predefined mathematical operations or functions are available for use in expressions. The programs for evaluating these standard functions have already been written and are stored as part of your Pascal system.

For example

```
    x := 4.0;
    writeln( sqrt(x) )
```

prints the value 2.00;

and

```
    y := 5.66;
    writeln( trunc(y) )
```

prints the value 5.

"Sqrt" is the name of the standard function which performs the
operation "finding the square root of". "Trunc" is the name of the
standard function which performs the operation "truncate", i.e. it
removes the fractional part from a real number to give an integer.

When you refer to a function you use its name and enclose
within round brackets the value to which the function is to be
applied. This value, which is called a parameter, can be any
arithmetic expression of a type appropriate to the particular
function.

For example:

```
    x := sqrt(16);
         .
         .
    x := sqrt(y);
         .
         .
    x := sqrt(3*y/z);
         .
         .
    x := 15.6 + sqrt(3*y/z);
         .
         .
```

Because parameters can be arithmetic expressions, a function can
be used in the expression which is the parameter of another
function:

```
    writeln( trunc(sqrt(17.3)))
```

prints 4.

```
    writeln( sqrt(sqrt(16)))
```

prints 2.00.

```
    theta := 3.142/3;
    writeln(sqrt(sin(theta) + cos(theta)))
```

prints 1.17.

You must ensure that the parameter given to a function, whether
it is a constant, a variable, or an expression, has the required
type. If you are assigning the result of a function to a variable,
the type of the variable must correspond to the type of the
function result.

For example you cannot write:

```
VAR x : integer;

BEGIN
    x := sqrt(16);
      .
      .
      .
```

because the type of the result of "sqrt" is classified as real.

There is a complete list of standard functions in Appendix 3, together with information on the types of parameters required and the types of results produced.

Program 1.7

For a standard "inverted v" shaped roof, this program works out the area of roof covering required, given the length and width of the building and the angular pitch of the roof.

```
PROGRAM roof(input,output);

VAR pitch, length, width, areaofroof : real;

BEGIN

    writeln('type in pitch of roof(degrees),',
            ' length and width');
    read(pitch, length, width);

    pitch := pitch * 3.14159/180;
    areaofroof := width/cos(pitch) * length;

    writeln('area of roof covering required is ',
            areaofroof, ' sq.m.')
END.
```

You should note that while people usually work in degrees, the parameters of trigonometric functions in Pascal have to be given in radians, hence the conversion in the above example.

Program 1.8

Converts degrees Centigrade to degrees Fahrenheit.

```
      PROGRAM conversion(input,output);

      VAR cdegrees, fdegrees : real;

      BEGIN
         read(cdegrees);
         fdegrees := cdegrees * 9/5 + 32;
         writeln(cdegrees, 'c = ', fdegrees, 'f or approx ',
                           round(fdegrees), 'f')
      END.
```

This will produce, for example:

21.50c = 70.70f or approx 71f

The following program demonstrates how the functions "trunc" and "round" can be used to convert times expressed as a real number of hours into hours and minutes (to the nearest minute).

Program 1.9

Given a distance between two towns, a speed in miles per hour and a departure time from one town, the program prints the arrival time at the other town. Times are input as, for example, 0845 or 1357 and are output as, for example, 8-45 and 13-57. We assume that the journey takes place in one day.

```
      PROGRAM journey(input,output);

      VAR dist, mph, startime, hours, mins : integer;
          realhours : real;

      BEGIN
         read(dist, mph, startime);

         hours     := startime DIV 100;
         mins      := startime MOD 100;
         realhours:= hours + mins/60;

         { next statement calculates time of arrival }
         { as a real number of hours after midnight }

         realhours:= realhours + dist/mph;

         { time now converted back into hours and mins }

         hours     := trunc(realhours);
         mins      := round((realhours - hours)*60);
         write(' arrival time: ', hours, '-', mins)
      END.
```

One further feature has been introduced in the above program. We

have inserted comments which explain to the human reader what the
program is supposed to be doing. Any group of characters enclosed
between { and } is printed as part of the program but has no
effect on its behaviour when it is obeyed. Such comments should be
inserted in a program where they make the program easier for the
human reader to understand. This would be important if someone
else is likely to have to take over your program and modify it, or
if you yourself are likely to have to modify it at some future
date when the details of how it works have been forgotten. If your
keyboard does not provide {...} brackets, then you can enclose a
comment between (* and *).

The need for comments in Pascal is generally much less than in
the equivalent code written in BASIC or FORTRAN. The use of
explicit control structures and mnemonic names should make the
program readable and obviate the need for excessive comments,
except perhaps as a prelude to a program module.

1.10 Raising a number to a power

Note that for various reasons there is no "raising to the power
of" operator in Pascal. If we wanted to raise "x" to the 8th power
for example, we could write:

    x := sqr(sqr(sqr(x)))

and to the 9th power:

    x := x*sqr(sqr(sqr(x)))

More generally, "x" to the power 3.4 could be calculated by:

    x := exp(3.4*ln(x))

1.11 Named constants

Named constants are boxes into which a value is put before a
program is obeyed. This value remains unchanged during the
execution of the program and cannot be altered.

Program 1.10

This program prints the area and circumference of a circle of
given radius.

```
PROGRAM areaofcircle(input,output);

CONST pi = 3.14159;
VAR radius : real;

BEGIN
   read(radius);
   writeln('the cicumference is ', 2*pi*radius);
   writeln('the area is        ', pi*radius*radius)
END.
```

You can see from this that named constants are declared before variables and that the declaration takes the form of a name, equals sign and value.

If several constants were to be declared, then the declaration might take the form:

```
CONST pi = 3.14159;
      g = 981.181;    { at NPL, London}
      joulespercalorie = 4.2;
```

Giving names to values like these makes a program more readable. Also, if at some future date we need to run our program with a more accurate value for "pi", we do not need to search through the program for all occurrences of the value 3.14159, possibly missing some. Only the constant declaration needs to be changed.

Finally, an expression cannot be used to specify a value for a constant. We **cannot** write a constant declaration such as

```
CONST increase = 12.5/100;
```

but must write instead

```
CONST increase = 0.125;
```


Exercises

(7) Write a program that, given a number as input, prints its square, cube and fourth power without doing any unnecessary calculations.

(8) Extend Program 1.5 so that when the program has read the coefficients of the equations, it prints the equations in full before printing the solution.

(9) In Program 1.5, the denominator of the expression for x is the same as the denominator of the expression for y, apart for a change of sign. Use this fact to reduce the amount of

arithmetic done by the program.

(10) Write a program that reads the coefficients of the equation

$$ax^2 + bx + c = 0$$

and prints the two roots of the equation. Assume that the equation has real roots. Note the need for brackets round the denominator when evaluating an expression of the form

(...)/(2*a)

(11) Write a program that accepts as input the lengths a, b and c of a triangle. The program should output the area of the triangle.

(area^2 = s(s-a)(s-b)(s-c) where s=(a+b+c)/2)

(12) Write a program which accepts as input the amount of cash (a real number of pounds or dollars) to be enclosed in an employee's pay packet. The program should do a "coin and note analysis" and print the number of coins and notes, of each available denomination, which are to be included in the pay packet. Hint: Use the techniques illustrated in Program 1.9 to separate the cash amount into pounds and pence, or dollars and cents. Then deal separately with the two amounts as illustrated in Program 1.6.

2 Control statements

Up to now we have met assignment statements that make the computer perform arithmetic, and input-output statements that deal with information transfer to and from the computer. If these were the only facilities available in a programming language then the implementation of a task would be tedious indeed. A **control statement** in a computer language is a statement that controls the order of execution of the assignment and input-output statements. These are the 'drone' statements that perform the labour and the control statements organize or marshal the labour. The ability to impose an organization framework on the 'drone' statements enables quite complex tasks to be easily implemented in a computer program. The common control frameworks involve making the computer obey a section of a program over and over again - a looping facility, and making the computer select one out of a number of alternative courses of action. These two general facilities used alone, or together in various combinations, make up the organizational framework of all computer programs.

2.1 Loops - a preliminary example

It is important at this stage to realize that a variable is just what the term **variable** says it is - its value can change while a program is being obeyed. Consider the following program.

Program 2.1

Adds three numbers together.

```
PROGRAM add3(input,output);

VAR next, sum : integer;

BEGIN
  sum:=0;

  read(next);    sum := sum + next;

  read(next);    sum := sum + next;

  read(next);    sum := sum + next;

  writeln(sum)
END.
```

27

Let us assume that the program is provided with input:

    36 7 19

When the first two statements have been obeyed, we have the situation:

sum | 0 | next | 36 |

When the assignment statement on this line is obeyed, the expression on the right is evaluated first, regardless of what appears on the left. At this stage "sum + next" has the value 36 and this value is placed in the variable "sum", destroying or overwriting the value previously stored there:

sum | 36 | next | 36 |

The next read statement causes the next number in the input to be stored in the variable "next", again overwriting the value previously stored there. "sum + next" now has the value 43 and this value is now placed in "sum".

sum | 43 | next | 7 |

After obeying the next two statements we have the situation

sum | 62 | next | 19 |

Thus "sum" holds four different values while the program is being obeyed and "next" holds three. The net effect of the program is to add together the three numbers presented in the input. This is done by repeatedly obeying the two statements:

```
read(next);
sum := sum + next
```

In the above program two Pascal statements are repeated three times. A loop statement allows a programmer to write the two statements **once** and explicitly instruct the computer to execute the statements several times.

2.2 Deterministic loops

Looping structures in programming fall into one of two categories. If the program knows in advance how many times the loop is to be executed we use a deterministic facility, otherwise a non-deterministic facility is employed. The first Pascal loop structure that is introduced is a **deterministic** statement.

2.2.1 Simple FOR statements

We now present the first of the three looping statements available
in Pascal. These are all used to tell the computer to obey a group
of one or more statements again and again. For example, instead of
writing the above three statements in full three times, we can
tell the computer to obey these statements three times by using a
FOR statement:

Program 2.2

Equivalent in effect to Program 2.1.

```
PROGRAM add3(input,output);

VAR next, sum, count : integer;

BEGIN
   sum:=0;
   FOR count:= 1 TO 3 DO
   BEGIN
      read(next);
      sum:= sum + next
   END;
   writeln(sum)
END.
```

There are several points to note here:

(1) The FOR statement tells the computer to obey the statement
    after the word DO three times before carrying on to the next
    statement.

(2) After the word DO, BEGIN and END have been used to bracket a
    group of statements to show that they belong together and
    are to be thought of as a single **compound statement**. Between
    BEGIN and END we always have a list of statements (two in
    this case), separated from each other by semicolons. Thus,
    in this example, the complete sequence of statements between
    the inner BEGIN and END is obeyed three times before the
    write statement is obeyed.

(3) "Count" is an integer variable which is given the value 1
    the first time the compound statement is obeyed, 2 the
    second time and 3 the third time. The computer uses this
    variable to count the number of times the compound statement
    has been obeyed. "Count" is called the **control variable** of
    the FOR statement. For the time being, the control variable
    will always be an integer variable and must be declared as
    such. As you will see shortly, there is no special
    significance in the name "count" - we could have given the
    control variable any name we chose.

(4) Remember that a semicolon is used to separate one complete

statement from the next. There is no semicolon after DO in the above example because the FOR statement is not complete until the end of the statement after DO. A semicolon is used after the compound statement to separate the completed FOR statement from the write statement on the next line.

The behaviour of the FOR statement when obeyed can be illustrated diagrammatically by

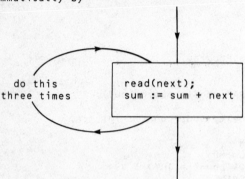

```
        do this          read(next);
      three times         sum := sum + next
```

hence the use of the term **loop**.

It is instructive to consider the effect of omitting the BEGIN and END brackets after the DO in the above program.

```
sum:=0;

FOR count := 1 TO 3 DO
    read(next);

sum := sum + next
```

Only the statement following DO is obeyed repeatedly and in the absence of BEGIN and END this consists only of:

```
read(next)
```

Thus the above is equivalent in effect to

```
sum:=0;
read(next);
read(next);
read(next);
sum := sum + next
```

This reads a number into "next", then reads another, overwriting the previous one, then reads a third. Only the third number is added onto the variable "sum".

It is sensible to type the program in such a way that the meaning is made clear to the human reader. A few extra spaces are usually inserted before the lines containing statements which are to be obeyed repeatedly, thus making these statements stand out in the text. You should remember, however, that this use of layout

30

does not affect the meaning of the program as far as the computer is concerned.

Our FOR statement which adds three numbers can be easily modified so as to add together ten numbers, say.

```
FOR count := 1 TO 10 DO
BEGIN
    read(next);
    sum := sum + next
END
```

We need not even commit ourselves to a fixed number of values to be added together. If the input supplied to the program starts with an integer telling the program how many numbers are to be added together, we could write

```
read(numberofvalues);  sum := 0;

FOR count := 1 TO numberofvalues DO
BEGIN
    read(next);  sum := sum + next
END
```

This program would then accept input such as

    5   26 72 41 32 61

and would add together the last 5 numbers. Input of

    2   15 42

would result in the addition of the 2 numbers 15 and 42.

The next program is a straightforward illustration of the use of a FOR statement.

Program 2.3

In sinking a well the rate of drilling is 20 metres per hour for the first hour. For each subsequent hour the depth sunk is 8 per cent less than in the previous hour. The program calculates the depth reached after 10 hours.

```
PROGRAM well(input, output);

VAR   hoursdepth, totaldepth : real;
      hour : integer;
BEGIN
  hoursdepth := 20; totaldepth := 0;
  FOR hour := 1 TO 10 DO
    BEGIN
        totaldepth := totaldepth + hoursdepth;
        hoursdepth := hoursdepth - 0.08*hoursdepth
    END;
  writeln('depth after 10 hours is', totaldepth)
END.
```

Note that in this program the order of the two assignment
statements within the loop is important.

2.2.2 Making use of the control variable

As we have already remarked, the control variable is used by the
computer to count how many times the statement following the DO
has been obeyed. However, there is no reason why the programmer
should not also make use of the value of this variable. As a
simple example, the statement:

```
FOR i := 1 TO 10 DO write(i:3)
```

will print the integers from 1 to 10 all on one line. Our last
program for calculating drilling depths could be changed to print
out a table showing the depth after each hour as follows:

Program 2.4

As Program 2.3 except that the output is to be in the form of a
table showing the depth drilled in each hour and the depth reached
after each hour.

```
PROGRAM well(input, output);

VAR   hoursdepth, totaldepth : real;
      hour : integer;
BEGIN
  hoursdepth := 20; totaldepth := 0;
  writeln('hour','depth drilled':16,'depth reached':16);
  FOR hour := 1 TO 10 DO
    BEGIN
        totaldepth := totaldepth + hoursdepth;
        writeln(hour:4, hoursdepth:16:2, totaldepth:16:2);
        hoursdepth := hoursdepth - 0.08*hoursdepth
    END
END.
```

32

This program will print the following table:

hour	depth drilled	depth reached
1	20.00	20.00
2	18.40	38.40
3	16.93	55.33
4	15.57	70.90
5	14.33	85.23
6	13.18	98.41
7	12.13	110.54
8	11.16	121.70
9	10.26	131.96
10	9.44	141.40

The first time the statement

```
writeln(hour:4, hoursdepth:16:2, totaldepth:16:2)
```

is obeyed "hour" has the value 1, the second time it has the value 2 and so on. The formatting information in this statement has been chosen so that each time the statement is obeyed, the three values printed are lined up below the three headings that were output by the statement:

```
writeln('hour', 'depth drilled':16, depth reached':16)
```

The use of formatting information is explained in Appendix 4. Again note the order of the statements within the loop. Updating of the variable "hoursdepth" must come immediately before the end of the loop.

A program can use a control variable in any way we like while the corresponding loop is being obeyed, except that the program must not attempt to change the control variable. This would be unreasonable because it would interfere, perhaps disastrously, with the only record there is of how many times the loop statement has been obeyed. In particular, this means that inside the loop the control variable must not appear on the left of any assignment statement or as a parameter of a read statement. Once the loop has been obeyed the appropriate number of times, the control variable no longer has a defined value, and the statements following the FOR statement should not assume that it still has a value. The variable can of course be given a new value or it can be used as the control variable of a subsequent FOR statement.

2.2.3 Other features of the FOR statement

Some further points about FOR statements are illustrated by the following examples.

```
FOR number := -8 TO 5 DO write(number:4)
```

When obeyed, this statement will output

```
  -8  -7  -6  -5  -4  -3  -2  -1   0   1   2   3   4   5
```

The   control variable can go up only in steps of 1. In order to
print all the even numbers from 2 to 100 we can use

        FOR n := 1 TO 50 DO writeln(n*2:3)

The odd numbers from 1 to 99 could be output by

        FOR n := 1 TO 50 DO writeln(n*2-1:2)

or by

        FOR n := 0 TO 49 DO writeln(n*2+1:2)

    We can use any expression we like to specify the starting and
finishing values for the control variable. For example, given two
integers m and n (both greater than 1), we can print all the
integers from m+n to m*n by

        FOR next := m+n TO m*n DO writeln(next)

    Finally, the control variable can be made to take values which
decrease in steps of 1. For example, we can print the integers
from 0 to 100 in reverse order by

        FOR k := 100 DOWNTO 0 DO writeln(k:3)

    Further use of these possibilities will be illustrated in later
chapters.

    In general, the FOR statement has one of the two forms

        FOR **variable** := **expression**   TO   **expression** DO

                    ┌─────────────────────┐
                    │   **statement**   │
                    └─────────────────────┘

or

        FOR **variable** := **expression** DOWNTO **expression** DO

                    ┌─────────────────────┐
                    │   **statement**   │
                    └─────────────────────┘

2.2.4 FOR loops with non-unit increment

Quite often in practical programming a situation is encountered
where we would like the control variable to be incremented in
steps other than unity. For example in the previous program we may

34

have wanted a table giving information every half hour or every two hours. Unfortunately Pascal only allows increments or decrements of unity. There is a good reason for this which is to do with using types other than integer as a control variable, a requirement not much encountered in scientific programming. This means that any non-unity stepping has to be handled explicitly by the programmer using another variable.

Say for example in the previous program we required the tabulated output to be every two hours.

```
totaldepth := 0;  hoursdepth := 10;
hours := 0;

FOR interval := 1 TO 5 DO
  BEGIN
    hours := hours + 2;
    intervaldepth := hoursdepth + 0.92*hoursdepth;
    totaldepth := totaldepth + intervaldepth;
    writeln(hours:4, intervaldepth:16:2, totaldepth:16:2);
    hoursdepth := 0.92*0.92*hoursdepth;
  END;
```

In this program we require a table that produces 5 rows of 2-hourly reports. We therefore need a control variable that goes from 1 to 5, and a separate variable "hours" that increments by 2 each time.

The lack of a non-unit loop increment would probably be considered by most programmers to be an omission in the language. It is an unfortunate side effect of generality in the syntax of Pascal. If we could increment the control variable by non-unity steps then a separate variable (in the above - "hours") would not be necessary. Such a requirement is common in mathematical programming and its non-availability in Pascal is unfortunate.

Exercises

(1) Write a program which reads and adds 15 real numbers and then prints their average.

(2) Write a program which reads and multiplies together 20 real numbers.

(3) Write a program to print a "4 times table" in the form

```
1 x 4 =  4
2 x 4 =  8
3 x 4 = 12
    etc.
```

(4) Write a program which reads an integer, n say, and prints an "n times table".

(5) Write a program which prints all multiples of 3 from 3 to 90.

(6) "n factorial" is defined as n*(n-1)*(n-2)*...*3*2*1. Write a program which reads a value for n and calculates n factorial.

(7) Write a program which reads an integer n followed by n real numbers. The program should calculate and print the average of the numbers.

(8) The statement "writeln('*':i)" will print a star preceded by i-1 spaces. In fact any integer expression can be used in place of "i". Write a program to read an integer n and print a large "7" occupying n lines. For example, with n=6 output should be

(9) Write a program to draw a triangle occupying n lines where n is supplied as input. For example, with n = 4

(10) An electricity board has previous and present meter readings for a known number of customers. Write a program which will read the appropriate number of pairs of readings and print a bill for each customer. (Make up your own rules for calculating the bill.)

(11) 20 candidates have each taken two examination papers, paper 1 and paper 2. The marks obtained are to be typed as input for a computer program. The first two numbers typed are the marks obtained by the first candidate, the next two numbers are the marks obtained by the second candidate, and so on. Write a program which prints the total mark obtained by each candidate over the two exam papers. The program should also calculate and print the overall average mark for paper 1, the overall average mark for paper 2 and the overall average total mark.

(12) Write a program that will read an integer n, an initial radius r of a pipe (in metres), an increment h for r, and a rate of flow of liquid in the pipe (in metres/s). The program should tabulate rates of flow in cubic metres/s for pipes of radii r, r+h, r+2h.., .r+nh.

(13) The Fibonacci sequence is:

0, 1, 1, 2, 3, 5, 8, 13, ...

Each number is the sum of the two previous ones. Write a program that generates the first n numbers in this sequence.

2.3 Selecting alternatives

We now introduce two control structures that are used to specify alternative courses of action. The courses of action are to obey one section of a program or another and the selection of an alternative is made on the outcome of a test set up by the programmer. Values of variables or expressions that can only be determined during execution are then effectively used to control the progress of the program.

2.3.1 Selecting one out of two alternatives

In the first instance we consider that one of the alternatives is to do nothing. A statement is either obeyed or ignored depending on the outcome of a test.

Consider the following simple examples:

```
IF previousconvictions > 3 THEN
    fine := fine*2
```

```
IF total > 100 THEN
    total := total - 0.10*total
```

The form of each of these examples is:

IF **condition** THEN **statement**

A simple condition relates two quantities using one of a number of relational operators. The particular relational operator we used above was ">" which means "greater than".

The complete list of relational operators is:

operator	meaning
>	greater than
>=	greater than or equal to
<	less than
<=	less than or equal to
=	equal to
<>	not equal to

The operators >=, <= and <> are single operators written in this way because of the limited number of characters usually available on a keyboard.

The following examples use these operators:

```
IF age >= 18 THEN
    write('eligible for jury service')


IF i <> j THEN
    write('i and j are unequal')
```

In general, real numbers should not be compared using = or <>. Two values which we think should be identical may differ very slightly when represented inside the computer. For example, because of the limited space available for storing a real, "1/3" might be stored as 0.3333333 and "1/3*3" would therefore be stored as 0.9999999. The computer does not actually work in decimal and the same problem arises in less obvious contexts. You will find that, for example "1/10*10" is not equal to 1. We can make the computer test whether whether two values are very close to each other by, for example:

```
IF abs(x-y) < 0.0001 THEN
    writeln('x and y are almost equal')
```

We can test whether a value is close to zero by, for example:

```
IF abs(determinant) < 0.0001 THEN
    writeln('Determinant is close to zero.')
```

The behaviour of a simple IF-THEN statement can be illustrated as follows:

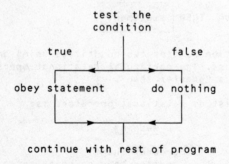

The branch taken depends on the outcome of the test. If the condition is satisfied then the left-hand branch is followed, otherwise the right-hand branch is taken. We say that the outcome of a test is the value "true" or the value "false" and this is a concept of which we shall make frequent use later.

Now consider the following examples:

```
IF total > 100 THEN
    total := total - 0.10*total
ELSE
    total := total - 0.05*total


IF age > 60 THEN
    benefit := (age - 60)*annualrate
ELSE
    write('no benefit payable')


IF currentreading > previousreading THEN
    unitsused := currentreading - previousreading
ELSE
    unitsused := 10000 - previousreading + currentreading


IF i <> j THEN
    write('i and j are unequal')
ELSE
    write('i and j are equal')
```

In each of the above examples the general form is:

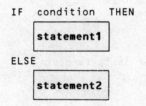

```
IF   condition   THEN

    statement1

ELSE

    statement2
```

The behaviour of such an IF-THEN-ELSE statement can be illustrated as follows:

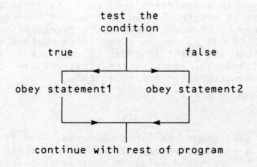

Again we are selecting one out of two alternatives but this time the second alternative, instead of being to do nothing, is another statement. Again the selection is dependent on the outcome of the test which can be either "true" or "false". Technically we say that the condition has a value "true" or "false". Statement1 is executed if (the value of) the condition is "true", otherwise statement2 is executed because (the value of) the condition is "false".

Here is a complete program illustrating these mechanisms.

Program 2.5

This program reads three numbers and prints the largest.

```
PROGRAM largest(input,output);

VAR first, second, third, largestsofar, largest : real;

BEGIN
    read(first, second, third);

    IF first > second THEN
        largestsofar := first
    ELSE
        largestsofar := second;

    IF largestsofar > third THEN
        largest := largestsofar
    ELSE
        largest := third;

    writeln('biggest number is ', largest)
END.
```

2.3.2 About semicolons

An IF-THEN-ELSE statement is a single statement. Thus a semicolon, which is technically a statement separator, is not inserted before an ELSE. Refer to Program 2.5 which contains two consecutive IF-THEN-ELSE statements. You will see that there is no semicolon before either ELSE but of course a semicolon appears at the end of each IF-THEN-ELSE statement in order to separate it from the next statement. Incidentally, you will find that you **are** permitted to insert a redundant semicolon before an END.

Program 2.6

Four numbers are input to this program. The first number is interpreted as a standard value and the three further values are compared with this standard value. A message is printed indicating how many of these three values are within 0.1 of the standard value.

```
PROGRAM tolerance(input,output);

VAR standard, next : real;  numberclose : integer;

BEGIN
   numberclose := 0;
   read(standard);

   read(next);
   IF abs(standard - next) < 0.1 THEN
      numberclose := numberclose + 1;

   read(next);
   IF abs(standard - next) < 0.1 THEN
      numberclose := numberclose + 1;

   read(next);
   IF abs(standard - next) < 0.1 THEN
      numberclose := numberclose + 1;

   writeln(numberclose,
            ' values are near the standard')
END.
```

For example, if the input is:

   3.156   3.051 3.152 3.091

the output will be:

   2 values are near the standard

In Program 2.6 the same operations are being performed three times over. A more elegant way of writing this program would be to put the repeated statements inside a loop. We shall do this in Chapter 3 which deals in detail with the techniques of nesting control statements, or putting control statements inside other control statements.

2.3.3 The use of compound statements

Now it may be that the action to be selected according to the outcome of a test comprises a number of statements rather than a single statement. In this case such statements are bracketed together using the BEGIN...END brackets introduced earlier in this chapter.

Program 2.7

This program finds the sum and difference of two numbers ensuring that the larger of the two numbers ends up in variable "larger" and the smaller in variable "smaller". Here we read the two numbers, in the first instance, into variables "larger" and "smaller" and swap the contents of the variables if necessary.

```
PROGRAM twonumbers(input,output);

VAR larger, smaller, temporary, sum,
        difference : integer;

BEGIN
   read(larger, smaller);

   IF larger < smaller THEN
   BEGIN
      temporary := larger;
      larger    := smaller;
      smaller   := temporary
   END;

   sum        := larger + smaller;
   difference := larger - smaller;

   writeln('the sum is ', sum);
   writeln('the difference is ', difference);
   writeln('nos. in order are ', larger, smaller)
END.
```

Note that the action to be performed if the outcome of the test is "true" now consists of three statements bracketed together to form a single compound statement. Also note that to swap over the contents of two variables you need three assignment statements and one extra variable. You should examine what would happen if we had written:

```
larger := smaller;
smaller := larger
```

2.3.4 More complicated conditions

The simple conditions we have used so far have been composed of two quantities related by a relational operator:

| quantity1 | relational operator | quantity2 |

The quantities we have used have been variables and constants but they can also be arithmetic expressions:

```
IF sum1 + sum2 - credit > 250 THEN
   write('limit exceeded')
```

We can combine more than one condition in an IF statement by joining conditions together using the words AND and OR.

Consider the following examples:

```
IF (previousconvictions > 3) AND (timespread < 1.5) THEN
   fine := fine * 4

IF (x=y) AND (x > 0) AND (y > 0) THEN
   write('x and y are equal and positive')
```

Note that individual conditions involving relational operators must be enclosed in round brackets. The words AND and OR join individual conditions together to make a more complex condition. Technically a condition is called a boolean expression.

A common mistake made by new programmers is to write:

```
IF (x > 0) AND < 10 THEN...
```

instead of:

```
IF (x > 0) AND (x < 10) THEN...
```

You should see from this that each constituent simple condition involving a relational operator must be complete.

2.3.5 Definition of AND and OR

When an IF statement contains a condition involving AND and OR, the meaning of the condition is usually clear from reading the program. However, here we tabulate the possible values of a composite condition involving two subsidiary conditions:

IF **condition1** AND **condition2** THEN...

condition1	condition2	composite condition
false	false	false
false	true	false
true	false	false
true	true	true

```
IF  condition1   OR   condition2   THEN...
```

condition1	condition2	composite condition
false	false	false
false	true	true
true	false	true
true	true	true

Try making up your own examples using combinations of AND and OR. The words AND and OR are called boolean operators and they join conditions or boolean expressions together, just as arithmetic operators join arithmetic expressions together.

The other boolean operator we use is NOT. Its use can be illustrated by a simple example:

```
IF NOT (x = y) THEN
    write('x and y are unequal')
```

is exactly equivalent to:

```
IF (x <> y) THEN
    write('x and y are unequal')
```

As with arithmetic operators there is an order of priority. In the case of boolean operators the order of priority is NOT, AND, OR. Thus:

```
IF (calories>2000) OR (weight>200) AND (height<1.7)  THEN
    write('you are overeating')
```

is equivalent to:

```
IF (calories>2000) OR ((weight>200) AND (height<1.7)) THEN
    write('you are overeating')
```

Remember: if in doubt, use extra brackets to make your intentions clear.

2.4 Boolean types and variables

Up to now we have been able to tell the computer that the contents of a storage location or variable are going to be of integer or real type. We now introduce a new type - boolean. A boolean variable can contain only one of the two values "true" or "false". Boolean variables are declared just like other variables:

```
VAR heavy, bright : boolean;

    ⋮
    heavy := true;
    bright:= false
```

In the above example "heavy" and "bright" are the names of storage locations into which the program places the values "true" and "false" respectively.

heavy | true | bright | false |

The use of a boolean variable is illustrated by the following fragment of program which prints out part of a menu. The dishes listed on the menu are to vary according to whether or not it is a summer month.

```
VAR month : integer;  itsasummermonth : boolean;

BEGIN
    read(month);
    itsasummermonth := (month >= 5) AND (month <= 8);

    writeln('menu');  writeln;

    IF itsasummermonth THEN writeln('melon')
                       ELSE writeln('oysters');
    writeln;
    write('roast chicken with ');
    IF itsasummermonth THEN writeln('green salad')
                       ELSE writeln('two veg.');
    :
```

When the program is being obeyed, the value of the condition

```
(month >= 5) AND (month <= 8)
```

is "true" or "false". This value is stored in the boolean variable "itsasummermonth". The program can then refer to the value of the condition as often as is necessary without having to perform the test again. The use of boolean variables in examples like this can improve the readability of the program, particularly when the result of a test is to be used more than once. As another example, consider:

```
VAR height, weight : real;
    tall,  heavy  : boolean;
BEGIN
    read(height, weight);
    tall  := height > 1.8;
    heavy := weight > 200;

    IF tall AND heavy THEN
        writeln('you are big enough to be a policeman.');

    IF NOT tall AND NOT heavy THEN
        writeln('have you thought about being a jockey?');
    :
```

Program 2.8

An insurance broker wishes to implement the following guidance table in a program, so that when he types in an age, engine capacity, and number of convictions the appropriate message is typed.

age	engine size	convictions	message
>=21	>=2000	>=3	policy loaded by 45%
>=21	>=2000	< 3	policy loaded by 15%
>=21	< 2000	>=3	policy loaded by 30%
>=21	< 2000	< 3	no loading
< 21	>=2000	>=3	no policy to be issued
< 21	>=2000	< 3	policy loaded by 60%
< 21	< 2000	>=3	policy loaded by 50%
< 21	< 2000	< 3	policy loaded by 10%

```
PROGRAM policy(input,output);

VAR over21 , largecar , riskdriver : boolean;
        age , cc , convictions : integer;
BEGIN
    read(age,cc,convictions);
    over21 := age >= 21;
    largecar:= cc >= 2000;
    riskdriver:= convictions >= 3;

    IF over21      AND      largecar AND      riskdriver
    THEN writeln('policy loaded by 45 percent');

    IF over21      AND      largecar AND NOT riskdriver
    THEN writeln('policy loaded by 15 percent');

    IF over21      AND NOT largecar AND      riskdriver
    THEN writeln('policy loaded by 30 percent');

    IF over21      AND NOT largecar AND NOT riskdriver
    THEN writeln('no loading');

    IF NOT over21 AND      largecar AND      riskdriver
    THEN writeln('no policy to be issued');

    IF NOT over21 AND      largecar AND NOT riskdriver
    THEN writeln('policy loaded by 60 percent');

    IF NOT over21 AND NOT largecar AND      riskdriver
    THEN writeln('policy loaded by 50 percent');

    IF NOT over21 AND NOT largecar AND NOT riskdriver
    THEN writeln('policy loaded by 10 percent')
END.
```

It must be pointed out that this is a rather inefficient program which on average results in a lot of wasteful testing (consider the case when the last row in the table is to be selected). In Chapter 3 we will be looking at how we can further develop our IF-THEN-ELSE structure and a more efficient and more elegant version of this program will be presented.

There are a number of standard functions which produce as their result the value "true" or "false". A boolean function can be used wherever the computer expects a boolean expression. The only boolean function we mention at this stage is "odd". Its use is illustrated in the following program fragment:

```
    VAR i, j, k : integer;

BEGIN
    read(i);
    IF odd(i) THEN writeln('that integer is odd.')
    ELSE writeln('that integer is even.');

    read(j, k);
    IF odd(j) AND odd(k) THEN
        writeln('these two integers are both odd.')
        .
        .
        .
```

2.5 Selecting one of many alternatives - CASE statement

There are many contexts in which we require a statement to select one out of a number of alternatives, rather than one out of two alternatives. One way of doing this can be represented diagrammatically as:

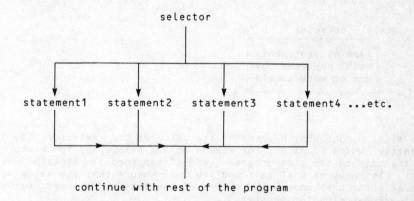

We have replaced a condition which could have one of two values - "true" or "false" - with a more general selector. The two valued condition which selected one out of two branches has been replaced by an entity which can select one out of a number of branches. Consider the following program fragment which could be part of a program for controlling a coin in the slot machine. Depending on

the denomination or weight of the coin one out of six totalizing
instructions is selected and obeyed.

```
read(weight);

CASE weight OF
    35 : amountinserted := amountinserted + 50;
    16 : amountinserted := amountinserted + 10;
    9  : amountinserted := amountinserted + 5;
    7  : amountinserted := amountinserted + 2;
    3  : amountinserted := amountinserted + 1;
    1  : amountinserted := amountinserted + 0.5
END
```

We are assuming that coins of denomination 50,10,5,2,1 and 0.5
have weights of 35,16,9,7,3 and 1 respectively. The structure is
called a CASE statement and in this example the selector is (the
value of) "weight" which is an integer variable. "weight" must
contain either 35,16,9,7,3 or 1. If it contains 9 then the third
statement is selected. If it contains 1 then the last statement is
selected. Thus one statement is selected - the statement whose
label corresponds to the value of the selector. More than one
label can be associated with a statement:

```
read(month);

CASE month OF
    1,2,11,12  : writeln('low season rate');
    3,4,5,10   : writeln('mid season rate');
    6,7,8,9    : writeln('peak season rate')
END
```

The general form is:

```
CASE   selector   OF
```
```
List of statements
each  preceded  by
one or more labels
```
```
END
```

You might wonder what happens if the value of the selector is a
quantity which does not correspond to any label. Say for example
in the coin in the slot program "weight" happened to contain 40.
Well the program will fail and you must ensure that the value of
the selector does correspond to one of the labels. Ways of doing
this are described in Chapter 3.

The selector need not necessarily be a variable, it can be an
arithmetic expression. The next program illustrates a context in
which an expression would be employed. You should note that the
expression must not be real. In the program below the expression
being used as a selector has type integer.

Program 2.9

This program determines in which of the four quadrants an angle
lies, where

   0 <= angle <= 360 degrees

```
                PROGRAM quadrant(input, output);

                VAR angle : real;
                BEGIN
                   read(angle);
                   write('angle is in the');
                   CASE trunc(angle/90) OF
                      0 : write('first');
                      1 : write('second');
                      2 : write('third');
                      3 : write('fourth');
                   END;
                   writeln(' quadrant');
                END.
```

   If one of the actions to be selected in a CASE statement
involves obeying more than one Pascal statement, then a group of
statements can, as usual, be bracketed together by using
BEGIN...END.

   Finally, a boolean expression can be used as a selector in a
case statement. Thus a case statement can be used as an
alternative to an IF-THEN-ELSE statement. For example, in Program
2.5 we could have used

```
    CASE first > second OF
       true : largestsofar := first;
       false: largestsofar := second
    END;

    CASE largestsofar > third OF
       true : largest := largestsofar;
       false: largest := third
    END;

    writeln('largest value is ', largest)
```

Exercises

(13) Write an electricity bill program similar in specification to
     Program 1.7 but take into account the fact that a meter goes
     back to zero after reaching 9999 making the previous reading
     greater than the present.

(14) Write a program which calculates the discount, if any, on a sale. Sales of $100 and over are eligible for a 10% discount.

(15) Write a program which will read in the lengths of the three sides of a triangle and which will print out the lengths of the sides in descending order followed by a message to say whether the triangle is right angled. Include a test to check that the data does in fact specify a legal triangle.

(16) Write a program which accepts twenty examination marks and prints a "pass/fail" message depending on whether the average is greater than or equal to 50, or less than 50.

(17) Write a program to read in data a, b, c and compute the roots of a quadratic equation:

$$ax^2 + bx + c = 0$$

Your program should print out a message indicating whether the roots are real or imaginary, and should print separately the real and imaginary parts of an imaginary root.

(18) An educational establishment gives 10 courses numbered 1..10. Each course is given during two hourly periods and some courses take place concurrently as follows:

```
Course 1,2     thu  9am     fri 10am
Course   3     mon 10am     thu 10am
Course 4,5     mon 11am     tue 11am
Course 6,7     tue  9am     wed  2pm
Course   8     mon 12am     thu  9am
Course   9     tue 10am     wed 11am
Course  10     fri  9am     fri 11am
```

Write a timetable enquiry program which is to accept a course number and print a message giving the time periods at which the course is held.

(19) At the educational establishment of the previous exercise the days of the week are numbered 1..5 and the hours of each day are numbered 1..6. (Hour 1 is at 9am and Hour 6 is at 2pm.) A period is coded as a two digit integer where the first digit gives the day and the second digit gives the hour of a period. Thus, for example, 23 means Tuesday at 11am. Write a program which accepts as input a single integer period code and which outputs the numbers of any courses taking place during that period.

(20) Write a program which reads three integers representing an abbreviated date, for example:

    26 12 79

and which will print the date in full, for example:

    26th December 1979

Note that the day should be followed by an appropriate suffix, 'st', 'nd', 'rd' or 'th'.

(21) Write a program which will read the number of a month and, assuming that it is not a leap year, will print the number of days in the month.

(22) Extend your solution to Exercise 21 so that it accepts the number of a month and the number of a year (which may be a leap year). It should print the number of days in the month. Note: Your program should start with the statement:

```
IF    ((year MOD 4 = 0) AND (year MOD 100 <>0))
      OR (year MOD 400 = 0)
THEN daysinfeb := 29
ELSE daysinfeb := 28
```

2.6 Non-deterministic loops

As well as the deterministic loop facility introduced earlier Pascal provides two non-deterministic or conditional loop facilities. We frequently require the computer to obey a section of program repeatedly until, as a result of this repetition, some condition is satisfied. As a practical analogy, we might instruct a person to keep putting items in a container until the container is full.

To emphasize the difference between a deterministic and a non-deterministic or conditional loop consider the problem of a bouncing sphere dropped onto a horizontal surface, rebounding each time to 0.75 of its previous height. To write a program that would calculate the total distance travelled after n impacts, we would use a deterministic facility - a FOR statement. If however we wanted to calculate the number of impacts that occurred before it comes to rest we would have to use a conditional loop structure. We do not know in advance how many bounces will occur before it stops.

2.6.1 Simple REPEAT statements

The first program introduces the most commonly used conditional loop facility - a REPEAT statement.

Program 2.10

Starting from a predefined height the program calculates the number of bounces that occur before a ball stops, given that each time it bounces it reaches 0.75 of its previous height. The ball is deemed to have stopped if the height of a bounce is less than 0.5cms.

```
PROGRAM ball(input, output);

CONST initial = 10;  { centimetres }
VAR  height  : real; noofbounces : integer;
BEGIN
  height := initial;  noofbounces := 0;

  REPEAT
    height := 0.75*height;
    noofbounces := noofbounces + 1
  UNTIL height < 0.5;

  writeln('object stops after', noofbounces, 'bounces')
END.
```

When a REPEAT statement is obeyed, the computer starts by obeying any statements between the words REPEAT and UNTIL. The condition after the word UNTIL is then tested. Provided the outcome of the test is "false", the statements between REPEAT and UNTIL are obeyed again and the condition tested once more. As long as the outcome of the test is "false", the process is repeated. When the outcome of the test is discovered to be "true", the computer goes on to obey the next statement. This process can be illustrated diagrammatically as follows:

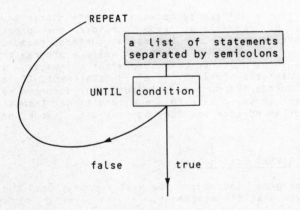

Note that in a REPEAT loop there is no record kept by the computer of the number of times the loop is obeyed. It is therefore very common to find a counting variable included in the loop. This variable will be initialized outside the loop and incremented within it. In the above example we have used a variable "noofbounces". Note also that the terminating test or condition must contain information that is being changed within the loop. If the terminating condition is independent of any calculations within the loop, the loop will not terminate and an infinite loop will occur. Clearly with a conditional loop the scope for an infinite loop error is vast. The above remarks on terminating condition may appear obvious but more subtle errors can easily arise.

```
VAR  x, y, : integer;
          :
          :
     x := 101;
     y := 4;
     REPEAT
       x := x-2
     UNTIL x = y
```

is a trivial example of a common error. "x" decreases towards "y" but never becomes equal to it. Whenever you intend to use the relational operator "=" in a condition, careful thought must be given to the loop statements that process the variables used in the relational expression. (Remember that in general it is unwise to ever use "=" with real variables or expressions.)

In a REPEAT statement, the two words REPEAT and UNTIL mark the beginning and end of the section of program which is to be obeyed repeatedly and, if more than one statement appears here, there is no need to bracket them with BEGIN and END.

The next example uses two variables within the loop, an accumulating variable "total" and a counting variable "days". Both of these require initialization just prior to entering the loop.

Program 2.11

A sequence of experimental readings has been taken at daily intervals. These values, (real numbers), are to be typed as input to this program. The readings are added together, one by one, and as soon as the total exceeds a specified threshold a message is printed indicating how many readings have been processed.

```
PROGRAM countdays(input,output);
CONST threshold=100;
VAR nextreading, total :real;
    days :integer;
BEGIN
    days := 0;  total := 0;

    REPEAT
       days := days + 1;
       read(nextreading);
       total := total + nextreading
    UNTIL total > threshold;

    writeln('threshold total of ', threshold,
            ' has been exceeded.');
    writeln('this occurred after ', days, ' days.')
END.
```

Now data does not always have to originate from a keyboard. In most computing systems, it will be possible to type information onto a magnetic disk or tape so that subsequently a program can read the information from the disk or tape. The data does not then have to be typed every time the program is obeyed. The way you arrange for a program to do this will depend on the computing system you are using. There will be little or no difference in the program itself but the commands used to tell the computer to obey the program may change. The reader is referred to Appendix 5 for more information on this (file) facility.

2.6.2 Iteration

The next program uses a process known as iteration - very common in numerical programming. An example of an iterative process is finding the square root of a number. If a variable r initially has the value a and the value of r is repeatedly replaced by the value of:

$$\frac{r}{2} + \frac{a}{2*r}$$

the values produced get closer and closer to the square root of a.

Program 2.12

This program accepts two positive values for "a" and "e" and uses the above technique to compute "r" such that:

    abs(r*r - a) <= e

"r" is then an **approximation** to the square root of "a". (The smaller the value of "e" chosen, the closer will be the approximation.)

```
        PROGRAM squareroot(input, output);

        CONST e = 0.01;
        VAR  r, a : real;
        BEGIN
          read(a);
          r := a;
          REPEAT
            r := r/2 + a/(2*r);
          UNTIL abs(r*r - a) <= e;
          writeln('The square root of', a, 'is approx.', r)
        END.
```

54

2.6.3 Simple WHILE statements

A loop using a WHILE statement is in most contexts identical in effect to a REPEAT-UNTIL loop, and in fact the two facilities can be interchanged mostly with impunity. The important difference is that in a WHILE loop the condition is tested **before** the loop is entered. In a REPEAT-UNTIL loop the terminating condition is tested **after** the statements within the loop have been obeyed. This means that the statements within the REPEAT-UNTIL loop **are always obeyed at least once** whereas the statements within the WHILE loop need not necessarily be obeyed at all. Thus a WHILE loop will not be entered at all if the terminating condition is initially false. Examples where this requirement is necessary are few. Perhaps a good one is the following.

Program 2.13

This program types out a simple sum for the person sitting at the keyboard to attempt. The program then reads the answer which is typed. As long as the answer is wrong, the person sitting at the keyboard is asked to try again. An appropriate message is output when the correct answer has eventually been typed.

```
PROGRAM arithmetictest(input,output);

CONST a = 16;  b = 25;

VAR nooftries, answer :integer;

BEGIN
    writeln('lets test your arithmetic.');
    writeln('type the answer to the following sum.');
    write(a, ' + ', b, ' = ');
    read(answer);  nooftries :=1;

    WHILE answer <> a+b DO
    BEGIN
        writeln;  writeln('wrong - try again.');
        write(a, ' + ', b, ' = ');
        read(answer);  nooftries := nooftries + 1
    END;

    writeln;
    IF nooftries = 1 THEN
        writeln('very good, got it in one!')
    ELSE writeln('got it at last!');
    writeln('bye for now!')
END.
```

When executed, this program might produce a display such as

```
lets test your arithmetic.
type the answer to the following sum.
16 + 25 = 42

wrong - try again.
16 + 25 = 41

got it at last!
bye for now!
```

The numbers 42 and 41 have been typed by the user, and the rest by
the program. If the user types the correct answer the first time,
it would clearly be unsatisfactory for the statements in the loop
to be obeyed at all. This is a trivial example of a Computer
Assisted Learning (CAL) program. A more realistic program would
generate random numbers for "a" and "b" and would then use these
numbers.

When a WHILE statement is obeyed, the computer starts by
testing the condition after the word WHILE. If the outcome is
"true", the statement after the word DO is obeyed and the
condition after the word WHILE is tested again. The process is
repeated as long as the outcome of the test is "true". As soon as
the outcome of the test is "false", the computer goes on and obeys
the next statement.

Diagrammatically we have

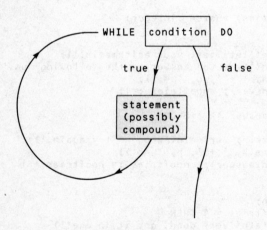

Note that in Program 2.13, the loop statements had to be
bracketed together into a single compound statement by using BEGIN
and END. This is necessary because the condition used to control
the WHILE statement is written before the loop statement and there
is no natural terminator as there is in a REPEAT statement.

2.6.4 Comparison of REPEAT statements and WHILE statements

In the following table we summarize the main differences between REPEAT statements and WHILE statements.

REPEAT	WHILE
The loop statements are obeyed at least once.	The loop statements may not be obeyed at all.
When the loop condition is "true", the computer stops obeying the loop.	As long as loop condition is "true" the computer keeps obeying the loop.
The words REPEAT and UNTIL act as brackets between which we can write as many statements as we like.	If more than one statement is to be obeyed repeatedly these must be bracketed together between BEGIN and END

In some examples, the choice of which statement to use is largely a matter of personal taste. For example, the loop in Program 2.11 could have been equally well expressed as

```
WHILE total <= threshold DO
BEGIN
   days := days + 1;
   read(nextreading);  total := total + nextreading
END
```

In such cases, the authors prefer the use of the REPEAT statement.

In some examples where we could use either statement, the use of a WHILE statement is a little clumsy. For example, if we wish to search through the input ignoring values until an odd number is found, we might have:

```
REPEAT
   read(next);
UNTIL odd(next);
```

or

```
read(next);
WHILE NOT odd(next) DO
   read(next);
```

When using a WHILE statement, we need to insert an extra read so that the WHILE condition can be evaluated first time round. In this example the use of 'negative' logic can also be confusing. Note that BEGIN...END are not necessary after the WHILE, as only a single statement is being obeyed repeatedly.

Finally, there are some examples in which only the WHILE statement is satisfactory. This was the case in Program 2.13.

2.6.5 Multiple terminating conditions

Up to now we have looked at examples of conditional loops where there has been one terminating condition. A fairly common situation that occurs in many practical contexts is when there are a number of terminating conditions. These of course can easily be combined using the logical operators OR or AND depending on the context:

```
REPEAT
   .
   .
UNTIL condA OR condB OR condC etc.


REPEAT
   .
   .
UNTIL condA AND condB AND condC etc.
```

However this is usually not the end of the story. In the case of the ORed terminating condition it is common for the program to want to know which condition caused the termination:

```
REPEAT
   .
   .
UNTIL condA OR condB OR condC;

IF condA THEN write('process terminated because of A');
IF condB THEN write('process terminated because of B');
IF condC THEN write('process terminated because of C');
```

The first example illustrates this point using both AND and OR operators in the terminating condition. Consider the problem of a meteorologist who requires programs which can be used to analyze the weather readings for a particular year.

Program 2.14

This reads input which consists of 365 pairs of values, one pair for each day of the year. The first number in each pair is the average temperature for the day and the second is the number of hours of sunshine for the day. The program counts how many days elapsed before the first day on which both the average temperature exceeded 15 degrees and the number of hours of sunshine exceeded 10. The program caters for the possibility that there is no such day.

```
PROGRAM heatwave(input,output);

CONST tempthreshold = 15;  sunthreshold =10;

VAR nexttemp, nextsun :real;
    day :integer;

BEGIN
   day := 0;

   REPEAT
      day := day + 1;
      read(nexttemp, nextsun)
   UNTIL (nexttemp > tempthreshold)  AND
         (nextsun > sunthreshold)  OR
         (day = 365);

   IF (nexttemp > tempthreshold) AND
      (nextsun > sunthreshold)
   THEN writeln('there were ', day-1,
                ' days before the first good day.')
   ELSE writeln('that was an exceptionally bad year.')
END.
```

In the above example, there are two reasons why the program might
stop obeying the loop. In order to test why the loop terminated
and print an appropriate message, the program had to re-test the
main stopping condition with an IF statement. Note that it would
have been wrong for the IF statement to use the condition
"day <> 365" instead, as this would not result in an appropriate
message in the case where the last day of the year was found to
satisfy the temperature and sunshine requirements. Neater ways of
dealing with this will be discussed later.

A multiple terminating requirement is often met in iterative
numerical programs where it is not known in advance if an
iteration will converge. To illustrate this point we will revisit
Program 2.12. This obviously does converge but we can make it more
realistic by reducing "e"

Program 2.15

As Program 2.12 except that the process is to terminate either if
the root is found or if the number of iterations becomes
excessive.

```
PROGRAM squareroot2(input, output);

VAR  e, r, a : real;
     noofiterations   : integer;
BEGIN
    writeln('type number and "e"');
    read(a, e);
    r := a;  noofiterations := 0;
    REPEAT
      noofiterations := noofiterations + 1;
      r := r/2 + a/(2*r);
    UNTIL (abs(r*r - a) <= e) OR
          (noofiterations >= 10);
    IF (abs(r*r-a) <= e) THEN
     writeln('Square root of', a, 'is approx.', r)
    ELSE  writeln('process does not converge');
END.
```

Again note that the condition:

```
IF noofiterations >= 10 THEN
  writeln('process does not converge')
ELSE writln('Square root of', a, 'is approx.', r);
```

would be inappropriate. The process may have converged on the 10th iteration! (See remarks on previous program).

2.6.6 Data terminators

When a computer reads from a source that produces many data items, a loop framework controls the number of reads that the computer performs. Previously we have introduced two mechanisms. Firstly inserting a constant in the program:

```
FOR i := 1 TO 3 DO
    read(x);
```

   data: X X X   (X represents a data item)

Secondly this constant can appear in the data:

```
read(n)
FOR i := 1 TO n DO
    read(x);
```

   data: 4 X X X X (the data now contains an integer
                          specifying the number of data items following)

and this is a more flexible facility than the first. Both require explicit knowledge of the number of items in the data set. This can be rather inconvenient if large data sets are to be frequently processed, and a widely used alternative approach is to insert a special value - a data terminator or sentinel at the end ot the data set. The only requirement now is that this value must not be contained in the data itself. No knowledge of the size of the data set is required.

```
    REPEAT
        read(x)
    UNTIL Y occurs;
```

   data: X X X ... X Y   (Y is the data terminator or
                                        senitel)

The first program introduces a slight complication often met when using this facility.

Program 2.16

This program reads and adds a sequence of positive real numbers (at least one). In this program the data terminator is any negative number. This program illustrates a common feature of conditional loops: the next value to be processed is obtained at the end of the loop so that this value is tested before it is processed. This necessitates obtaining the first value before entering the loop.

```
PROGRAM add(input,output);

VAR sum, next :real;

BEGIN
    sum := 0;

    read(next);
    REPEAT
        sum := sum + next;
        read(next)
    UNTIL next < 0;

    writeln('sum is ', sum)
END.
```

   It is interesting to consider a number of alternative constructions for the loop in Program 2.16, all of which are occasionally produced by beginners and all of which are **wrong**.

```
    sum := 0;
    REPEAT
        read(next);
        sum := sum + next
    UNTIL next < 0
```

This would add the data terminator, which is a negative number, to the total.

```
      sum := 0;
      read(next);
      REPEAT
         read(next);
         sum := sum + next
      UNTIL next < 0
```

This would not add the first number onto the total and would again
add the data terminator onto the total.

```
      sum := 0;
      REPEAT
         read(next);
         sum := sum + next;
         read(next)
      UNTIL next > 0
```

This version adds together the first, third, fifth, etc. numbers
in the data and tests the second, fourth, sixth, etc.

   If the numbers in the input are being handled in groups of two
or more, care has to be taken in handling data terminators. The
neatest solution is to insert a group of data terminators which
contains the same number of values as the groups into which the
rest of the data is organized.

Program 2.17

Voting takes place for two political parties in a number of
constituencies. The two vote-totals for each constituency are
typed in pairs as input to a program and two negative numbers are
typed in the input when all pairs of totals have been typed. This
program adds up the overall totals for the two parties and reports
the overall result.

```
      PROGRAM election(input,output);

      VAR party1next, party2next,
          party1overall, party2overall :integer;

      BEGIN
         party1overall := 0;  party2overall := 0;

         read(party1next, party2next);
         REPEAT
            party1overall := party1overall + party1next;
            party2overall := party2overall + party2next;
            read(party1next, party2next)
         UNTIL party1next < 0;

         writeln('party1: ', party1overall, '    ',
                 'party2: ', party2ovarall)
      END.
```

62

If presented with the input:

```
 3  7
 5  9
 4  2
-1 -1
```

this program will output

    party1: 12   party2: 18

The logical structure of this program is the same as that of Program 2.16, except that the input values are processed in pairs. Two data terminators are needed in order that they can be read by the same statement that reads the other pairs of values. (The test for termination of the loop needs to examine only the first value of each pair.) If we wish to type only one negative value at the end of the input data, a slightly more difficult structure is required for the loop:

```
    read(party1next);
    REPEAT
       read(party2next);
       party1overall := party1overall + party1next;
       party2overall := party2overall + party2next;
       read(party1next)
    UNTIL party1next < 0
```

This version reads only one number at the end of the loop and tests it. Only if this value is not the terminator can a second value be safely read.

    Finally, we present a program in which two REPEAT statements are used one after the other.

Program 2.18

This program adds up the overall totals for the two parties in an election, but the constituency subtotals for one party are all typed first in the input and are terminated by a negative number. The subtotals for the second party are then typed and are also terminated by a negative number.

```
PROGRAM election2(input,output);

VAR party1next, party1overall,
    party2next, party2overall :integer;

BEGIN
    party1overall := 0;
    read(party1next);
    REPEAT
        party1overall := party1overall + party1next;
        read(party1next)
    UNTIL party1next < 0;

    party2overall := 0;
    read(party2next);
    REPEAT
        party2overall := party2overall + party2next;
        read(party2next)
    UNTIL party2next < 0;

    writeln('party1: ', party1overall, '   ',
            'party2: ', party2overall)
END.
```

The second loop is not encountered until the first loop has been
obeyed the appropriate number of times. The first REPEAT loop is
obeyed until the first negative number is read and only then can
the program carry on to obey the next loop. The input for the
program will take the form

```
3  5  4  -1
7  9  2  -1
```

or even

```
2  3  7  9  4  -1
1  7  6  -1
```

if candidates for party 1 are standing for election in more
constituencies than are candidates for party 2.

2.6.7 Character markers

Although the processing of input on a character by character basis
is not extensively covered in this book, you will find that a
useful alternative to a numerical data terminator is a 'character
marker'. For example, the following program fragment adds together
a sequence of numbers, the last number being marked by the
character '*' typed immediately after the number:

```
        sum := 0;
        REPEAT
           read(next);
           sum := sum + next
        UNTIL input↑ = '*';
                { input↑ looks ahead at the next unread character }
        get(input)    { removes the next character from the input }
```

The expression "input↑" has as its value the next character in the
stream of characters being supplied as input to the program. Using
input↑ does not remove the next character from the input and if
further reading of numbers is to take place in the same program,
then it is necessary to remove the character from the input before
such reading takes place. The standard procedure "get" can be used
for this purpose.

2.6.8 Use of boolean variables

A boolean variable often provides a neat way for a programmer to
express the terminating condition for a loop, and to test
subsequently why the loop was terminated. As an example, we shall
rewrite Program 2.14 to use a boolean variable in this way.

Program 2.19

An alternative version of Program 2.14 using a boolean variable.

```
        PROGRAM heatwave2(input,output);
        CONST tempthreshold = 15;   sunthreshold =10;
        VAR nexttemp, nextsun :real;
            day :integer;
            warmdayfound :boolean;
        BEGIN
            day := 0;
            warmdayfound := false;

            REPEAT
                day := day + 1;
                read(nexttemp, nextsun);
                warmdayfound := (nexttemp > tempthreshold)  AND
                                (nextsun > sunthreshold)
            UNTIL warmdayfound OR (day = 365);

            IF warmdayfound THEN
                writeln('there were ', day-1,
                        ' days before the first good day.')
            ELSE
                writeln('that was an exceptionally bad year.')
        END.
```

Further examples of this approach will appear in later chapters.

Exercises

(23) The equation:

$$x^3 - 16x^2 + 32x + 256 = 0$$

has a solution that is a small positive integer. Write a program that finds a solution by trying in turn x = 1, 2, 3, ...

(24) Write a program that reads a real value s (>=1.5) and finds the smallest integer n such that:

1 + 1/2 + 1/3 + 1/4 + ... + 1/n > s.

(25) Write a program that calculates the smallest power of 2 not exceeding a bound input to the program. For example for an input of 21 the program should output:

smallest power of 2 greater than 21 is 5.
2 raised to the power of 5 is 32.

(26) 365 figures representing the rainfall in millimetres for consecutive days in a year are available. Write a program which counts how many days elapsed before the total rainfall for the year up to that point exceeded 250 millimetres. Allow for the possibility of a very dry year.

(27) In a board game for three players, the players take turns at making a move, and a player scores a variable number of points for each move made. Write a program which accepts, as input, the separate move scores and announces each player's total score. Assume that the scores are supplied to the program three at a time and that the input is terminated by three zeros.

(28) A machine is manufacturing ball-bearings and, at equal time-intervals during a production run, a ball-bearing is sampled and its diameter measured. A sequence of such measurements terminated by a negative number is available for input to a computer program. A similar sequence of measurements is available from a production run on a second machine. Each ball-bearing should have a diameter of 2.0mm. Write a program which reads the two separate sets of measurements and reports which machine is producing samples whose average diameter is closer to the ideal value.

(29) Write a program which accepts as input a set of sample diameter measurements from a production run on one of the machines described in Exercise 28. The program should report whether the sample contained any ball-bearings that were excessively large (>2.05) or excessively small (<1.95). The program should not waste time reading further input if such a value is found in the sample.

3 Statements within statements

Sometimes a control structure needs to be included inside another. For example it is possible to have a conditional statement inside a loop, a loop within a conditional statement and loops within loops. In this chapter we demonstrate how to write programs involving nested control structures. We shall use examples of some of the most commonly occurring structures.

A particular programming problem will require a combination of control structures that may not necessarily be illustrated in this chapter. However, those that are illustrated are very typical and should enable you to gain expertise in setting up your own structures.

3.1 IF statements within loops

We have seen in Chapter 2 that a FOR statement can take the form

FOR **variable** := **expression** TO **expression** DO

> **statement**

The statement to be obeyed repeatedly can in fact be any Pascal statement. We now illustrate the case where an IF statement is obeyed repeatedly by writing a program to print all the integers between 2 and 9 which divide exactly into a given integer. We can describe in outline what the program must do as follows:

        read(giveninteger);

        FOR i := 2 TO 9 DO

            **statement to test whether i divides
            exactly into the given integer**

In order to test whether an integer "i" divides exactly into "giveninteger" we can use

        IF giveninteger MOD i = 0 THEN
            writeln(i, ' divides into the given integer.')

and this is the statement which must follow the DO of the above FOR statement:

Program 3.1

To print all the positive integers under 10 which divide exactly into a given number.

```
PROGRAM factors(input, output);

VAR giveninteger, i : integer;

BEGIN
    read(giveninteger);

    FOR i := 2 TO 9 DO

        IF giveninteger MOD i = 0 THEN
            writeln(i, ' divides into the given integer.')
END.
```

The FOR statement in the above program will behave as if a sequence of eight separate IF statements were obeyed:

```
IF giveninteger MOD 2 = 0 THEN
    writeln(2, ' divides into the given integer.');
IF giveninteger MOD 3 = 0 THEN
    writeln(3, ' divides into the given integer.');
        :
IF giveninteger MOD 9 = 0 THEN
    writeln(9, ' divides into the given integer.')
```

Thus, given input of 18, the program will print

```
2 divides into the given integer.
3 divides into the given integer.
6 divides into the given integer.
9 divides into the given integer.
```

In Program 2.6, the same test was applied to three input values by using three separate occurrences of the same IF statement. Such a process is better structured as a loop:

```
FOR count := 1 TO 3 DO

        process the next
        value in the input
```

The statement following the DO can be a compound statement and it can be as complicated as we like; in this example it must read the next value in the input and then test it as in the following version of the program:

Program 3.2

Four numbers are input to this program. The first number is interpreted as a standard value and the three further values are compared with this standard value. A message is printed indicating how many of these three values are within 0.1 of the standard value.

```
PROGRAM tolerance2(input,output);

VAR standard, next : real;
    numberclose, count : integer;

BEGIN
    numberclose := 0;
    read(standard);

    FOR count := 1 TO 3 DO
    BEGIN
        read(next);
        IF abs(standard - next) < 0.1 THEN
            numberclose := numberclose + 1
    END;

    writeln(numberclose, ' values are near the standard.')
END.
```

Program 3.3

This is an elaboration of Program 3.2. Numbers are input to a program from a length-measuring device which measures the length of a manufactured component on a production line. The program counts the number of components within 0.1 of a standard length of 6.37 and the number of components outside this tolerance. The program terminates when it receives any negative number. We simulate input from the length measuring device by using "read" and the keyboard.

```
PROGRAM tolerance3(input,output);

CONST standard = 6.37;
VAR length : real;
    nowithin, nowithout : integer;

BEGIN
   nowithin := 0;
   nowithout:= 0;

   read(length);

   REPEAT
      IF abs(length - standard) < 0.1 THEN
         nowithin := nowithin + 1
      ELSE
         nowithout:= nowithout + 1;

      read(length)
   UNTIL length < 0;

   writeln(nowithin,  ' values are within  tolerance.');
   writeln(nowithout, ' values are outside tolerance.')
END.
```

3.2 Loops within loops

One loop inside another loop is a nested structure frequently
encountered in programs. This is because so much data analyzed by
computer programs is organized in the form of tables.

Consider the problem of processing the 5 examination marks
obtained by each of 25 candidates. The structure required is a
loop of the form

FOR candidate := 1 TO 25 DO

process the marks obtained
by the   next   candidate

Processing one candidate's marks might involve reading the 5 marks
obtained by the candidate, computing his average and testing for a
pass or fail:

```
total := 0;

FOR exam := 1 TO 5 DO
BEGIN
    read(mark);
    total := total + mark
END;

average := total/5;
IF average >= 50 THEN
    writeln('passed, average is ', average)
ELSE
    writeln('failed, average is ', average)
```

and a segment of program like this must be obeyed 25 times. This can be achieved by bracketing it into a single compound statement and inserting it into the previous FOR statement.

Program 3.4

Data for this program consists of 25 rows of 5 exam marks, each row representing the performance of one candidate in 5 exams. The program outputs a reference number, a pass/fail message and an average mark for each of the 25 candidates.

```
PROGRAM examarks(input,output);
VAR candidate, exam, total, mark : integer;
    average : real;
BEGIN
    FOR candidate := 1 TO 25 DO
    BEGIN
        total := 0;
        FOR exam := 1 TO 5 DO
        BEGIN
            read(mark);
            total := total + mark
        END;
        average := total/5;
        IF average >= 50 THEN
            writeln('candidate ', candidate,
                    ' passed, average is ', average)
        ELSE
            writeln('candidate ', candidate,
                    ' failed, average is ', average)
    END
END.
```

In the above program the outer loop is executed 25 times. Each time the computer enters the inner loop, it stays there until this loop has been executed 5 times. The innermost instructions are executed a total of 25x5 times and 125 marks would be supplied as input data in the form of 25 groups of 5 marks. If we imagine a counter associated with each loop then the "exam" counter would be turning 5 times as fast as the "candidate" counter, resetting to 1 for each new candidate.

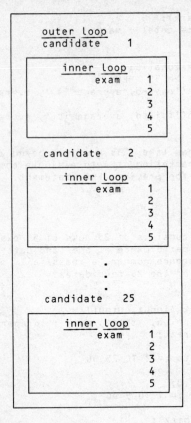

Note that, within the scope of the outermost loop, statements can be executed **before** entering the innermost loop and **after** exiting from the innermost loop.

To improve your understanding of the idea of a nested loop, you should examine the difference in behaviour between the following two fragments of program:

```
FOR i := 1 TO 3 DO

    FOR j := 1 TO 3 DO
        writeln(i, ' ', j)
```

which prints

```
1 1
1 2
1 3
2 1
2 2
2 3
3 1
3 2
3 3
```

and

```
FOR i := 1 TO 3 DO
    writeln(i);

FOR j := 1 TO 3 DO
    writeln(j)
```

which prints

```
1
2
3
1
2
3
```

The first fragment is of course a nested structure, whereas the second is just two consecutive loops.

The final example in this section involves an IF statement inside a REPEAT statement inside a FOR statement.

A traffic survey has been carried out at each of 27 survey points in a large town. A program is required to analyze the data obtained and report on the number of long vehicles (over 5 metres long) that passed each survey point. Before we consider the layout of the data in detail, we can see that the outline structure of the program will be:

```
FOR surveypoint := 1 TO 27 DO

    analyze the data from one survey point
```

The input for each survey point consists of a list of numbers representing the approximate lengths of each vehicle that passed the survey point during the period of the survey. Each such list is terminated by a negative value. The data for **one** survey point can thus be analyzed by:

```
        longvehicles := 0;
        read(nextlength);

        REPEAT

            test next length for long vehicle

            read(nextlength)
        UNTIL nextlength < 0;

        writeln('Survey point:', surveypoint:2, '    ',
                'Long vehicles:', longvehicles:4)
```

Filling in the rest of the details, we get:

Program 3.5

Counts the number of long vehicles that passed each of 27 survey
points during a traffic survey.

```
        PROGRAM longvehicles(input,output);

        CONST long = 5.0;

        VAR surveypoint, longvehicles : integer;
            nextlength : real;

        BEGIN
            FOR surveypoint := 1 TO 27 DO
            BEGIN
                longvehicles := 0;
                read(nextlength);

                REPEAT
                    IF nextlength >= long THEN
                        longvehicles := longvehicles + 1;
                    read(nextlength)
                UNTIL nextlength < 0;

                writeln('Survey point:', surveypoint:2, '    ',
                        'Long vehicles:', longvehicles:4)
            END
        END.
```


3.3 Nested IF statements

Consider the following sequence of 3 IF statements for testing the
'determinant' of a quadratic equation:

```
IF determinant = 0 THEN
    writeln('Equation has two equal real roots.');

IF determinant > 0 THEN
    writeln('Equation has two distinct real roots.');

IF determinant < 0 THEN
    writeln('Equation has two imaginary roots.')
```

Here three consecutive IF statements are used to select one of
three possible courses of action. The three conditions used are
such that one and only one of them must be true. However, even if
the condition in the first IF statement is true, the computer will
still waste time testing the conditions in the remaining two IF
statements. If the conditions in the first two IF statements are
false, the condition in the third must be true and the computer
will again waste time testing it. These inefficiencies can be
eliminated by using a more appropriate IF statement structure for
making the tests involved. Let us start by noting that if the
determinant is zero then the first write statement should be
obeyed and no further tests made. This can be achieved by using an
IF-THEN-ELSE structure. Use of this structure also allows us to
replace the test "determinant=0" by a more appropriate test to see
if the determinant is **close** to zero.

```
IF abs(determinant) < 0.0001 THEN
    writeln('Equation has two equal real roots.');
ELSE
```

            statement to be obeyed
        only if abs(determinant) >= 0.0001

Any statement inserted after the ELSE will be obeyed **only** if the
determinant is not close to zero. In this example we can obtain
the effect we require by making the statement after the ELSE a
further IF statement which distinguishes the cases determinant > 0
and determinant < 0:

```
IF abs(determinant) < 0.0001 THEN
    writeln('Equation has two equal real roots.');
ELSE
    IF determinant > 0 THEN
        writeln('Equation has two distinct real roots.')
    ELSE
        writeln('Equation has two imaginary roots.')
```

This version of the program will not test the second condition if
the first is satisfied and will automatically obey the third write
statement if the first two conditions are false. We can illustrate
the behaviour of this nested IF statement as follows:

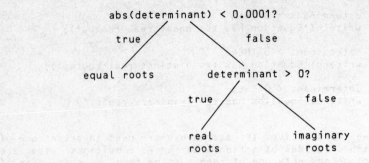

abs(determinant) < 0.0001?

true / \ false

equal roots   determinant > 0?

true / \ false

real   imaginary
roots   roots

We can imagine the computer following one path from the top of this diagram and carrying out the action at the end of that path.

Program 3.6

This is a more efficient version of Program 2.8, which selected one out of 8 messages to be typed according to 3 items of information input - age, size of car and conviction record.

```
PROGRAM policy2(input,output);

CONST p45 = 'policy loaded by 45 percent';
      p15 = 'policy loaded by 15 percent';
      p30 = 'policy loaded by 30 per cent';
      ok  = 'no loading';
      no  = 'no policy to be issued';
      p60 = 'policy loaded by 60 percent';
      p50 = 'policy loaded by 50 percent';
      p10 = 'policy loaded by 10 percent';
VAR over21, largecar, riskdriver : boolean;
    age, cc,convictions : integer;

BEGIN
   read(age,cc,convictions);
   over21 := age >= 21;
   largecar := cc >= 2000;
   riskdriver := convictions >= 3;

   IF over21 THEN
      IF largecar THEN
         IF riskdriver THEN writeln(p45)
         ELSE               writeln(p15)
      ELSE
         IF riskdriver THEN writeln(p30)
         ELSE               writeln(ok)
   ELSE
      IF largecar THEN
         IF riskdriver THEN writeln(no)
         ELSE               writeln(p60)
      ELSE
         IF riskdriver THEN writeln(p50)
         ELSE               writeln(p10)
END.
```

Note the use of **string constants** in this program.

   You should now compare the structure of this program with
Program 2.8, which is identical in effect, and by constructing a
tree diagram appreciate the difference between the two structures.
An alternative way of implementing the nested IF statement in this
program is to use a nested CASE statement as follows:

```
CASE over21 OF

    true :   CASE largecar OF
             true :   CASE riskdriver OF
                      true : writeln(p45);
                      false: writeln(p15)
                      END;
             false:   CASE riskdriver OF
                      true : writeln(p30);
                      false: writeln(ok)
                      END
             END;

    false:   similar structure for dealing
             with    other   possibilities

    END
```

The next program illustrates the use of a nested IF statement within a loop.

Program 3.7

This is an elaboration of Program 3.3. The program counts the number of components within 0.1 of a standard length of 6.37, the number of components whose length is too high and the number whose length is too low. As before, we have the outline structure:

```
read(length);
REPEAT

    test length;

    read(length)
UNTIL length < 0
```

To test a length, we require to distinguish three separate possibilities as follows:

```
IF abs(length - standard) < 0.1 THEN
   nowithin := nowithin + 1
ELSE
   IF length - standard >= 0.1 THEN
      noabove := noabove + 1
   ELSE
      nobelow := nobelow + 1
```

The complete program therefore becomes:

```
PROGRAM tolerance4(input,output);
CONST standard = 6.37;
VAR length : real;
    noabove, nobelow, nowithin : integer;
BEGIN
   nowithin := 0;  noabove := 0;
   nobelow := 0;   read(length);

   REPEAT
      IF abs(length - standard) < 0.1 THEN
         nowithin := nowithin + 1
      ELSE
         IF length - standard >= 0.1 THEN
            noabove := noabove + 1
         ELSE
            nobelow := nobelow + 1;
      read(length)
   UNTIL length < 0;

   writeln(nowithin, ' values are within tolerance.');
   writeln(noabove,  ' values are too large.');
   writeln(nobelow,  ' values are too small.')
END.
```

We finish this section by drawing your attention to a minor difficulty which can arise when nesting IF statements, some of which have no ELSE part. The computer always assumes that an ELSE belongs to the nearest unterminated IF...THEN. Thus in:

```
IF  condition1  THEN
   IF  condition2  THEN  statementa
   ELSE  statementb
```

the ELSE belongs to the second IF and the computer will behave as follows:

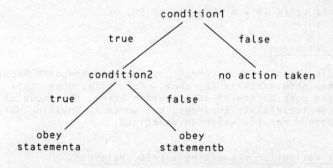

For example, when the computer obeys the statement

```
IF x > 50 THEN
   IF y > 50 THEN writeln('both values > 50')
   ELSE writeln('only the first value is > 50')
```

no action at all is taken if x <= 50.

    If necessary, BEGIN...END brackets can be used to terminate an
IF...THEN as follows:

```
    IF  condition1  THEN
    BEGIN
        IF  condition2  THEN  statementa
    END
    ELSE statementb
```

The BEGIN...END indicate that the enclosed IF-THEN statement is
complete and the following ELSE is taken as belonging to the first
IF. In this case the computer behaves as follows:

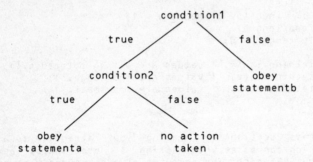

For example, if the computer obeys the statement:

```
    IF x > 50 THEN
    BEGIN
        IF y > 50 THEN writeln('both values are > 50')
    END
    ELSE writeln('the first value is not > 50')
```

no action is taken if x > 50 and y <= 50.

3.4 Data validation

When it is possible to check or validate the data input to a
program this should always be done. Not only does this guard
against the possibility of an execution error, the cause of which
might not be immediately apparent, but worse - invalid data may
cause erroneous results which go unnoticed.

3.4.1 Data validation - guarding a CASE statement

In Chapter 2 when CASE statements were introduced we mentioned
that if the selector did not contain one of the labels in the CASE
statement, the program would fail. This is obviously undesirable
and in Pascal it is the programmer's responsibility to guard
against such an eventuality. In practice this means that a CASE
statement may have to be protected by a structure which ensures

that the CASE statement is not obeyed unless the value of the
selector does correspond to one of the labels:

IF selector has a sensible value THEN

      CASE statement

ELSE write an error message

The next program uses this structure.

Program 3.8

This is a program which is to control a "coin in the slot"
machine. We assume that coins of denomination 50, 10, 5, 2, and 1
have weights of 35, 16, 9, 7 and 3 respectively. Also we are
simulating a single coin being put in th slot by "read(weight)".
The program is to print a message as soon as at least $1.23 has
been inserted, calculating any change due.

```
PROGRAM coins(input,output);
VAR weight : integer;
    total : real;
BEGIN
   total := 0;

   REPEAT
      read(weight);

      IF weight IN [35,16,9,7,3] THEN
         CASE weight OF
            35 : total := total + 50;
            16 : total := total + 10;
             9 : total := total +  5;
             7 : total := total +  2;
             3 : total := total +  1
         END
      ELSE writeln('coin rejected')

   UNTIL total >= 123;

   write('coins accepted.');
   IF total > 123 THEN
      writeln(' change due: ', total - 123)
END.
```

In the above program, we have informally introduced the operator
IN which can be used to test whether a value is one of a given set
of values. A test such as

   (weight = 35) OR (weight = 16) OR (weight) = 9) OR
   (weight = 7) OR (weight = 3)

is rather cumbersome. This condition is more concisely expressed as

    weight IN [35, 16, 9, 7, 3]

We can test whether a given integer is in the range 1 to 10 by using a condition such as

    (1 <= i) AND (i <= 10)

but this can also be more concisely expressed in set notation as

    i IN [1..10]

The elements of a set in the above sense can not be real numbers and you may find that your Pascal system imposes some further restrictions on the range of values which can appear in a set (inside the square brackets). This is a consequence of the way such a set is represented inside the computer.

3.4.2 Data validation - guarding a program

In simple cases, we can protect a complete program from faulty data by using a structure such as:

> **read data;**
>
> IF **data is ok** THEN
>
> > **main part**
> > **of program**
>
> ELSE **write error message**

The following program uses this structure. The individual CASE statements do not need guarding because in each the selector has already been checked.

Program 3.9

This program calculates the cost of a holiday by multiplying the duration in days by a daily rate which is seasonally dependant. The input data is two dates in the form day, month and we assume that the months are either going to be identical or consecutive. Also we assume that it is the second month that determines the seasonal rate.

```
PROGRAM holiday(input,output);

CONST lowrate = 57;
      midrate = 72;
      peakrate= 87;
VAR day1, month1, day2, month2, duration,
    tillendofmonth, cost : integer;

BEGIN
   read(day1,month1,day2,month2);

   IF (day1 IN [1..31]) AND (day2 IN [1..31])
      AND (month1 IN [1..12]) AND (month2 IN [1..12])
      AND (month1 <= month2)   THEN

   BEGIN
      IF month1 = month2 THEN
         duration := day2 - day1 +1
      ELSE
      BEGIN
         CASE month1 OF
                   2 : tillendofmonth := 28 - day1;
            9,4,6,11 : tillendofmonth := 30 - day1;
            1,3,5,7,
             8,10,12 : tillendofmonth := 31 - day1
         END;
         duration := day2 + tillendofmonth + 1
      END;

      CASE month2 OF
      1,2,11,12 : cost := duration*lowrate;
      3,4,5,10  : cost := duration*midrate;
      6,7,8,9   : cost := duration*peakrate
      END;

      write('cost of holiday is ', cost)
   END

   ELSE write('you have typed erroneous dates')

END.
```

In this example we have simplified the input data check (not every month has 31 days!); but comprehensive validation would be too lengthy for the purpose of this demonstration.

The main part of the program is entered only if the data is acceptable (within the limits of the test used). If the data is erroneous the computer will have to be told to execute the program again. If a program is required automatically to request more input until a correct set of data values has been typed, then the following structure can be used:

```
read data;

WHILE  data is faulty  DO
BEGIN
   write a message requesting data to be retyped;
   read data
END;

main  part
of program
```

For example, a program that requires input of a date (day, month, year) before carrying out some operation might make use of this structure as follows:

```
readln(day, month, year);
WHILE  NOT ((day IN [1..31]) AND (month IN [1..12])
                             AND (year  IN [80..89]) )  DO
BEGIN
   writeln('Erroneous date.');
   write('Please retype - day,month,year:');
   readln(day, month, year)
END;

remainder of program
```

3.5 Stepwise refinement

In writing some of the programs in this chapter, we have informally introduced the technique that is sometimes termed **stepwise refinement** or **top-down program design.** Instead of attempting to write down a complete Pascal program in one step, we first decide what the outermost control structure in the program should be. For example, in writing Program 3.5, we can see immediately that we have to analyze data from 27 traffic survey points. Giving a brief English description to the process of analyzing the data from one survey point enabled us to write down an outline of this loop:

```
FOR surveypoint := 1 TO 27 DO

     analyze the data from one survey point
```

Having got this clear in our minds, we then concentrated on the rather easier sub-problem of analyzing the data from one survey point and the program for doing this was eventually inserted in the above structure. This sub-problem was of course tackled by a further application of stepwise refinement.

Such an approach enables the construction of a complex nested control structure to be broken down into a number of simpler programming tasks that are more or less independent of each other. This is just one aspect of the set of programming techniques known as **structured programming**.

Stepwise refinement is discussed further in Chapter 5.

Exercises

(1) Write a program that outputs **all** the factors of a given positive integer.

(2) Given input data consisting of 30 numbers, some of which are positive and some of which are negative, write a program which finds the average of the positive numbers and the average of the negative numbers.

(3) Write a program that accepts as input a set of sample diameter readings from one of the ball-bearing machines described in Exercise 28, Chapter 2. A ball-bearing is classified as faulty if its diameter is less than 1.99mm or greater than 2.01 mm. Your program should report the percentage of faulty ball-bearings in the sample.
    Now extend your program to accept two successive sets of readings from two machines and to report which machine is producing the smaller proportion of faulty samples.

(4) Write a program to accept a single integer and print a multipication table for all the positive integers up to the one specified as input.

(5) Write a program that will read the lengths of three sides of a triangle (three integers) and which will print the lengths of the sides in descending order followed by a message to say whether the triangle is right-angled.

(6) Extend your solution to Exercise 5 to include a test to check that the data does in fact specify a legal triangle. (The sum of the two smallest sides must be greater than the largest side.)

(7) Write a program that solves a quadratic equation given the three coefficients. The program should distinguish the three cases: distinct real roots; coincident real roots; imaginary roots. In the case of imaginary roots, the real and imaginary parts of the roots should be output separately.

(8) Write a program that accepts as input two coordinates x and y (x<>0, y<>0). The program should output a message indicating whether the point (x,y) is in the first, second, third or fourth quadrant of the coordinate plane.

(9) If we start with two different integers and repeatedly replace the larger value by the magnitude of their difference, stopping when both numbers are the same, this

final value is the highest common factor (HCF) of the two
original numbers. Write a program that prints the HCF of two
given integers.

(10) Write a program that will read a real number x and will then
read positive real numbers until a negative one is read. A
message should be printed indicating which of these numbers
is closest to x.

(11) Write a program that accepts as input the numbers of two
months (in the same year) followed by the number of the year,
and outputs the total number of days from the beginning of
the first month to the end of the second month.

(12) Extend your solution to Exercise 11 so that it accepts two
dates in the form, for example:

13 6
25 12

where the first number in each pair is a day and the second
is a month. Again assume that both dates are in the same
year. The dates will be followed in the input by the number
of the year. The program should print the number of days from
the first date to the second date.

4 Arrays

If a program systematically processes a collection of variables, it may not be convenient for the programmer to give each of these variables a different name. For example it would be rather tedious to write:

```
totalprice := priceofhammer + priceofsaw   +
              priceofaxe    + priceofplane +
              priceofchisel + priceofvice  +
              priceofscrewd + priceofspanner;
```

Instead of giving such a group of variables separate names, it is often more convenient to give them a collective name and to refer to the individual variables in the collection by subscripts, where the subscripts may be numbers.

4.1 One dimensional arrays

A one-dimensional array is a set of storage locations or variables all of the same type which share the same name, but have different subscripts. For example the information:

name of variable	content
priceofhammer	5.77
priceofsaw	3.15
priceofaxe	2.50
priceofplane	16.33
priceofchisel	2.50
priceofvice	13.45
priceofscrewd	.86
priceofspanner	1.98

could be stored in a one-dimensional array:

name of variable	content
priceof[1]	5.77
priceof[2]	3.15
priceof[3]	2.50
priceof[4]	16.33
priceof[5]	2.50
priceof[6]	13.45
priceof[7]	.86
priceof[8]	1.98

The numbers in square brackets are the distinguishing subscripts, that enable the programmer to refer to individual elements. Arrays have to be declared, and for our example the declarations could be:

```
VAR   priceof : ARRAY [1..8] OF real;
```

In this declaration "priceof" is the name of the array. The numbers in square brackets are the least and greatest subscripts separated by two dots. "OF real" means that the variables are to contain reals. In a program, the subscript used to select a location of the above array can be an integer constant, an integer variable, or indeed any integer expression as long as the value of the subscript is in the range 1..8. This has the advantage that we can use a loop to systematically process all the values in the array (a point we shall return to later). For example:

```
totalprice := 0;
FOR itemno := 1 TO 8 DO
  totalprice := totalprice + priceof[itemno]
```

The variables that make up an array are called array elements. Array elements can be manipulated just like simple variables. For example:

```
read(price[1], price[2], price[3], price[4]);
read(price[5], price[6], price[7], price[8]);
writeln('the price of item 2 is ',price[2]);
writeln('the price of item 4 is ',price[4]);

writeln('Price difference between items 1 and 2 is ',
        abs(price[1] - price[2]));

difference := price[1] - price[2];
IF difference > 0 THEN
 writeln('item 1 costs ', difference,
         ' more than item 2.')
ELSE  IF difference < 0 THEN
        writeln('item 2 costs ', -difference,
                ' more than item 1.')
```

4.1.1 Sequential access to one-dimensional arrays

In the following example we have declared an array of ten integer locations all named "number".

Program 4.1

This program reads ten integers and prints them in reverse order.

```
PROGRAM reverse(input,output);

VAR number : ARRAY [1..10] OF integer;
    position : integer;

BEGIN
   FOR position := 1 TO 10 DO
      read(number[position]);

   FOR position := 10 DOWNTO 1 DO
      writeln(number[position])
END.
```

In Program 4.1 the array elements are accessed systematically one
after another. This is a very simple example of sequential access.
The program reads input integers into successive locations. It
then starts at the tenth location and fetches the integers in
reverse order printing them as it goes. A control structure
appropriate for these actions is a FOR statement and we use the
control variable "position" as an array subscript. The execution
of the first FOR statement proceeds as follows:

value of "position"	statement obeyed
1	read(number[1])
2	read(number[2])
3	read(number[3])
⋮	⋮

It is important to note that each array location has two
quantities associated with it:

    (1) the subscript,
    (2) the contents of the location.

Program 4.2

Given a set of data comprising 10 temperature readings the program
evaluates the average temperature and then finds the number
of occurrences of temperatures greater than twice the average.

```
        PROGRAM temps(input, output);
        VAR temp : ARRAY[1..10] OF real;
            noofhightemps, i : integer;
            hightemp, average, total : real;

        BEGIN
            total := 0;  noofhightemps := 0;
            FOR i := 1 TO 10 DO
             BEGIN
               read(temp[i]);
               total := total + temp[i]
             END;
            average := total/10; hightemp := 2*average;
            FOR i := 1 TO 10 DO
               IF temp[i] > hightemp THEN
                                noofhightemps := noofhightemps + 1;

            writeln('no. of occurrences of high temperatures is',
                                   noofhightemps)
        END.
```

In Program 4.1 we used an array of integers and in Program 4.2 an array of reals.

When an array element is referred to in a program, the value of the subscript must always be within the subscript range that has been declared. Let us consider what would have happened in Program 4.2 if we had typed:

        for i := 1 to 20 do

At one stage, the computer would attempt to refer to "temp[11]" which does not exist and the program would fail during execution. If the program is required to store 20 temperatures, the array should be declared as:

        VAR temp : ARRAY[1..20] OF real;

4.1.2 Random access to one-dimensional arrays

The following program illustrates the use of an array where the elements are being accessed randomly rather than in a sequential manner.

Program 4.3

Given two item numbers in the range 1-4 the program prints the corresponding prices.

```
PROGRAM prices2(input,output);

VAR priceof : ARRAY [1..4] OF real;
    itema, itemb : integer;

BEGIN

    priceof[1] := 5.77;
    priceof[2] := 3.15;
    priceof[3] := 2.50;
    priceof[4] := 1.35;

    read(itema, itemb);
    writeln('item no. ', itema, ' costs ', priceof[itema]);
    writeln('item no. ', itemb, ' costs ', priceof[itemb])

END.
```

In this program the two elements are not accessed in any
particular order. When the program is executed, we could type 3
followed by 1. The program would then access "priceof[3]" followed
by "priceof[1]". We say that the array has been accessed randomly.
The process can be illustrated diagramatically as:

The two numbers typed from the keyboard are placed in the integer
variables "itema" and "itemb". The contents of "itema" are used to
select one of the 4 elements of "price". The process is then
repeated for "itemb". In this case, output would be:

    item no. 3 costs 2.50
    item no. 1 costs 5.77

In this case, if a number other than 1,2,3 or 4 had been typed as
input, the program would have failed.

    The next two programs use a mixture of sequential and random
access.

Program 4.4

Six candidates in an election have reference numbers 1,2,3,...6. A
list of votes (terminated by -1) takes the form of a list of such
reference numbers For example:

number typed

```
       5         means 1 vote for candidate 5
       3         means 1 vote for candidate 3
       1         means 1 vote for candidate 1
       3         means 1 more vote for candidate 3
       .
       .
      -1         means "end of list"
```

The program totalizes the votes for each candidate and finds the winner. The structure used in this program is commonly used in programs accumulating data and constructing frequency distributions or histograms.

```
PROGRAM votes(input,output);

VAR candidate, mostvotesofar, winner : integer;
    votesfor : ARRAY [1..6] OF integer;

BEGIN
   FOR candidate := 1 TO 6 DO
      votesfor[candidate] := 0;

   read(candidate);
   REPEAT
      votesfor[candidate] := votesfor[candidate] + 1;
      read(candidate);
   UNTIL candidate = -1;

   mostvotesofar := 0;
   FOR candidate := 1 TO 6 DO
      IF votesfor[candidate] > mostvotesofar THEN
         BEGIN
            mostvotesofar := votesfor[candidate];
            winner := candidate
         END;

   writeln('winner is candidate no. ',winner)
END.
```

In the first loop the 6 elements of "votesfor" are initialized to zero using sequential access. In the second loop each number typed in from the list determines which of the 6 elements is to be incremented - random access. The third loop finds the element that now contains the highest integer.

Program 4.5

Reads 2 dates each in the form day, month, and calculates the number of days from one day to the next. It is assumed that the dates are sensible and that they lie in the same year which is not a leap year.

```
PROGRAM days(input,output);

VAR month, daystogo, firstday,
    firstmonth, secondday, secondmonth : integer;
    daysin : ARRAY [1..12] OF integer;

BEGIN
   FOR month := 1 TO 12 DO
      CASE month OF
                    2: daysin[month] := 28;
           9,4,6,11: daysin[month] := 30;
      1,3,5,7,8,10,12: daysin[month] := 31
      END;

   read(firstday,firstmonth,secondday,secondmonth);
   IF firstmonth = secondmonth THEN
      daystogo := secondday - firstday
   ELSE
   BEGIN
      daystogo := daysin[firstmonth] - firstday;

      FOR month := firstmonth + 1 TO secondmonth - 1 DO
         daystogo := daystogo + daysin[month];

      daystogo := daystogo + secondday
   END;

   writeln('days to go:', daystogo)
END.
```

In this program the initialization of "daysin" is achieved by a
CASE statement inside a FOR statement. The FOR statement controls
the sequential access and the CASE statement selects the
appropriate value for each element. If the two days are not in the
same month then the program calculates the number of days to go by
adding 3 fragments to "daystogo". For example if the input was:

5   2
20   5

the program would select the appropriate numbers as follows:

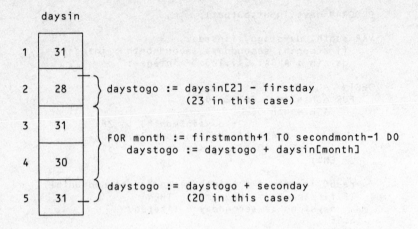

daysin

1	31
2	28	daystogo := daysin[2] - firstday
(23 in this case)
3	31
		FOR month := firstmonth+1 TO secondmonth-1 DO
daystogo := daystogo + daysin[month]
4	30
5	31	daystogo := daystogo + seconday
(20 in this case)

Program 4.6

The following table indicates the maximum permitted span for each available size of floor joists (with joists spaced 600mm apart).

cross section (mm x mm)	maximum span (metres)
50 x 75	0.92
50 x 100	1.55
50 x 125	2.29
50 x 150	2.81
50 x 175	3.27
50 x 200	3.72
50 x 225	4.18

The program is to accept as input a value representing a required span and then uses the above table to find the minimum size of joist which can be employed. The table is assumed to be stored in a text file from which it can be read each time the program is obeyed (see Appendix 5).

```
      PROGRAM spans(input, output, maxspan);
      VAR maxspan : text;
          xsect    : ARRAY[1..7] OF integer;
          span    : ARRAY[1..7] OF real;
          requiredspan : real; i : integer;
      BEGIN
        reset(maxspan);
        FOR i := 1 TO 7 DO
         read(maxspan, xsect[i], span[i]);

        read(requiredspan);
        i := 0;
        REPEAT
         i := i + 1
        UNTIL  requiredspan <= span[i];

        writeln('xsect required for a span of', requiredspan,
               'is 50x',xsect[i])
      END.
```

Strictly speaking as it stands this program does not require the
use of an array. The data could be read directly each time from a
file. However, it could be part of a much larger program other
parts of which used the same data.

4.2 Two-dimensional arrays

Many techniques in science, engineering and commerce deal with
data which is organized in two dimensions. Pictures from
interplanetary explorers, for example, are enhanced and analyzed
by computer. The pictures are represented inside the computer as a
two-dimensional table of numbers. Each number corresponds to the
brightness of a picture element or point. A picture is converted
into a table of numbers by a special input device and after it is
processed, it is converted back into a picture by a special output
device. It is much easier and more natural for a programmer to
think in terms of a two-dimensional set of picture elements - the
picture retaining its two-dimensional form when referred to in the
program - than it would be if the picture elements were strung out
row-wise or column-wise into a one-dimensional array or list.

   Consider a simpler example - an 8x10 table of numbers (8 rows,
10 columns), where each number represents the population of the
corresponding zone of an 8x10 square mile map. We can retain the
two-dimensional nature of the data by storing it in a two-
dimensional array "popmap". First of all let us see how we declare
such an array.

      VAR popmap : ARRAY [1..8, 1..10] OF integer;

This declaration has set up a two-dimensional structure of integer
variables into which we can place the data. It is usual to picture
a two-dimensional array as a collection of variables, all of the
same type, organized into rows and columns.

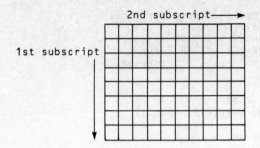

1st subscript

2nd subscript——————▶

where the first subscript determines a row and the second subscript determines a column. For example "popmap[3,7]" refers to the location in the 3rd row and the 7th column of the array. Thus the declared array corresponds in size and shape to the table of data that we are considering. It is equally valid to set up a two-dimensional array in Pascal as an array of arrays:

```
    VAR  popmap : ARRAY[1..8] OF ARRAY[1..10] OF integer;
```

but perhaps most engineering pragmatists would prefer the former declaration.

To do something systematically with all the locations of a two-dimensional array, we need to use a nested FOR statement. For example, if we wish to deal with the array a row at a time we need the outline structure:

```
    FOR row := 1 TO 8 DO

        deal with row
```

and dealing with a row involves a further loop:

```
    FOR column := 1 TO 10 DO

        deal with the location popmap[row,column]
```

The next example illustrates this.

Program 4.7

This program reads the population table described above (from a text file), stores it in a suitable array, calculates the total population and prints a copy of the population table.

```
PROGRAM population(popfile, output);

VAR popmap : ARRAY [1..8,1..10] OF integer;
    popfile: text;
    row, column, total : integer;

BEGIN
    reset(popfile);
    FOR row := 1 TO 8 DO
        FOR column := 1 TO 10 DO
            read(popfile, popmap[row,column]);

    total := 0;
    FOR row := 1 TO 8 DO
        FOR column := 1 TO 10 DO
            total := total + popmap[row,column];

    writeln('total population is ', total);  writeln;

    writeln('populations of individual zones are:');
    FOR row := 1 TO 8 DO
    BEGIN
        writeln;
        FOR column := 1 TO 10 DO
            write(popmap[row,column])
    END
END.
```

The first nested FOR statement causes the data to be read into the
two-dimensional array "popmap", the second accesses the array,
performing the required calculation, and the third causes the
contents of the array to be printed. When the data file for this
program is set up, the 10 numbers in the first row of the table
are typed first and these will be stored in the first row of the
array. Then the 10 numbers in the second row are typed, and so on.
Incidentally, the processes of reading the data and accumulating
the total could have been carried out simultaneously, the first
two nested loops being merged into a single nested loop. This
could not be easily done in the next program.

Program 4.8

Reads data as in Program 4.7. In addition it reads four numbers
defining a sub-region on the map over which the population is to
be added. For example, input of 2 6 3 5 specifies the region
lying between rows 2 and 6 and between columns 3 and 5:

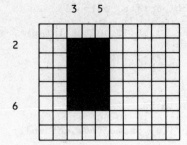

```
PROGRAM popmap2(popfile, output);

VAR popmap : ARRAY [1..8,1..10] OF integer;
    popfile: text;
    row, col, rowa, cola, rowb, colb, subtotal : integer;

BEGIN
   reset(popfile);
   FOR row := 1 TO 8 DO
      FOR col := 1 TO 10 DO
         read(popfile, popmap[row,col]);

   subtotal := 0;
   read(rowa, rowb, cola, colb);

   FOR row := rowa TO rowb DO
      FOR col := cola TO colb DO
         subtotal := subtotal + popmap[row,col];

   writeln('population of sub-zone is ', subtotal)
END.
```

Program 4.9

Reads data as in Program 4.7 and finds every zone with a
population less than half the average of its north, south, east
and west neighbours.

```
PROGRAM popmap3(input,output);

VAR popmap : ARRAY [1..8,1..10] OF integer;
    row, col : integer;  average : real;

BEGIN
   FOR row := 1 TO 8 DO
      FOR col := 1 TO 10 DO
      read(popmap[row,col]);

   FOR row := 2 TO 7 DO
      FOR col := 2 TO 9 DO
      BEGIN
         average := (popmap[row-1,col]
                    +popmap[row+1,col]
                    +popmap[row,col-1]
                    +popmap[row,col+1])/4;
         IF popmap[row,col] < average/2
         THEN writeln('the region ', row, col,
                      ' is underpopulated')
      END
END.
```

The next program illustrates random access to a two-dimensional
array.

Program 4.10

A student's week is divided up into 5 days, each of 6 periods
numbered 1..6. He must attend 20 lectures during each week. The
program reads a list of his lecture times and places. Each lecture
time is represented by two integers giving the day (1..5) and the
period (1..6) and these two integers are followed by the number of
the room (a positive integer) in which the lecture takes place.

The program prints a timetable for the student in the form:

			period			
	1	2	3	4	5	6
mon	3	1	2	9		
tue	6	6	5	7	6	
wed		2	1			
thu	5	2	5		8	7
fri	3	2	1	3		

where the entry for each period represents the room number in
which he should be. We assume that the input data is such that
there are no timetable clashes.

```
PROGRAM times(input,output);

VAR day, period, room, lecture : integer;
    place : ARRAY [1..5,1..6] OF integer;

BEGIN

{ use zeros to mark all periods as free }
    FOR day := 1 TO 5 DO
        FOR period := 1 TO 6 DO
            place[day,period] := 0;

{ now fill in appropriate periods with room number }
    FOR lecture := 1 TO 20 DO
    BEGIN
        read(day,period,room);
        place[day,period] := room;
    END;

{ now print the timetable }
    writeln('period':28);
    writeln('1  2  3  4  5  6':34);
    writeln('----------------':34);

    FOR day := 1 TO 5 DO
    BEGIN
        CASE day OF
            1 : write('mon');
            2 : write('tue');
            3 : write('wed');
            4 : write('thu');
            5 : write('fri')
        END;

        write('       ');
        FOR period := 1 TO 6 DO
            IF place[day,period] = 0 THEN
                        write('   ')
            ELSE  write(place[day,period]:3);

        writeln
    END
END.
```

4.3 More about subscripts

Previously we have utilized arrays with the subscript range
starting at 1. There are many contexts in which we may require a
subscript range to start at some integer other than 1. Consider
again our price list example:

    VAR priceof : ARRAY [1..100] OF real;

Such a declaration would mean that we could use in our program the

100

integers 1..100 as reference numbers. However, the following declaration:

```
VAR priceof : ARRAY [99..199] OF real;
```

would mean that we could use the integers 99..199 as reference numbers.

Program 4.11

A mail order company stocks 563 different items with reference numbers 3001 to 3563. The program reads a list of prices in order of reference number. The program then reads a list of items required by a customer. Each item is specified by a reference number followed by the quantity required, and the last item is followed immediately by the terminating character '*'. The total cost of the customer's order is printed.

```
PROGRAM sale(input,output);

CONST minref = 3001; maxref = 3563;
VAR priceof : ARRAY [minref..maxref] OF real;
    ref, nextref, quantity : integer;
    totalprice : real; nextch : char;

BEGIN
   FOR nextref := minref TO maxref DO
      read(priceof[nextref]);

   totalprice := 0;
   REPEAT
      read(ref,quantity);
      totalprice := totalprice + priceof[ref]*quantity;
      read(nextch)
   UNTIL nextch = '*';

   writeln('total cost of order is ', totalprice)
END.
```

Note that in this example we have used two named constants to define the subscript range. A subscript range must be defined in terms of **constant** values, named or otherwise.

4.4 Matrix operations

There are no predefined matrix operations available in Pascal (as there are for example in BASIC) so these have to be programmed in full using FOR statements. The only exception to this is assignment. Arrays can be assigned by referring to the array name only, but the two arrays must be identical both in subscript range and component type. Thus:

```
CONST  min = 1;  max = 500;
VAR    x, y : ARRAY[min..max] OF real;
         .
         .
         .
       x := y
```

is a valid assignment in Pascal.

The main properties of matrices required in practice are those of inversion, addition, subtraction, multiplication and transposition. Inversion is covered in one of the exercises for Chapter 9. Addition is defined as:

C = A + B

where

$$c_{ij} = a_{ij} + b_{ij}$$

Matrices A and B must be of the same order (same number of rows and columns). The Pascal is straightforward:

```
VAR a, b, c : ARRAY[1..m, 1..n] OF real;
         .
         .
         .
FOR i := 1 TO m DO
  FOR j := 1 TO n DO
    c[i,j] := a[i,j] + b[i,j];
```

The transpose of matrix A called A' is derived from A by interchanging rows and columns:

$$a'_{ji} = a_{ij}$$

For example:

```
VAR a  : ARRAY[1..m, 1..n] OF real;
    at : ARRAY[1..n, 1..m] OF real;
         .
         .
         .
FOR i := 1 TO m DO
  FOR j := 1 TO n DO
    at[j,i] := a[i,j];
```

Finally the product of two matrices A(lxm) and B(mxn) is a matrix C(lxn) where:

$$c_{ij} = \sum_{k=1}^{m} a_{ik} b_{kj}$$

This operation of course requires three nested FOR statements:

```
    VAR a : ARRAY[1..l, 1..m] OF real;
        b : ARRAY[1..m, 1..n] OF real;
        c : ARRAY[1..l, 1..n] OF real;
        :
        :
    FOR i := 1 TO l DO
      FOR j := 1 TO n DO
      sum := 0;
      BEGIN
        FOR k := 1 TO m DO
          sum := sum + a[i,k]*b[k,j];
        c[i,j] := sum;
      END;
```

Exercises

(1) Write a program that reads a price list for 100 items from a
    text file. The program is then to read a list of quantities
    required by a customer, for example:

5	means 5 of item 1
10	means 10 of item 2
0	means 0 of item 3
12	means 12 of item 4
.	.
.	.
27	means 27 of item 100

The program should calculate the total cost of the customer's
order.

(2) As Exercise 1 but this time the customer's order is specified
    as a list of pairs where each pair contains an item number
    followed by the quantity required. The last quantity is
    followed immediately by the character '*'. The item numbers
    appear in any order. The program should check that each item
    number input does in fact exist.

(3) Write a program that accepts input from a file of thirty
    daily temperature readings in the range -20 to 40. The
    program is to draw a graph of the following form:

```
        1                    +   *
        2                    + *
        3                    *+
        4                *   +
        5                *+
        6                 +   *
        7                 +      *
             etc.
```

where the distance of a '*' from the left represents a

temperature reading and the position of the '+'s represents the average reading over the whole period.

(4) A text file contains 20 real values that represent the standard thicknesses (in millimetres) in which a sheet material is manufactured. Write a program that uses this file to initialise an array. The program should then repeatedly read a required thickness from the keyboard and report the closest available standard thickness.

(5) Write a program that accepts input of 30 vectors, each consisting of 10 values. The program should output the sum vector, where the first value in the sum vector is the sum of the first values in the input vectors, the second value in the sum vector is the sum of the second values in the input vectors, and so on.

(6) Each day in a college's weekly timetable is divided into seven periods. The timetable for a course consists of a list of five periods during which the course is given, where a period is represented by two numbers, the first giving the day of the week (1 = Monday, 2 = Tuesday, etc.) and the second giving the number of the period on that day.

Write a program that accepts as input the timetables for the 6 courses a pupil wishes to attend, and which tells him whether he has any timetable clashes.

(7) Write a program that will read and add fifteen 10x10 matrices.

(8) A particular photo-micrograph contains a single simple convex shape, such as a circle, represented as a dark area on a light background. Such images are commonly represented in computers as two-dimensional arrays, where each element has the value 1 or 0. A dark area on a light background becomes a group of 1's surrounded by 0's.

Write a program that will accept such an array as input. The program should display the shape of the dark region by printing the points on the boundary as 1's and the background and interior points as spaces. Test your program on a 10x10 array.
Hint: Scan the image row-wise or column-wise. For a given 1, if any of the surrounding points are 0's, then that 1 represents a boundary point.

(9) Write a program that accepts as input a photomicrograph of the type described in Exercise 8. The program should calculate the ratio of the area of the dark region to its perimeter. As a measure of the area, count the number of ones. A (rather inaccurate) measure of the perimeter can be obtained by counting the number of boundary points and you should use this in your program. As a more difficult exercise, you might like to think about how to obtain a more accurate measure of the length of the boundary. (Two diagonally adjacent boundary points would make a contribution

of sqrt(2) to such a measure.)

(10) Write a program that will read an integer n (n<=40) followed
by a matrix of 'bits' representing information about
electrical connections between n terminals numbered 1 to n.
Each bit is either 1 or 0 where a 1 in row i and column j
indicates that terminal i is directly connected to terminal
j. Each terminal is treated as being directly connected to
itself. The program is to construct and print a new matrix
where element i,j in the new matrix is 1 if terminals i and j
are either directly connected or connected indirectly via a
single intermediate terminal.
Hint: The process required to form the new matrix is very
similar to the process of matrix multiplication.

5 Procedures and functions

A procedure is a section of program to which a name has been given. The programmer can then write the name of the procedure wherever he wants that section of program to be obeyed. This has two main advantages:

Firstly, if the named operation has to be carried out at several different places in a large program, we avoid writing out the same section of program in full at each place.

Secondly, careful use of procedures can make a large program easier to write and easier for other people to read. For example, in a payroll program we might have a sequence of operations such as

```
addnormalhourspay;
addovertimehourspay;
deductincometax
```

where the details of each named operation are defined elsewhere. This makes it much easier to understand what the program is doing than would be the case if the program text for each calculation were written out in full here.

5.1 Introductory example

We shall introduce the idea of giving a name to a section of Pascal program by writing a program that solves three separate pairs of simultaneous equations in two variables. An outline what the program will do is as follows:

```
writeln('First pair of equations:');
SolveEquations;
writeln; writeln('Second pair of equations:');
SolveEquations;
writeln; writeln('Third pair of equations:');
SolveEquations
```

We could of course have organized this as a loop to be executed three times, but for the purpose of introducing procedures we prefer to use the above structure. The process that we call "SolveEquations" will be the same as that used in Program 1.5, except that in this case, this process is used at three different places in our program. Each occurrence of "SolveEquations" in the outline program could be replaced in full by a copy of the statements that were used in Program 1.5 to solve a pair of simultaneous equations. Instead of repeating these statements three times, we shall give a name to this section of program by writing it separately as a **procedure declaration:**

Program 5.1

Solves three pairs of simultaneous linear equations.

```
PROGRAM threepairs(input, output);

   PROCEDURE SolveEquations;
     VAR a1,b1,c1, a2,b2,c2, x, y : real;
   BEGIN
      write('Equation 1 coefficients:');  readln(a1, b1, c1);
      write('Equation 2 coefficients:');  readln(a2, b2, c2);
      x := (b1*c2 - b2*c1)/(a2*b1 - a1*b2);
      y := (a1*c2 - a2*c1)/(a1*b2 - a2*b1);
      writeln('x = ', x:6:2, ',  y = ', y:6:2)
   END;

   BEGIN
      writeln('First pair of equations:');
      SolveEquations;
      writeln;  writeln('Second pair of equations:');
      SolveEquations;
      writeln;  writeln('Third pair of equations:');
      SolveEquations
   END.
```

The procedure definition or **declaration** has been inserted after the variable declarations at the start of the program. "SolveEquations" is the name of the procedure and we can insert an instruction to go and obey the procedure at any point in the program by simply writing the name of the procedure. Such an instruction is known as a **procedure call.**

When the computer executes this program, the first statement obeyed is the first statement in the list between the main BEGIN...END of the program. The instructions within the procedure declaration are not obeyed until a procedure call is encountered. Thus the above program behaves as if the text of the procedure definition were substituted in place of each call of the procedure.

Notice that the structure of a procedure declaration is exactly like that of a miniature program. In fact, the only difference between Program 1.5 and the procedure of Program 5.1 is the heading. A procedure can contain declarations of constants and variables intended for use only within itself. It can even contain another procedure declaration. The following program further illustrates the declaration and use of variables within a procedure.

Program 5.2

A manufacturer has two identical machines, each of which is producing ball-bearings. The diameters of a sample of 10 ball bearings from the first machine are to be typed as input to a computer program and are to be followed by the diameters of a sample of 10 ball-bearings from the second machine. This program accepts the two sets of 10 measurements. It calculates and prints the average of the first 10 values, the average of the second 10 values and then prints the overall average for the 20 values supplied.

```
PROGRAM average20(input,output);

VAR overallsum : real;

    PROCEDURE average10;
    VAR count : integer;  next, sum10 : real;
    BEGIN
        sum10 := 0;
        FOR count := 1 TO 10 DO
        BEGIN
            read(next);
            sum10 := sum10 + next
        END;
        writeln('average of 10 readings :', sum10/10);
        overallsum := overallsum + sum10
    END;

BEGIN
    overallsum := 0;
    average10;
    average10;
    writeln('overall average :', overallsum/20)
END.
```

In the above program, the variable "overallsum" is declared at the start of the program and can be used anywhere in the program, even within the procedure. Such a variable is called a **global** variable. The variables "count", "next", and "sum10" on the other hand are used only within the procedure "average10" and are therefore declared within this procedure. Variables declared at the start of a procedure in this way **cannot** be used outside the procedure definition. We describe the variables "count", "next" and "sum10" as being **local** to the procedure. Storage space for these variables is allocated each time the procedure is called and the space is freed for possible use by other variables elsewhere in the program when the procedure terminates. It is recommended that any variable which is used only within a particular procedure should be declared locally to that procedure. The computer will then ensure that the programmer does not accidentally use the same variable for conflicting purposes in different parts of a large program. In fact, any variable used as a control variable in a FOR loop **must** be declared locally - for example "count" in the above program.

In the above programs, defining a procedure saved us from writing exactly the same piece of program out in detail twice. We shall explain later how a procedure can be given **parameters** telling it which values or variables to process on a particular occasion. The same procedure can then be used to perform similar, but not necessarily identical, operations on different occasions. We first draw attention to an important application of simple procedures - their use in making programs easier to write and easier to read.

5.2 The use of simple procedures in stepwise refinement

It was suggested in Chapter 3 that we should start planning a program by writing an outline description of the process that we want carried out, giving meaningful names to any sub-processes involved. Programming these sub-processes can then be tackled in the same way, almost as if they were separate programming problems. By adopting this technique of stepwise refinement, we never get involved in considering a program or section of program in more detail than our minds can cope with at one time.

For example, the outline description of our program for analyzing traffic data (Program 3.5) was as follows:

FOR surveypoint := 1 TO 27 DO

analyze the data from one survey point

The outline program for analyzing the data from one survey point included a line that referred to a further sub-process:

test next length for long vehicle

Previously, the complete program was written by replacing the line

analyze the data from one survey point

by the more detailed Pascal description, in which the line

test next length for long vehicle

was in turn replaced by an appropriate IF statement. We now demonstrate how we could instead make the structure of the program match the way in which it was designed. Each process, to which a name was given while planning the program, is defined as a separate procedure. This makes the program considerably easier to understand or modify at a later date, because the different stages involved in planning the program correspond clearly to separate sections of the text of the program. This is particularly important if, as is often the case, the person responsible for maintaining and modifying a program is not the original programmer.

Program 5.3

A version of Program 3.5 in which named procedures are used to make clear the stepwise refinement process used in designing the program.

```
PROGRAM longvehicles(input,output);

CONST long = 5.0;

VAR surveypoint, longvehicles : integer;
    nextlength : real;

  PROCEDURE checksurveypoint;

    PROCEDURE testnextvehicle;
    BEGIN
        IF nextlength >= long THEN
            longvehicles := longvehicles + 1;
    END;

  BEGIN { checksurveypoint }
      longvehicles := 0;
      read(nextlength);

      REPEAT
          testnextvehicle;
          read(nextlength)
      UNTIL nextlength < 0;

      writeln('Survey point:', surveypoint:2, '    ',
              'Long vehicles:', longvehicles:4)
  END;

BEGIN  { main program }
    FOR surveypoint := 1 TO 27 DO
        checksurveypoint
END.
```

When attempting to read and understand a program like the above, always start by looking at the main **block** of the program between the main BEGIN...END. Once you understand the outline structure of the program, you can then go on to examine any procedures that are called from the main block. These procedures should be read in the same way - first read the main block of the procedure definition and then go on to look at the definitions of the procedures that are used there. By doing this you will be working through the program in the same order as that in which it was originally written. Finally, note the way in which comments have been inserted after two of the BEGINs in order to make it clearer to the human reader which BEGIN belongs to which procedure.

Exercises

(1) Rewrite Program 3.4, using procedures to reflect its logical structure.

(2) Rewrite Program 3.9, using procedures to reflect its logical structure.

(3) Write a program that solves a quadratic equation, given the coefficients as input. The main block of the program should include the statement:

```
IF abs(determinant) < 0.0001 THEN equalroots
ELSE IF determinant > 0 THEN realroots
                              ELSE imaginaryroots
```

where the three procedures are defined appropriately.

5.3 Simple parameters

We have seen how simple procedures can be used to enable a program to carry out the **same** operation at different points in a program. A much more common requirement is for **similar,** but not necessarily identical, operations to be carried out at different points in a program.

For example, in Program 1.6, the operation used to calculate the number of 50p pieces to be included in the change was very similar to the operation used for each of the other coin denominations. We can reprogram this process using a procedure as follows:

```
write('Change?');  readln(change);

howmany(50);  howmany(20);
howmany(10);  howmany( 5);
howmany( 2);  howmany( 1)
```

The intention here is that "howmany" is the name of a procedure that is going to be used six times. Each time the procedure is called, it is supplied with a **parameter** in brackets telling it which denomination of coin to deal with next. The complete program is as follows:

Program 5.4

An alternative version of Program 1.6.

```
PROGRAM coinanalysis(input, output);
VAR change : integer;

    PROCEDURE howmany(denomination : integer);
    VAR noofcoins : integer;
    BEGIN
        noofcoins := change DIV denomination;
        change := change MOD denomination;
        writeln('No of ', denomination:2, 's ', noofcoins)
    END;

BEGIN
    write('Change?'); readln(change);
    howmany(50); howmany(20);
    howmany(10); howmany( 5);
    howmany( 2); howmany( 1)
END.
```

In the procedure definition, or declaration, the operation to be carried out by the procedure is specified in terms of "denomination", which is a parameter. When the procedure is called, this parameter is given an actual value which is to be used when the procedure is obeyed. Thus, obeying the statement

        howmany(50)

causes the procedure definition to be obeyed with the parameter "denomination" set to the value 50. Similarily, obeying the statement

        howmany(20)

causes the procedure to be obeyed with the parameter "denomination" set to the value 20.

A parameter supplied in brackets when the procedure is called is usually referred to as an **actual parameter.**

A procedure with parameters will perform some general task defined in terms of these parameters. When the parameters are given actual values, the procedure performs a particular version of the general task. Such a facility is extremely important in modern programming.

As an example of a procedure with two parameters, consider:

```
PROCEDURE tabulate(x : real; n : integer);
VAR i : integer;
BEGIN
    writeln('Table of multiples of ', x:6:2);  writeln;
    FOR i := 1 TO n DO writeln(i*x :6:2);
    writeln
END;
```

This procedure is defined in terms of two parameters, "x" and "n".
In this case, these are of different types, and parameters of
different types must be separated from each other in the procedure
heading by semicolons.

When this procedure is called, multiples of the real supplied
as its first parameter are printed, the number of multiples being
specified as a value for the second parameter. For example, if we
call the procedure as follows:

```
tabulate(3.72, 4)
```

"x" is given the value 3.72, "n" is given the value 4 and the
procedure definition is obeyed. Output is therefore:

```
Table of multiples of   3.72

 3.72
 7.44
11.16
14.88
```

Notice that when a procedure is called, the actual parameters used
in the procedure call are always separated by commas.

The actual parameters supplied to this procedure can in fact be
any two expressions of appropriate type. For example, if "r" is a
real variable and "noofmultiples" is an integer variable, then the
fragment:

```
r := 4.3; noofmultiples := 5;
tabulate(r, noofmultiples);
tabulate(sqr(sqr(r)), 2*noofmultiples)
```

will tabulate the first 5 multiples of 4.3 and the first 10
multiples of the fourth power of 4.3.

If "a" is an "ARRAY[1..4] OF real", then the fragment:

```
FOR i := 1 TO 4 DO
    tabulate(a[i], 10)
```

will call the procedure 4 times and output 4 tables, one for each
entry in the array "a".

As we have seen, the type of each parameter of a procedure must
be specified in the procedure heading. However, when a procedure

involves a group of parameters of the same type, the names of these parameters can be listed together, separated by commas, with the type specified once at the end of the list. Parameters of different types still have to be separated from each other by semicolons. The following example of a procedure heading should make this clear:

```
PROCEDURE demo(i,j :integer;  x,y,z,t :real;  b :boolean);

BEGIN

        definition of the procedure

END;
```

Remember that all parameters are separated by commas when the procedure is called. This procedure could be called as follows:

```
demo(256, 73, 26.45, 72.6, 18.253, 3.142, true)
```

As we mentioned earlier, a procedure definition can include declarations of other procedures, for its own local use:

Program 5.5

This program reads two positive integers and prints them in descending order. The integers are to be output on separate lines and, when an integer is output, the millions are to be followed by a comma and the thousands are to be followed by a comma. Thus, instead of writing 5674251 the program should write 5,671,251 (This program will not work on a Pascal system where the maximum permitted integer is less than 1000000.)

```
        PROGRAM compare(input,output);

        VAR first, second : integer;

            PROCEDURE commawrite(n : integer);
            VAR millions, thousands, units : integer;

                PROCEDURE zerowrite(m : integer);
                BEGIN
                    IF m < 100 THEN write('0');
                    IF m < 10 THEN write('0');
                    write(m:1)
                END;
```

```
BEGIN { commawrite }
    millions := n DIV 1000000;
    thousands := (n MOD 1000000) DIV 1000;
    units := n MOD 1000;
    IF millions > 0 THEN
    BEGIN
        write(millions:1, ',');
        zerowrite(thousands); write(',');
        zerowrite(units)
    END
    ELSE
        IF thousands > 0 THEN
        BEGIN
            write(thousands:1, ',');
            zerowrite(units)
        END
        ELSE write(units:1);

    writeln
END; { commawrite }

BEGIN { main program }
    read(first, second);
    IF first > second THEN
    BEGIN
        commawrite(first);  commawrite(second)
    END
    ELSE
    BEGIN
        commawrite(second);  commawrite(first)
    END
END.
```

Remember to read the main block of the program first. In this case, the main block is straightforward, provided that we avoid getting bogged down in the problems involved in printing a number with the commas inserted. Designing the procedure "commawrite" can then be viewed as a programming problem which is rather easier than the original problem. The need for the procedure "zerowrite" arises because, for example, a number of thousands has to be written with a full three digits in the context of a number like 2,067,003. In the number 67,003 the thousands are printed with no extra zeros, and a normal write statement is used. The format ":1" is used to ensure that an integer is printed with no extra spaces. This is explained in Appendix 4.

5.4 Variable parameters

In the procedures of the previous two sections, a parameter was always used for specifying a **value** which was to be processed when the procedure is called. As another example of this, consider the following procedure declaration:

```
      PROCEDURE process(x : integer);
      BEGIN
         writeln(x);
         writeln(x*x)
      END;
```

When this procedure is called, the parameter corresponding to "x"
can be any expression representing an integer **value**. For example,
provided that the variable "a" and the array location "mark[2,3]"
each contain an integer value, then each of the following
statements are valid calls of this procedure:

```
      process(5742);
      process(a);
      process(a*5 + 32);
      process(mark[2,3]);
      process(mark[2,3]*3 + 564)
```

Such parameters are known as **value parameters.**

   When a procedure is called, a value parameter can be used only
for transferring information **into** the procedure. We sometimes
require to use a parameter to transfer information **out** of the
procedure back to the calling section of program. This is done by
giving the procedure a **variable** parameter which tells the
procedure where to put the required information.

   We illustrate the use of a variable parameter by writing a
program that reads two lists of sample values (the results of two
surveys perhaps). The mean of the first set of values is to be
compared with the mean of the second set of values and a message
output indicating which sample had the larger mean. An outline of
what the program must do is as follows:

      **Calculate the mean of the first sample and
         put the result in** "sample1mean";

      **Calculate the mean of the second sample and
         put the result in** "sample2mean";

      IF sample1mean > sample2mean THEN
         writeln('Sample 1 has the larger mean.')
      ELSE
         :
         :

we shall define a procedure "calculateaverage" which can be used
as follows:

```
      writeln('First sample:');
      calculateaverage(sample1mean);

      writeln('Second sample:');
      calculateaverage(sample2mean);
```

Here, we require the procedure to place a value in a **variable,**
which is supplied as a parameter when the procedure is called, and

116

this has to be indicated in the procedure heading.

Program 5.6

Compares the means of two separate sets of sample values. Each sample is terminated by a '*'.

```
PROGRAM CompareSamples(input, output);

VAR sample1mean, sample2mean : real;

    PROCEDURE calculateaverage(VAR mean : real);
    VAR next, total : real;  count : integer;
    BEGIN
       count := 0;  total := 0;
       REPEAT
          read(next);
          count := count+1;
          total := total + next
       UNTIL input↑ = '*';
       get(input);
       mean := total/count
    END;

BEGIN { main program }

    writeln('First sample:');
    calculateaverage(sample1mean);

    writeln('Second sample:');
    calculateaverage(sample2mean);

    IF sample1mean > sample2mean THEN
       writeln('Sample 1 has the larger mean.')
    ELSE IF sample2mean > sample1mean THEN
          writeln('Sample 2 has the larger mean.')
       ELSE writeln('Samples have the same mean.')
             { The last possibility is highly unlikely }
             { to occur when processing real data.     }
END.
```


In general, if a procedure is to be called with the intention of changing one of its parameters by assigning a value to that parameter or by reading a value into it, then that parameter must be preceded by the word VAR in the procedure heading. This is the case with the parameter "mean" in the above program. When the procedure is called by

    calculateaverage(sample1mean);

the procedure is obeyed with "mean" referring to the same storage location as "sample1mean". Thus, when the statement

```
mean := total/count
```

is obeyed, the computer behaves on this occasion as if it was obeying

```
sample1mean := total/count
```

The result of obeying the procedure on this occasion is to place the mean of the first sample in the variable "sample1mean". Later, when the procedure is obeyed as a result of

```
calculateaverage(sample2mean)
```

the reference to "mean" behaves like a reference to "sample2mean". This call of the procedure places the mean of the second sample in the variable "sample2mean".

It would clearly be **wrong** for a call of the procedure "calculateaverage" to have a constant or expression as its parameter.

```
calculateaverage(2)
```

or
```
calculateaverage(sample1mean + sample2mean)
```

would be silly. The procedure expects to be told **where to put** a value and must therefore be given the name of a variable or an array location as its actual parameter. We could declare an array such as

```
VAR samplemean : ARRAY[1..3] OF real;
```

and call the procedure by, for example,

```
calculateaverage(samplemean[1]);
calculateaverage(samplemean[2]);
calculateaverage(samplemean[3]);
```

or equivalently

```
FOR s := 1 TO 3 DO
    calculateaverage(samplemean[s]);
```

In this case, three sets of sample values would have to be supplied as input.

There is no reason why a procedure should not be supplied with an actual VAR parameter which already has a value stored in it. Any such value can be operated on during the execution of the procedure. As an example, we will write a program which reads three numbers and prints them in descending order. To do this, the numbers will be read and stored in the order in which they are input in three variables: "first", "second" and "third". The program will then rearrange the numbers as follows:

order the two numbers in "first" **and** "second";
{ this may involve swapping their contents }

order the two numbers now in "first" **and** "third";
{ "first" now contains the largest number }

order the two numbers now in "second" **and** "third"

We shall define a procedure which will examine the contents of two specified variables and, if necessary, swap their contents so as to ensure that the larger number is in the first variable and the smaller number is in the other. This procedure will be used as follows:

```
order(first, second);
order(first, third);
order(second, third)
```

Program 5.7

Reads three numbers and prints them in descending order.

```
PROGRAM sort3numbers(input,output);

VAR first, second, third : integer;

    PROCEDURE order(VAR a,b : integer);
    VAR temp : integer;
    BEGIN
       IF a < b THEN
       BEGIN
          temp := a;
          a := b;
          b := temp
       END
    END;

BEGIN
    read(first, second, third);
    order(first, second);
    order(first, third);
    order(second, third);
    writeln(first:6, second:6, third:6)
END.
```

Finally, note that in a procedure heading variable parameters must be grouped separately from other parameters, the groups being separated from each other by semicolons. The following procedure takes two values and puts their sum in one variable and their product in another:

```
      PROCEDURE addandmultiply(value1, value2 : real;
                              VAR sum, product : real);
      BEGIN
         sum := value1 + value2;
         product := value1 * value2
      END;
```

This procedure might be called as follows:

```
      VAR x, y, sum1, prod1 : real;
         a, b : ARRAY [1..10] OF real;
         ⋮
         ⋮
         addandmultiply(3.4, 7.2, x, y);
         addandmultiply(x + 3.7, y + 4.3, sum1, prod1);
         addandmultiply(23.72, 63.15, a[1], b[1])
         ⋮
         ⋮
```

To summarize:

A value parameter can be used only for transmitting information
into a procedure.

A variable parameter is used when we require information to be
transmitted out of the procedure.

5.5 Array parameters

In this section, we describe how an array can be used as the
parameter of a procedure. To introduce the techniques required,
consider the following simple problem.

Fred and Joe have each taken six examination papers. Write a
program which will read the six marks obtained by Fred followed by
the six marks obtained by Joe. The program should calculate the
total marks obtained by each candidate and should then print the
six individual paper marks and the total mark for each candidate.
The marks for the candidate with the higher total mark should be
printed first.

The outline structure of this program will be as follows:

```
        VAR fredsmarks, joesmarks : ARRAY [1..6] OF integer;
            fredstotal, joestotal : integer;
              :
    BEGIN
        readandadd(fredsmarks, fredstotal);
        readandadd(joesmarks, joestotal);
        IF fredstotal > joestotal THEN
        BEGIN
            write('fred: '); writeout(fredsmarks, fredstotal);
            write('joe:  '); writeout(joesmarks,  joestotal )
        END
        ELSE
        BEGIN
            write('joe:  '); writeout(joesmarks,  joestotal );
            write('fred: '); writeout(fredsmarks, fredstotal)
        END
    END.
```

The procedure call

```
    readandadd(fredsmarks, fredstotal)
```

is intended to read 6 numbers into the array "fredsmarks" and add
these numbers together, putting the total in "fredstotal". This
procedure will be defined in terms of two parameters – an array of
six locations and an integer variable – and in the procedure
declaration, these parameters must be specified as such. However,
a complex type description such as "array[1..6] OF integer" must
not be used to specify the type of a procedure parameter. Only
named types can be used in procedure headings and the above type
must be given a name by inserting a line such as

```
    TYPE marklist = ARRAY [1..6] OF integer;
```

at the start of the program. The name "marklist" can then be used
throughout the rest of the program to describe such an array of
six integers.

Program 5.8


```
    PROGRAM exam(input, output);

    TYPE marklist = ARRAY[1..6] OF integer;

    VAR fredsmarks, joesmarks : marklist;
        fredstotal, joestotal : integer;
```

```
         PROCEDURE readandadd(VAR markfor : marklist;
                              VAR total : integer);
     VAR nextpaper : integer;
     BEGIN
        total := 0;
        FOR nextpaper := 1 TO 6 DO
        BEGIN
           read(markfor[nextpaper]);
           total := total + markfor[nextpaper]
        END;
        writeln;  writeln
     END;

         PROCEDURE writeout(VAR markfor : marklist;
                            total : integer);
     VAR nextpaper : integer;
     BEGIN
        FOR nextpaper := 1 TO 6 DO
           write(markfor[nextpaper] : 3);
        writeln('   total: ', total)
     END;

  BEGIN  { main program }
     write('Freds marks?');   readandadd(fredsmarks, fredstotal);
     write('Joes  marks?');   readandadd(joesmarks, joestotal);
     IF fredstotal > joestotal THEN
     BEGIN
        write('Fred: ');  writeout(fredsmarks, fredstotal);
        write('Joe:  ');  writeout(joesmarks,  joestotal )
     END
     ELSE
     BEGIN
        write('Joe:  ');  writeout(joesmarks,  joestotal );
        write('Fred: ');  writeout(fredsmarks, fredstotal)
     END
  END.
```

For various reasons, an array parameter should always be
specified as a VAR parameter, except in rare circumstances, a
discussion of which is beyond the scope of this book. The effect
of this is that a procedure is always told **where to find** an array
rather than being given copies of all the values stored in it.

Finally, note that the declarations at the head of a program or
at the head of a procedure or function (see next section) must be
in the following order:

(1) CONST declarations
(2) TYPE declarations
(3) VAR   declarations
(4) PROCEDURE and FUNCTION declarations.

5.6 Functions

If the result of some process is a single value then a function is sometimes an elegant alternative to a procedure. We have already seen how to use the standard functions "sqrt", "sqr", "sin", "cos" and so on.

First let us look at the ways in which a function differs from a procedure. Certainly, they are both separate modules of program text referred to by name, but they differ in the way in which they are called. Functions are called by using them in arithmetic expressions - that is the first difference. The second difference is that the result of obeying the function is a single value which replaces the function call in the originating expression. Let us illustrate this by considering:

    y := x + sqrt(2)

When this statement is being obeyed, the computer obeys the definition of the function "sqrt", and a number - the result of obeying the function - replaces the subexpression "sqrt(2)". In the case of a standard function like "sqrt", the definition of the function is already stored as part of the Pascal system, but it is also possible for the programmer to define his own functions. They are declared at the start of a program in a way similar to that in which procedures are declared. A function declared in this way can then be used in exactly the same way as the standard functions.

Program 5.9

This program reads 3 pairs of numbers and adds the larger of the first pair, the larger of the second pair and the larger of the third pair.

```
PROGRAM add(input,output);

VAR a,b,p,q,x,y : real;

   FUNCTION max(first,second : real) : real;
   BEGIN
      IF first > second THEN max := first
      ELSE max := second
   END { of max };

BEGIN
   read(a,b, p,q, x,y);
   writeln(max(a,b) + max(p,q) + max(x,y) :6:2)
END.
```

The effect of calling a function is the calculation of a single result. The result has a type which must be specified. This is done by writing the name of this type after the parameter list in the function heading. The Pascal system can use this type information to ensure that the function is subsequently used in an appropriate context.

Since calling a function produces a single result, we must indicate, somewhere in the function definition, what this result is to be. In the function definition the name of the function is used as if it were the name of a variable to which values can be assigned. When the function is being obeyed, any value assigned to the name of the function is returned as the value of the sub-expression used to call the function.

When the above program is obeyed, evaluation of the sub-expression "max(a,b)" causes the function definition to be obeyed with "first" set to the value of "a" and "second" set to the value of "b". If the function is called when we have the situation

a | 4.79 | b | 5.64 |

then the function definition is obeyed with

first | 4.79 | second | 5.64 |

and the statement

    max := second

is obeyed as a result of obeying the IF statement. The value of the sub-expression "max(a,b)" will therefore be 5.64 and this is the value which will be used in subsequent evaluation of the larger expression:

    max(a,b) + max(p,q) + max(x,y)

If the main body of the program had included a statement such as

        writeln(max(63.45, 61.23))

the function would have been obeyed with

first | 63.45 | second | 61.23 |

and the value returned as the result of the function in this case would be 63.45, this value being printed by the writeln statement. The actual parameters can of course be any expressions that will have real values when the program is obeyed. This means that the actual parameters in a call of the function can themselves involve further function calls. We have already seen how we can do this with the standard functions:

    z := sqrt(sqr(x) + sqr(y));
    writeln(sqr(sqr(sqr(z))))

Our function "max" can be used in the same way:

```
writeln(max(sqrt(2), sqrt(3)))
```

will print

1.73

and

```
writeln( max(max(6.2, 7.4), max(2.3, 9.5)) )
```

will print

9.5

In the last case, the function calls are evaluated as follows:

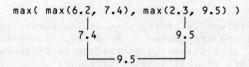

Note that in a function definition you should not attempt to use the name of the function anywhere except on the left of an assignment statement. The use of the function name in any other way within the function definition has a special meaning which is beyond the scope of this book.

The result of a function cannot be a structured type such as an array or a record (see next chapter). Functions can also have variable parameters, but the use of this facility is looked upon as being bad programming practice. A function is intended to be a module of program that operates on actual values and returns a single result. In a context where several results are to be returned via variable parameters, a procedure should be used.

5.7 A final example

As a final illustration of the use of procedures and functions, we present a program that evaluates a polynomial in x for a given value of x and evaluates the derivative of the polynomial for the same value of x.

The following is an outline of what the program will do:

Obtain polynomial coefficients from a file;
Differentiate the polynomial;
write('x = ');   readln(x);
Evaluate and print P(x);
Evaluate and print P'(x)

To evaluate a polynomial, we shall use the technique known as nested multiplication. Given a polynomial of the form:

$$P(x) = a_n x^n + a_{n-1} x^{n-1} + \ldots + a_1 x + a_0$$

it can be most efficiently and conveniently evaluated by rewriting it in the form:

$$P(x) = (\ldots(((a_n x + a_{n-1})x + a_{n-2})x + a_{n-3})x + \ldots + a_1)x + a_0$$

To evaluate the polynomial, we then calculate:

$$s_n = a_n$$
$$s_{n-1} = s_n x + a_{n-1}$$
$$s_{n-2} = s_{n-1} x + a_{n-2}$$
$$\vdots$$
$$P = s_0 = s_1 x + a_0$$

We shall define a function "ValueOfPoly" that implements the above method where the a-values are stored in an array. Differentiating the above polynomial involves reducing the number of terms by one and generating a new set of coefficients given by:

$$P'(x) = n a_n x^{n-1} + (n-1) a_{n-1} x^{n-2} + \ldots + 2 a_2 x + a_1$$

A procedure will be used to generate a new array of coefficients representing the derivative of the polynomial.

Program 5.10


```
PROGRAM EvaluatePolynomial(input, output, polyfile);

CONST degree = 10;

TYPE   terms = 0..degree;
       polynomials = ARRAY [terms] OF real;

VAR    i : terms;   x : real;
       p, pdiff : polynomials;
       polyfile : text;

    FUNCTION ValueOfPoly(VAR a : polynomials;
                             n : terms;  x : real): real;
    VAR total : real; i : terms;
    BEGIN
       total := a[n];
       FOR i := n-1 DOWNTO 0 DO
          total := total*x + a[i];
       ValueOfPoly := total
    END;
```

```
      PROCEDURE DiffPoly(VAR coeff, diffcoeff : polynomials;
                                           n : terms);
      VAR i : terms;
      BEGIN
         FOR i := n-1 DOWNTO 0 DO
            diffcoeff[i] := (i+1)*coeff[i+1]
      END;

   BEGIN  { main program }
      reset(polyfile);
      FOR i := degree DOWNTO 0 DO read(polyfile, p[i]);

      DiffPoly(p, pdiff, degree);

      write('x = ');  readln(x);  writeln;

      writeln('P(', x:5:2, ') = ',
                          ValueOfPoly(p, degree, x) :7:3);
      writeln('P''(', x:5:2, ') = ',
                          ValueOfPoly(pdiff,degree-1,x) :7:3)
   END.
```

Note that if we want a program to output a single quotation mark,
we need to insert two single quotation marks at the appropriate
point in the string. This is necessary to indicate that the
quotation mark does not represent the end of the string.

5.8 Procedure libraries

One of the most important uses of procedures and functions is in
the provision of libraries of useful programs for solving commonly
occurring problems. Such a library takes the form of a collection
of procedures and functions stored on file. A procedure from such
a library can then be incorporated in a user's program. All the
user has to do is to write a program that organizes his data and
calls the procedure with parameters of appropriate type.
Information about how to use a procedure from the procedure
library would be contained in the documentation for the computer
system being used.

    A typical computer system might have procedure libraries for
solving numerical problems, solving optimization problems, using
the graphics facilities on the computer system, performing
statistical analyses, and so on.

Exercises

(4) A motor rally takes place all on one day and, for each car, a
    start time and a finish time are recorded. Each car also has
    a handicap time which is to be subtracted from the true time
    taken for the rally in order to determine an adjusted time.
    Write a program which reads the start time, finish time and
    handicap time for one car and which prints the true time and

the adjusted time for that car. Each time is input as two integers (hours and minutes) separated by a space. The program should do all its calculations in minutes, the conversion from hours and minutes being done by a procedure "readtime" which reads a time in hours and minutes; and the conversion back to hours and minutes being done by a procedure "writetime".

(5) 'Tan' is not a standard Pascal function. Define a Pascal function for evaluating tan and use it in a program that repeatedly evaluates tan(x) for values of x that are input at the keyboard.

(6) Define three Pascal functions for evaluating sinh, cosh and tanh and use these functions in a program that tabulates sinh(x), cosh(x) and tanh(x) for values of x from 0 to 3.5 in steps of 0.1.

(7) Write a program to evaluate the expression

$$x^5 + y^4 + z^3$$

where "x", "y" and "z" are supplied as input. Your program should include a function "power" which can be used to raise a real number to an integer power. For example, the expression:

power(x, 5)

would have the value x^5.

(8) Write a program that accepts the coefficients of a polynomial as input and tabulates the values of the polynomial for values of x from 0 to 10 in steps of 0.2. Use the function of Program 5.10.

(9) Write a function that evaluates the HCF of two integers using the method of Chapter 3, Exercise 9 and use this function in a program that outputs the HCFs of three pairs of numbers.

(10) Given a set of n real values which are stored in an array and which are to be sorted into ascending order, the following Pascal fragment will move all the values in the array closer to their correct positions:

```
FOR i := 2 TO n DO
    IF a[i-1] and a[i] are in the wrong order
    THEN swap the contents of a[i-1] and a[i]
```

The largest value is moved into the last position in the array. If necessary, you should convince yourself that this is so by applying the process to a list of numbers on paper. Thus, if the above fragment is obeyed n-1 times, this will ensure that the contents of the array are in order. Implement this process, making use of a procedure similar to "order" defined in Program 5.7. (Note that this simple sorting technique could be considerably improved.)

(11) The measurement of various parts of a fingerprint results in a sequence of ten real values. Two such sets of measurements can be compared by counting the number of corresponding pairs of values which differ by less than 5% of the larger value. Two fingerprints are classified as similar if this comparison results in a count of seven or more. Write a program which reads a set of measurements for one fingerprint found on the scene of a crime and which then compares that fingerprint with the fingerprints of known criminals whose measurements are to be read as further input. For comparing two sets of fingerprint measurements, your program should use a boolean function which can be used as follows:

        IF similar(foundprint, knownprint) THEN
          .
          .

(12) The output from a black-and-white television camera is a sequence of pictures, and each picture can be digitized as an array of 400x600 integers, each integer indicating the brightness of one point on the picture.

Write a program which reads digitized pictures taken alternately from two cameras. The first camera is directed at a brightly lit object moving against a very dark background. A point on the background appears in a picture as a brightness value less than 5. The output from the program is to be a sequence of digitized pictures from the second camera with the brightly lit object from the first camera superimposed.

It might be convenient to test your program on smaller pictures, of size 4x6 say.

6 Types and data structures

6.1 Scalar types

A scalar type is a type that has a natural ordering imposed on it. Up to now the scalar types that we have met are integer and (trivially) boolean. A common scalar type available in many high level languages is a character.

6.1.1 Handling character data

Hitherto, characters typed as input to our programs have been numeric characters grouped together to represent numbers in the usual way. Many computer applications involve handling non-numeric data. For example, an organization may want to use a computer program to process a list of its customer's names and addresses; a telephone customer account number might be a combination of letters and digits which has to be handled by a computer program; a student of literature might use a computer program to analyze a piece of text that he is studying. Pascal programs usually have to store and process such non-numeric data one character at a time.

Although the Pascal facilities for manipulating character data are not used extensively by scientists and engineers, it is occasionally useful to be able store characters. In this section, we introduce briefly the Pascal type "char".

Program 6.1

This program reads three characters and writes these three characters in reverse order.

```
PROGRAM reverse(input,output);

VAR first, second, third : char;

BEGIN
    read(first, second, third);
    writeln(third, second, first)
END.
```

"First", "second" and "third" are variables in each of which a single character can be stored. If this program is supplied with input:

130

```
bat
```

then after obeying the read statement, the character variables
contain:

first `'b'`   second `'a'`   third `'t'`

As in the case of strings, character values are always written in
quotation marks to avoid confusion with the names of variables. On
this occasion, the write statement has the same effect as

```
write('t', 'a', 'b')
```

If the input is

```
467
```

then the write statement has the effect of

```
write('7', '6', '4')
```

In this last case, you should note that, although the three
characters in the input could be treated as making up a single
number, this program reads and stores the input as three separate
digits, each being stored in a separate character variable.

   Characters stored in character variables can be tested in
various ways. For example, they can be tested for equality or they
can be tested to see if they are in alphabetical order. We shall
not investigate the use of such facilities in detail. In a later
chapter on character graphics, use will be made of arrays of
characters or strings.

6.1.2 Scalar type functions

The function "pred" can be used to obtain the character that comes
immediately before a given character in the ordering - its
'predecessor'. For example

```
writeln(pred('b'), 'b')
```

will print

```
ab
```

Similarly, "succ" is used to obtain the 'successor' of a given
character.

```
ch := 'j';
writeln(pred(ch), ch, succ(ch))
```

will print

```
ijk
```

These two functions can be applied to any scalar type including those now dealt with.

6.1.3 Symbolic or enumerated types

A facility not often found in other scientific high level languages is symbolic types. Pragmatists would perhaps argue over their usefulness but their purpose is to improve program transparency and error protection and thus ease program development. They are sometimes referred to as enumerated types because all possible values are enumerated in a type declaration. For example:

```
TYPE  sex = (male, female);
      colour = (red yellow, blue, green);
      weekday = (sun, mon, tue, wed, thu, fri, sat);
```

These type definitions are then used to define variables:

```
VAR   person, employee : sex;
      birthday : weekday;
      colourofhouse, colourofroom : colour;
```

Error protection is then given by the compiler against such errors as the mis-assignments:

```
person : = 3;
person := yellow
```

where:

```
person := male;
person := female
```

are the only valid assignments. The mis-assignment of 3, say, to "person" is not an unlikely occurrence in a language where it is necessary to represent sex by the integer codes 1 and 2 say. It is also important that as many errors as possible are detected by the compiler. Execution errors are far more difficult to find and such mis-assignments as:

```
person := 3
```

in an inferior language may go completely undetected. Also several errors can be spotted during a compilation, but execution is terminated by a single run-time error. You can perhaps see that error protection by the compiler is not an academic nicety but, some would claim, a vital facility in a modern high level language. 'Narrowing' simple type definitions by enumeration of all values is a significant contribution to this philosophy.

As we have seen user defined types can be assigned to. They can also be used as procedure parameters and in loop control.

```
      drawahousein(red);
      drawahousein(yellow);
      drawahousein(blue);
      drawahousein(green)
```

is equivalent to:

```
      FOR col := red TO green DO
        drawahousein(col)
```

where "drawahousein" might be a procedure controlling a colour
graphics device:

```
      PROCEDURE drawahousein(finish : colour);
```

and "colour" is a symbolic type as introduced earlier.

   The only operators that can be applied to symbolic types are
the relational operators(<, >, =, <>, <=, >=) and set membership
(IN). For example:

```
      IF person = male THEN ...
```

seems a sensible use of the operator = in this context. The
relational operators act on the ordering associated with the
enumeration. Thus for example with the type "weekday" above
"tue > mon" has value TRUE.

```
      TYPE sex = (female, male);
      VAR person1, person2 : sex;
           .
           .
      IF person1 > person2 THEN write('sex of person 1 is male',
                                     'sex of person 2 is female')
```

is a rather meaningless (and contentious!) use of the operator >.
The usefulness of the semantics of the relational operators
depends on the implied semantics of the enumerated type and:

```
      TYPE weekday = (sun, mon, tue, wed, thu, fri, sat);
      VAR  day1, day2 : weekday;
           .
           .
      IF day1 > day2 THEN write('day1 is later in the week')
```

is perhaps a more meaningful use of >.

   Something that you cannot do with enumerated types is read an
enumerated value or write an enumerated value. Values listed for a
given type are simply codes that can be used only within a
program.

```
      day1 := tue;
      write(day1)
```

will produce an error message, as will

```
        read(day2)
```

This is a rather tedious restriction and output for example has to
be handled by a 'side' procedure involving say a CASE statement:

```
        PROCEDURE printday(day : weekday);
        BEGIN
             CASE day OF
               mon  : write('monday');
               tue  : write('tuesday');
                        .
                        .
                     etc.
```

a somewhat absurd state of affairs. Reading is even worse and
would involve character by character analysis of the input. This
is because the values of an enumerated type are stored internally
as numeric codes and the programmer is responsible for the
conversion of these codes into character strings and vice versa.

6.1.4 Subrange types

A subrange type is a facility whereby a user can narrow the
definition of a simple type (technically an ordinal type) such as
"integer" and "char" by defining his own subrange type. Again
error protection is the goal of this facility for the same reasons
given in the previous section. The practical difference between a
subrange type and an enumerated type is that the values of a
subrange type are consecutive or contiguous values taken from an
existing type.

```
        TYPE  year = 1800..2000;
              letter = 'a'..'z';
```

Subrange types are invaluable when working with arrays and this is
their commonest application. They protect against 'subscript out
of range' errors.

```
        CONST maxval   = 100; minval = 1;
        TYPE  bound    =  minval..maxval;
        VAR   data     : ARRAY[bound] OF real;
              i        : bound;
```

Any array subscript expression that is not of type "bound" or does
not evaluate to type "bound" is then erroneous. Note that in this
context:

```
        VAR j : integer;
                .
                .
        data[j] := 1.342
```

cannot be checked by the compiler, but can only be checked on
execution because "j" may or may not have a value in the subrange
defined. Finally for reasons that should now be obvious constants

must be declared before types which must be declared before variables. So the order is always CONST, TYPE, VAR.

6.1.5 State variables

One of the most useful applications of user defined types is as state variables in multi-exit loops. To illustrate this point we revisit Program 2.15 This consisted of a REPEAT loop with two exit conditions ORed together. After exit from the loop the program is to determine the reason for termination.

Program 6.2

As Program 2.15 except that a symbolic or enumerated type is used as a state variable to control the termination of the loop.

```
PROGRAM squareroot3(input, output);

TYPE state = (iterating, rootfound, excessiveiterations);
VAR e, r, a : real;
    noofiterations : integer;
    exitstate : state;
BEGIN
  writeln('type number and "e"');
  read(a, e);
  r := a; noofiterations := 0;
  exitstate := iterating;
  REPEAT
    noofiterations := noofiterations + 1;
    r := r/2  + a/(2*r);
    IF abs(r*r - a) <= e THEN exitstate := rootfound ELSE
    IF noofiterations >=10 THEN exitstate := excessiveiterations;
  UNTIL exitstate IN [rootfound, excessiveiterations];

  CASE exitstate OF
    excessiveiterations : writeln('excessive iterations');
    rootfound           : writeln('root of', a, 'is', r)
  END
END.
```

Note in the above program the initialization of "exitstate" to "iterating" outside the loop. It is perhaps debatable if this approach is worthwhile for a two exit loop, but it is an elegant solution in general for an n exit loop.

6.2 Files : their uses

A file is a data structure that is used whenever we wish to scan a sequence of values in one direction, examining each component in the sequence consecutively. Unlike an array, a file cannot be randomly accessed and this means that, for example, to read the value of a component halfway through the file all the other component values preceding that value must be read. A file, however, is commonly used to initialize a data structure that can be randomly accessed. Other common uses of files are as follows:

6.2.1 Input file - process - output file

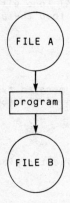

An external file supplies input data to a program which processes it and creates another external file. An example might be a list of personal records (names, addresses, dates of birth etc.) in File A. This list has to be sorted or ordered into a ranked sequence (alphabetic, by city or street are common examples) and the sorted list written to File B. Another common processing operation involving file input and output is merging. This could involve for example merging two alphabetically ordered lists into one master list. In this case there would be two input files and one output file.

6.2.2 Analysis of an input file

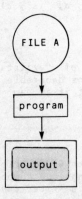

An external file supplies input data to a program that reduces the data to a few parameters that are displayed to the program user. (Technically even if there was only one result to be printed or displayed the program writes to a special file — the "output" file, but we will gloss over this detail.) For example File A could contain experimental readings that are summed and the average found.

6.2.3 Local or internal files

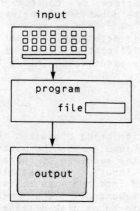

input

program

file

output

A file that is internal or local to the program is set up and used by the program. In the first example as we are reading personal records, we may want at the same time to extract the date of birth from each record and construct a file consisting solely of a sequence of ages for further analysis by the program. The file is not retained after the program has terminated.

6.2.4 Listing files

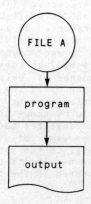

FILE A

program

output

An external file is simply listed by a program on a display. The only function of the program is to read from File A and write to the display unit. This is a familiar and common use of files in information systems. There are many variants on the above: reading from one file and creating n files, listing only a particular part of a file, etc.

6.2.5 Local and external files

A file can be external to the program , or it can be local only. We can define a local file as a structure or collection of component values that only 'live' for the duration of the program execution. An external file on the other hand is a permanent file that exists for all time (or until it is deleted by an operating system command). It can be accessed by different programs at any time. An external file can be made by association into a local file and vice versa.

6.2.6 Character and binary files

We have already met the idea of information being organized into a file or sequence of values. For example "input" is the standard name used in a program to refer to the sequence of characters being supplied as input to the program. "Input" is an example of an **external** file. The information read from the file comes from outside the program - almost always the keyboard in the case of "input". Other external files might be stored on disk or tape.

A file that stores codes representing a sequence of characters is known as a text file. The idea of text files was introduced in Chapter 2 and details of how such text files are declared and used appear in Appendix 5. The advantage of storing information in this form is that characters can be displayed on a screen or a printer and read by a person. A file of characters is the only form in which it is convenient for information to be transferred between people and computers. The disadvantage of a file of characters for storing numeric information is that the computer has to read the characters individually and work out what integer values or real values are represented by the sequence of characters. (This is done automatically by the read statement, but it still uses up computer time.) For example, an integer is represented as a single code inside the computer and that code is very different from the sequence of characters that we use to write an integer on paper or to type an integer at the keyboard. There are many circumstances in which a program needs to scan through a sequence of values in the order in which they are stored, and, in many cases the values are stored and read only by the program. The values can be stored in a file but there is no need for the values to be converted into character form when written to the file and converted back when read. Thus we have two different file formats or ways of storing information on a file: characters and binary. In the case of a binary file, the binary codes that the computer has in its primary memory to represent the information are also stored in the file.

6.2.7 File types and declarations

Clearly within the program we must have a way of telling the computer that the binary codes on the file represent characters, real numbers or integers. A file can be a sequence of items of any type (but all the items in one particular file must be of the same type). When we declare:

```
VAR   data : text;
```

this is equivalent to:

```
TYPE text = FILE OF char;
VAR  data : text;
```

The type "text" is required so often that it is available as a standard type. We can declare files of other types as follows:

```
VAR intfile : FILE OF integer;
    timefile: FILE OF real;
```

In fact we can have a file of almost any type of item we wish provided that all items within a particular file are of the same type. The main exception is that we cannot define a file of files. Let us illustrate the use of a file of reals by writing a program that accepts input of a sequence of experimental observations from the keyboard (or perhaps in practice a data logging device provided it supplies character codes in the form expected by the receiving program), calculates their average and counts the number of readings that were above the average. The program will proceed as follows:

```
Read values from the keyboard ( the file "input");
Add them up;
Calculate the average;
Count the values that are above the average
```

Clearly the program must store all the numbers read during the first stage of the above process so that it can look at them again during the last stage. The following program uses a local file of reals for this intermediate storage. As the numbers are read, and converted from the character form in which they appear in the "input" file ("input" is a text file), they are written into the file of reals. They can then be read back from this file when required.

Program 6.3

This program reads a sequence of reals from the keyboard, terminated by a "*" typed immediately after the last number. The program outputs the average of the reals and a count of how many of the input values are above the average.

139

```
PROGRAM experiment(input, output);
VAR  i, n, nabove : integer;
     observation, total, average : real;
     experimentfile : FILE OF real;
BEGIN
  rewrite(experimentfile);
  total := 0;  n := 0;
  REPEAT
    read(observation);
    n := n + 1;
    total := total + observation;
    write(experimentfile, observation)
  UNTIL input↑ = '*';

  average := total/n;
  writeln('average =', average);
  reset(experimentfile);
  nabove := 0;

  FOR  i := 1 TO n DO
   BEGIN
     read(experimentfile, observation);
     IF observation > average THEN nabove := nabove + 1
   END;

  writeln(nabove, 'readings were above the average')
END.
```

Note that the file "experimentfile" is a local file. Also we could
have declared it as a text file with no apparent difference in
program effect. The program would, however, have been much less
efficient for the reasons given above. Another point to note from
the program is that a file can be in only one of two possible
states or modes - read mode or write mode. A file is switched to
read mode by a call of "reset" and to write mode by a call of
"rewrite". The effect of "rewrite" is to destroy the previous
contents of the file (if any) and position the writing pointer at
the start of the file. The effect of the "reset" procedure is to
position the reading pointer at the start of the file. Thus you
could, for example, read part of the way through a file and return
to the beginning by using "reset".

6.2.8 Local-external association

In the above program, "experimentfile" was **local** to the program.
If the numerical values inserted in "experimentfile" were to be
preserved permanently then "experimentfile" would have to be made
into an **external** file by including it in the program heading.

        PROGRAM experiment(input, output, experimentfile);

The rest of the program would remain the same and once the program
has terminated, "experimentfile" remains in existence and could be
used subsequently by another program. Any other program that uses

140

this file would have to include the file name in the program
heading and the file would have to be declared in exactly the same
way as it was in the program that created the file. Note that
programs that subsequently process values in "experimentfile" no
longer need to include "input" in the program heading; we are no
longer taking information from the file "input" (keyboard).

6.2.9 A problem with read

Some Pascal systems restrict the use of "read" and "write" to text
files. Reading and writing information to and from non-text files
on such systems has to be done using "get" and "put". For example:

        write(experimentfile, observation)

is equivalent to:

        experimentfile↑ := observation;
        put(experimentfile)

and

        read(experimentfile, observation)

is equivalent to:

        observation := experimentfile↑;
        get(experimentfile)

"experimentfile↑" is the component that is currently being pointed
to in the file. Sometimes it is called a window to emphasize the
notion of a sequential scan that makes one component at a time
available to be seen or examined. The effect of "get" is to move
the window on one position and the assignment to the variable
"observation" makes this variable equal to the value in the
window. The effect of assigning a value to "experimentfile↑" is to
give the window a value that "put" transfers to the file.

6.2.10 The eof function

   A predefined function "eof" is available that enables a file to
be read until the end of the file is reached. This can be used
with a normal conditional loop structure in contexts where it is
not known in advance how many components are in the file. This
facility is used in the next program which accesses the file
created by the previous program.

Program 6.4

The file "experimentfile" is assumed to contain both the positive
and negative results. It is to be scanned and the number of zerocrossings (a transition through zero from a positive to a negative
reading) per unit of 10 readings found.

```
    PROGRAM zerocrossings(output, experimentfile);
    VAR  n, zerocross : integer;
         above        : boolean;
         observation  : real;
        experimentfile: FILE OF real;
    BEGIN
      reset(experimentfile);
      observation := experimentfile↑;
      get(experimentfile);
      IF observation > 0 THEN above := true
      ELSE                      above := false;
      n := 1;
      zerocross := 0;

      REPEAT
        observation := experimentfile↑;
        get(experimentfile);
        n := n + 1;
        IF above AND (observation < 0) THEN
                BEGIN
                    zerocross := zerocross + 1;
                    above := false
                END
        ELSE  IF NOT(above) AND (observation > 0) THEN
                BEGIN
                    zerocross := zerocross + 1;
                    above := true
                END
      UNTIL eof(experimentfile);

      zerocross := round(10*zerocross/n);
      writeln('zero crossings per unit length is', zerocross)
    END.
```

Note that in this program we have assumed that read is restricted
to use with text files and that we have used the necessary
equivalents described in the previous section. Also note that if a
WHILE loop was used rather than a REPEAT the situation of
"experimentfile" containing nothing after the first entry would be
catered for.

Finally there are problems concerning the use of "eof" in
conjunction with a text file. "Eof" is true only immediately after
the last end-of-line marker in the file, not after the last group
of numeric characters in the file.

6.2.11 Files as procedure parameters

The above process "zerocrossings" could have been written as a
procedure that is supplied with a file as a parameter. Say we have
3 files "exfilea", "exfileb" and "exfilec" that are to be analyzed
using this process:

```
        zerocrossings(exfilea);
        zerocrossings(exfileb);
        zerocrossings(exfilec)
```

The procedure would be declared as:

```
        PROGRAM zero(exfilea, exfileb, exfilec, output);
        TYPE exfile = FILE OF real;
        VAR exfilea, exfileb, exfilec : exfile;

            PROCEDURE zerocrossings(VAR experimentfile : exfile);
```

Note that the file parameter **must** be a VAR parameter. If this were
not the case, every time the procedure was activated all of
"exfilea", "exfileb" or "exfilec" would have to be copied into
"experimentfile".

6.2.12 Things you cannot do with files

Files cannot be compared:

```
        IF exfilea = exfileb THEN ..
```

is not allowed. Such an operation, used fairly frequently in
commercial programming, must be carried out on a component by
component basis. Also a file cannot be assigned to:

```
        exfilea := exfileb
```

is erroneous. Again such an operation must be carried out by
copying on a component by component basis.

6.3 Records and data structures

An array is a homogeneous collection of variables or components
all of which must be of the same type (although as we shall see
the component type itself can be a structure composed of entities
of different types). In many real life situations items or
entities of different types may be composed of components or sub-
entities of different types. A date for example is an entity
comprising an integer (1..31) followed by a string of characters
(the month) followed by another integer (1..2001 say). Now if we
are handling dates in a program it makes sense to be able to refer
both to a date as a single entity as well as being able to refer
to its sub-entities or component parts. We may have a collection
of dates of birth that have to be ranked in order of year. In such
an algorithm we would want to refer to the sub-entity year, to
control the sort process, but shift the whole entity when any
repositioning is to be performed. In an exchange sort, for
example, swapping a date of birth comprising three separate
variables with another would require 9 assignments. If the dates
could be referred to as single entities the swap would only
require 3 assignments. (See later for a full description of sort
algorithms.)

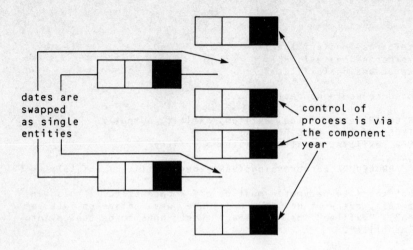

dates are
swapped
as single
entities

control of
process is via
the component
year

A record then is a structured grouping of sub-entities or
components of arbitrary type grouped into a single compound
entity.

6.3.1 Record declarations and fields

Records allow a programmer to group items of data together in some
way that reflects the external structure of the entity that the
data represent. This should produce an increase in program
transparency apart from the other obvious advantage expounded in
the previous section. The record facility allows us to make up a
single data entity out of a number of data types (usually
different). For example, as part of an architectural design
program we may wish to refer to the dimensions of a rectangular
shaped room as a single entity "roomdimension". This would be
accomplished as follows:

```
TYPE roomdimension = RECORD
                            length  :  3000..10000;
                            breadth :  2000..5000;
                            height  :  2300..3500;
                     END;
     VAR  room1, room2 : roomdimension;
```

Why not handle quantities such as length, breadth and height of a
room as independent single entities or as an array of 3 integers?
Well, apart from the assignment advantage, we can extend the
definition to include other types:

```
TYPE  roomdesign =  RECORD
                           length  : 3000..10000;
                           breadth : 2000..5000;
                           height  : 2300..3500;
                           colourcode : char;
                    END;
     VAR  room1, room2  : roomdesign;
```

144

Records are, of course, another level of abstraction in programming. There is no effect accomplished by using records that could not be achieved using arrays or single variables. But this is true of all high level language facilities. Abstraction is extremely important and the record facility allows a further level of abstraction in data just as procedures and functions facilitate higher levels of abstraction in the description of a task.

Now as we have discussed we can use the name of a record as a single entity in a program:

        room1 := room2

This will carry out 4 internal assignments with all the type protection brought into operation. Also we can have records as parameters of procedures and functions:

        heatingcost := unitcost*(volumeof(room1) + volumeof(room2))

and the function "volumeof" would be defined as follows:

        FUNCTION volumeof(room : roomdimension) : real;
          BEGIN
            volumeof := room.length * room.breadth * room.height
          END;

You might agree that we have achieved an obvious increase in transparency even at this rather trivial level. Using 3 single variables would mean that the function call would have been something like:

        heatingcost := unitcost*(volumeof(length1,breadth1,height1)+
                                 volumeof(length2,breadth2,height2))

and using an array would have meant that the function definition contains:

        volumeof := dim[1] * dim[2] * dim[3]

Now in the above function we have caused the **fields** of the record type "roomdimension" to be selected. Each variable of type "roomdimension" is of course a group of 3 entities:

	room1		room2
.length		.length	
.breadth		.breadth	
.height		.height	

and a particular field is selected by appending the field identifier to the record variable (with a dot in between).

        floorarea1 := room1.length * room1.breadth;
        perimeter2 := 2*(room2.length + room2.breadth)

This is analogous to the selection of array elements but we are using an identfier rather than a subscript; "room2.length" could be implemented, using an array, as "room2dim[1]".

A common example, widely used in commercial programming, is that old chestnut the date:

```
TYPE months = (jan, feb, mar, apr, may, jun,
               jul, aug, sep, oct, nov, dec );
     date   = RECORD
                 day   : 0..31
                 month : months;
                 year  : 1980..1999;
              END;
```

and the transparency of a holiday booking program would undoubtedly be improved as a result of using such an entity rather than 3 unconnected integers or 2 unconnected integers and a string. Such benefits cannot be over emphasized. An increase in transparency is not merely an academic nicety but it enables a programmer to proceed with a task at a higher level without bothering about details that should not concern him (in this case messing about with 3 entities rather than one). Such unnecessary details often place an artificial restriction on the complexity of the program being developed. "I cannot do this because it is too difficult" usually means "I cannot do this because it is too detailed, error prone and tedious".

6.3.2 The WITH statement

Another context in which the name of a record is used as a single entity is in conjunction with the WITH statement. This is just a shorthand facility and it allows for example the abbreviation of:

```
room1.length := 3520;
room1.breadth:= room2.breadth;
room1.height := 2400
```

to

```
WITH room1 DO
   BEGIN
     length := 3520;
     breadth:= room2.breadth;
     height := 2400
   END;
```

Thus any occurrence of a field name on its own within the scope of a WITH, whether on the right-hand side or the left-hand side of an assignment, is deemed to be a field of the record whose name appears after the word WITH. Note also that in the above example we can still refer to another record within the WITH scope.

6.3.3 Things you cannot do with RECORDS

On a negative note, it is fair to say that the the manipulation of a type "record" can sometimes be somewhat limited in scientific and engineering contexts. Here are 3 examples of things that you cannot do.

```
        (1)   IF room1 = room2 THEN WRITE('all dimensions are equal')
```

This is not allowed presumably for the sake of routine efficiency. Equality must be tested for on a field by field basis - a rather tedious operation if the records being compared are of any length. (Incidentally none of the other relational operators would make any sense in the context of records.)

```
        (2)   VAR  room1, room2, largerroom : roomdimension;
                  :
              largerroom := largerof( room1, room2 )
```

This is not allowed because a function cannot return anything other than a simple type. In this context we would have to use a procedure:

```
              findlarger(room1, room2, largerroom)
```

or pointers, a discussion of which is beyond the scope of this book.

```
        (3)   TYPE phasor = RECORD
                               realpart, imaginarypart : real;
                           END;
              VAR voltage, current, impedance : phasor;
                  :
              impedance := voltage/current
```

This is clearly a type error. Division is not defined for the type "phasor" and the details of how to divide "phasors" must be specified by the programmer.

6.3.4 Nested RECORDS

A RECORD can contain a field specification which is a reference to another record. This can be used to reflect the natural hierarchy in objects or data. Nesting a record means simply that record definitions can contain components that are also records.

```
      TYPE cylinder = RECORD
                           length : real;
                           radius : real;
                       END;
           workpiece =RECORD
                           barrel, rhshaft, lhshaft : cylinder;
                       END;
```

This is meant to represent such physical entities as:

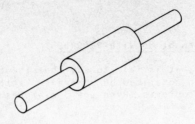

Note that the definition of "workpiece" must follow that of "cylinder" becauses it uses the definition of "cylinder".

```
startingdimension := workpiece.barrel.length
                   + workpiece.rhshaft.length
                   + workpiece.lhshaft.length
```

is an expression evaluating the length of the cylinder from which the workpiece is to be turned.

6.3.5 Records and files

Now, as we have already stressed, records are used to impose a structure on entities so that programming is more transparent and protected against errors. Let us consider a record defining the design of the front elevation of a small house:

```
TYPE  house = RECORD
                   elevation : RECORD
                                     length : real;
                                     breadth: real;
                                     finish : char;
                               END;
                   windows   : RECORD
                                     design : char;
                                     doubleglaze: boolean;
                               END;
                   doorstyle : char;
              END;
     VAR dunroamin : house;
```

And of course we could extend the declaration to a street of houses:

```
TYPE   house = ** as before **;
       street = ARRAY[1..6] OF house;
VAR    monoclassavenue, peytonplace : street;
```

This is another example of a nested record. The program sets up a hierarchical framework on data that can be exploited from within a program, and programs containing records, like programs containing arrays, tend to deal with large amounts of data.

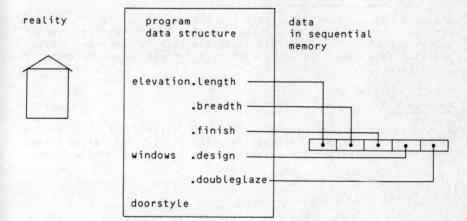

Numbers, codes or whatever appear in the computer memory as a sequence of binary codes, and the record facility imposes a structure on this information that makes programming easier. We might in the house design context have a program that creates values for a record. This may consider purchasers' and architects' requirements. A large number of such records can then be written to a file for future use. In reality the file is a sequence of binary codes, but it can be thought of as a file of records. A program containing an identical data structure can then be initialized from such a file. In the housing context this might be a program used by a quantity surveyor or a builder for interrogation or calculation. By this means a structuring imposed on the data is permanent via the file facility, and this technique of preserving a data structure is common in programs using arrays and records.

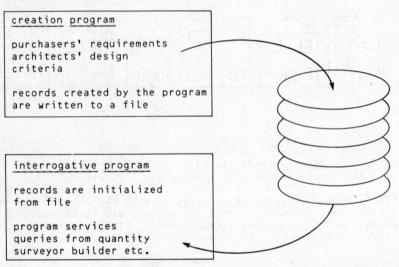

The next two programs illustrate the process of using files and records. In the first program a record is initialized from the keyboard or "input" file. This is to simulate a perhaps complex process that involves cost, architectural design and purchaser's requirements.

Program 6.5

A data structure that is an array of records is set up to represent a street of houses. The data structure is given values from the keyboard and the complete array is written onto a file.

```
PROGRAM street(input, streetfile);
CONST noofhouses = 10;
TYPE  house = RECORD
                    elevation : RECORD
                                      length : real;
                                      breadth: real;
                                      finish : char;
                                END;
                    windows   : RECORD
                                      design : char;
                                      doubleglaze : char;
                                END;
                    doorstyle : char;
              END;
      street = ARRAY[1..noofhouses] OF house;
VAR monoclassav : street;
    streetfile  : FILE OF street;
    unit : integer;
BEGIN
    FOR unit := 1 TO noofhouses DO
        WITH monoclassav[unit] DO
        BEGIN
            read(elevation.length, elevation.breadth,
                elevation.finish);
            read(windows.design, windows.doubleglaze);
            read(doorstyle)
        END;

    rewrite(streetfile);
    streetfile↑ := monoclassav;
    put(streetfile)
END.
```

Note that in this program we only need a single "write" to keep
the contents of the data structure on file. "Monoclassav" is of
type "street", an array of records, and we have declared that an
item in the file is of the same type. You should be able to work
out why we cannot do this with the file "input". Here we need a
WITH statement nested inside a FOR loop.

It may seem rather unusual to have a file with only one item or
component in it, but we are not processing the file directly. We
are using it to initialize a data structure that is processed.

The next program shows how the data structure is re-initialized
from a file.

Program 6.6

This program sets up an identical data structure to the previous
and initializes it from the file created by the previous program.
Some rudimentary 'interrogative' statements then follow that
perform calculations involving the data structure.

```
      PROGRAM street(output, streetfile);
      CONST windowproportion = 0.26;
            bricksperunitarea= 90;
            noofhouses = 10;
      TYPE  house = RECORD
                      elevation : RECORD
                                        length : real;
                                        breadth: real;
                                        finish : char;
                                  END;
                      windows   : RECORD
                                        design : char;
                                        doubleglaze : char;
                                  END;
                      doorstyle : char;
                  END;
        street = ARRAY[1..noofhouses] OF house;
      VAR monoclassav : street;
          streetfile  : FILE OF street;
          unit , noofgeorgiandoors, noofbricks : integer;
          totalarea : real;
      BEGIN
        totalarea := 0; noofgeorgiandoors := 0;
        reset(streetfile);
        monoclassav := streetfile↑;
        FOR unit := 1 TO noofhouses DO
            WITH monoclassav[unit] DO
              BEGIN
                totalarea := totalarea + elevation.length
                                        *elevation.breadth;
                IF doorstyle = 'g' THEN
                    noofgeorgiandoors := noofgeorgiandoors+1
              END;
        noofbricks := round(bricksperunitarea*
                      (totalarea - windowproportion * totalarea));
        writeln('bricks for Monoclass Av. is', noofbricks);
        writeln('georgian doors is', noofgeorgiandoors)
      END.
```

Finally records do not have to be used in conjunction with files
and vice versa. The above two programs merely demonstrate one
particular and common use of the record facility in Pascal.

6.4 Sorting algorithms

A problem frequently implemented using one-dimensional arrays of
simple types or one-dimensional arrays of records is sorting or
ranking data into some kind of order. If records are being sorted,
this ordering is usually determined by one of the record fields.
For example we could organize a list of records so that a
particular string field appears in alphabetic order. Alternatively
we might organize them so that a numeric field appears in
increasing or decreasing order.

152

As an example, consider the problem of sorting stock records so that the stock numbers are in increasing numerical order, where a stock record is:

```
TYPE   stockrecord = RECORD
                         deptcode : char;
                         stockno : integer;
                            price : real;
                      END;
```

Perhaps the simplest sort algorithm is the **exchange** sort. This can be described as follows:

```
Assume n records in array stock;
(i.e VAR stock : ARRAY[1..n] OF stockrecord;)

find the record with the smallest stock number;
swap it with the record in stock[1];
find the record with the second smallest stock number;
     { we need only look at stock[2] onwards }
swap it with the record in stock[2];
                  .
                  .
                etc.
```

The complete program is as follows.

Program 6.7

An array of 100 stock records is initialized from a file. The records are sorted so that the stock numbers are in increasing numerical order and the sorted data structure is written back into the same file.

```
PROGRAM sort(stockfile, output);
CONST max = 100;
TYPE stockrecord =  RECORD
                       deptcode : char;
                        stockno : integer;
                          price : real;
                    END;
         stock = ARRAY[1..max] OF stockrecord;
VAR stocklist : stock;
    stockfile : FILE OF stock;
        temp  : stockrecord;
    i, posnsmallest, next : integer;

BEGIN
   reset(stockfile);  stocklist := stockfile↑;

   FOR i := 1 TO max - 1 DO
     BEGIN
        posnsmallest := i;
        FOR next := i + 1 TO max DO
         IF stocklist[next].stockno < stocklist[posnsmallest]
                                     .stockno
         THEN posnsmallest := next;

         temp := stocklist[i];
         stocklist[i] := stocklist[posnsmallest];
         stocklist[posnsmallest] := temp
     END;

     rewrite(stockfile);  stockfile↑ := stocklist;
     put(stockfile)
END.
```

Note that "temp" is declared to be of type "stockrecord".

A sort algorithm that can be more efficient, is the so called
bubble sort. Consider the following fragment:

```
FOR i := 2 TO n DO
  IF stock[i].stockno < stock[i-1].stockno THEN
     BEGIN
         temp := stock[i];
        stock[i] := stock[i-1];
        stock[i-1] := temp
     END
```

If this fragment is executed once, the record with the largest
stock number will be picked up and carried to the end of the
array, and in the process some of the other records will be moved
closer to their correct position in the ordering. If we execute
the same fragment again, but for:

```
FOR i := 2 TO n-1 DO
```

then the record with the second largest stock number will be

154

carried to the second last position of the array. Repeated application of this process will eventually sort the records into order:

```
FOR lastonepossiblynotinorder := n DOWNTO 2 DO
   FOR i := 2 TO lastonepossiblynotinorder DO
      IF stock[i].stockno < stock[i-1].stockno THEN
         BEGIN
            temp := stock[i];
            stock[i] := stock[i-1];
            stock[i-1] := temp
         END;
```

This simple algorithm can be considerably improved. Each time the innermost loop is obeyed not only is one record certainly carried to its correct position, but other records may also be moved closer to their final positions. Thus the inner loop may not have to be obeyed n-1 times before the records are in order. If at some stage, obeying the inner loop does not move any of the records, they must already be in order and the process can be stopped.

Secondly, in obeying the inner loop, we may find that the "lastonepossiblynotinorder" is already in its correct position, and we in fact move an earlier record into its final position. This can be detected while the inner loop is being obeyed by keeping a note of the number of the last record moved down. Thus we get:

```
lastonepossiblynotinorder:= n;
REPEAT
   lastonemoveddown := 1;
   FOR i := 2 TO lastonepossiblynotinorder DO
      IF stock[i].stockno < stock[i-1].stockno THEN
         BEGIN
            temp := stock[i];
            stock[i] := stock[i-1];
            stock[i-1] := temp;
            lastonemoveddown := i-1
         END;
   lastonepossiblynotinorder := lastonemoveddown
UNTIL lastonepossiblynotinorder < 2;
```

This method is particularly effective when the data is already partially ordered for some reason. It will then take very few scans through the array to move every record into its correct position.

6.5 A comparison of files, arrays and arrays of records

Arrays and files are most similar; if we are processing 1000 experimental readings then we can declare:

```
VAR data : ARRAY[1..1000] OF real;
    datafile: FILE OF real;
```

One very important distinction is that arrays only 'live' for the duration of the program whereas a file can be made permanent by association. Another important difference is that the maximum memory allocated to a program by the operating system is fixed and this limit imposes an upper limit on the size of arrays. There is no limit (or practically a very large limit) on file size.

Arrays allow random access:

    x := data[999]

To fetch a corresponding element or component from a file means that the file must be 'unwound' or 'stepped' until the element or component is reached. We cannot read from a file until we have finished writing to it and we cannot write to a file until we have finished reading from it.

An array of records is used when the component data types have sub-components of different types:

```
TYPE stockrecord = RECORD
                    price    : real;
                    stockno  : integer;
                    deptcode : char;
                  END;
     stocklist  = ARRAY[1..n] OF stockrecord;
```

Although three 'parallel' arrays each of a single type could be used in this context, it would be less convenient and transparent from a programming point of view.

A common use of an array of records is in conjunction with a file:

    VAR datafile : FILE OF stocklist;

This is a convenient way of initializing such a structure and keeping the results of any manipulations on it.

Exercises

(1) Assuming the existence of:

```
        procedure drawablock(colour : colourcode;
                             pair : coordpair;
                             size : coordrange);
```

where "colourcode" is an enumerated type and "coordpair" a record, write a program that draws a chessboard in red and yellow, each square being of size 100x100.

(2) Write a program that accepts as input a date and prints out the date of the next day. **Complete** data validation should be built into the program using variables of an appropriate sub-range type for the day and month. Your program should incorporate the other necessary checks on the date.

156

(3) Write a program that accepts as input a file of students'
marks containing 100 real numbers. The program should scan
the file, find the average of the marks and then rescan the
file, counting the number of students whose mark was less
than the average mark, and the number of students whose mark
was greater than or equal to the average mark.

(4) Write a program to read a set of numbers from the keyboard,
sort them into ascending order, and create an output file
containing the sorted numbers.

(5) Write a program to 'merge' two files of integers, each
consisting of a sequence of integers in ascending order. The
'result' file is to contain all the integers from both files
in ascending order.

(6) Repeat Exercise 2 but this time use a record to store "date",
where "date.month" is a user defined type (jan, feb...etc.)
Note that you will now need an input and output procedure to
handle the month.

(7) Write a

        FUNCTION timebetween(date1, date2 : date) : integer;

that finds the number of days between two dates. "Date" is a
record.

(8) Write a set of procedures to add, subtract and multiply
complex numbers, so that an operation such as:

        c1 = c2 - c3*c4

can be programmed as:

        complexproduct(c3, c4, prod);
        complexsubtract(c2, prod, c1);

"c1", "c2", "c3", "c4" and "prod" are of type "complex",
which is a record.

(9) Elaborate the data structure given in Program 6.5 to include
more detail. Write a program that accesses this data
structure and outputs a table of materials and quantities
required for the construction of the street.

(10) Records are being collected on populations of a particular
plant. The information from each observation can be stored in
a Pascal record:

    TYPE poprecords= RECORD
                        height {metres above sea level} : real;
                        population {estimated in hundreds
                                per square kilometre } : integer;
                    END;

and data collected from one district is to be stored in a

file:

           district = FILE OF poprecords;

Write Pascal programs that can be used to

(a) set up a district file from keyboard input,

(b) display all the records in a file,

(c) sort a file into order of increasing height above sea level,

(d) 'merge' two sorted files to create one new file containing all the records from both the files in order of increasing height.

7 Functions and equations

We often need to use the computer to calculate values of some function for particular parameters in which we are interested. If the function can be represented by a straightforward algebraic expression, then that expression can be written into a program and its evaluation is straightforward. Similarly, when an equation has to be solved, an analysis of the equation often gives us an algebraic expression for the root or roots of the equation. If such an analytic solution exists then a straightforward program can be written to evaluate it. For example in Exercise 10, Chapter 1 you solved a quadratic equation by using the well-known formula for the roots.

In many situations, such convenient analytic solutions to problems involving functions and equations are not available. For example, the definition of a function may be such that it is difficult to evaluate. It will often be possible to obtain values of the function for some parameters, perhaps from a published table of values. These known values can be used to derive a simpler function that approximates the function in which we are interested. This simpler function can then be used in a program to calculate approximate function values for other parameters. Even if a fairly straightforward algebraic expression is available for a function, it may still be convenient to approximate the function by another that is easier to manipulate and this is the foundation of the techniques of numerical integration that are introduced in Chapter 8.

Similarly, many equations that occur in scientific and engineering applications do not lend themselves to convenient analytic solution and computer programs have to be used to obtain approximations to the required solution.

In this chapter, we introduce some numerical methods that can be used for evaluating functions and solving equations and we illustrate the Pascal programming techniques required to implement these methods.

7.1 Interpolation and extrapolation

7.1.1 Simple linear interpolation

Consider the following very simple situation. The precise nature of a function "f" of one variable is unknown, but values of $f(x)$ have been determined for $x=a$ and $x=b$. We require the value of $f(x)$ for a value of x such that $a<x<b$. Let us assume that evaluation of

f(x) is time-consuming and costly. We shall write a program that
uses the known values f(a) and f(b) to calculate an approximate
value for f(x). To do this we assume that the function is a
straight line between a and b and calculate a value for f(x) that
is based on this assumption. Figure 7.1 illustrates the idea.

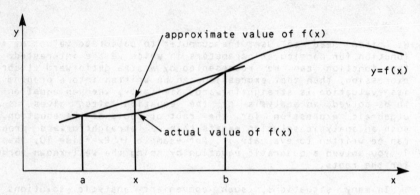

Figure 7.1   Approximation of a function by a straight line

The equation of the straight line between the points

$$(a, f(a)) \text{ and } (b, f(b))$$

can be written as

$$y = f(a) + \frac{f(b)-f(a)}{(b-a)}(x-a)$$

and we shall therefore use the right-hand side of the above
equation as an approximation to f(x). Notice that the equation of
the **same** straight line could have been written in many equivalent
ways, for example:

$$y = \frac{x-b}{a-b}f(a) + \frac{x-a}{b-a}f(b)$$

or

$$y = \frac{f(a)-f(b)}{a-b} x + \frac{a\ f(b)-b\ f(a)}{a-b}$$

Program 7.1

This program uses the two pairs of known values (a,f(a)) and
(b,f(b)) to calculate an approximation to f(x) for a value x
supplied at the keyboard.

160

```
PROGRAM LinearApprox(input, output);

CONST  a = 1.1;      b = 1.2;
       fa = 0.8912;  fb = 0.9320;

VAR x, fx : real;

BEGIN
   write('value of x:');  readln(x);
   fx := fa + (fb-fa)/(b-a)*(x-a);
   writeln('Approximation for f(', x:3:3, ') is ', fx:4:4)
END.
```

The accuracy of the above approximation will depend on the
behaviour of our function in the interval [a,b]. Problems can
arise if the unknown function is not continuous in the interval
(see Figure 7.2a) or if the points a and b are too far apart in
relation to the curvature of the function (see Figure 7.2b).

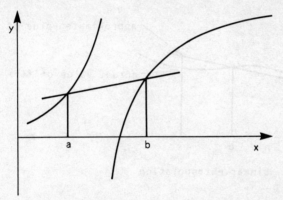

Figure 7.2(a) a discontinuous function

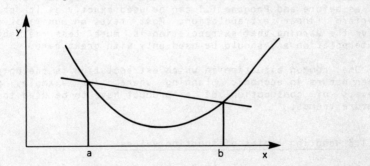

Figure 7.2(b) too large an interval [a,b]

161

For further reading on techniques for estimating the error in an approximation, the reader is referred to the Bibliography. We shall confine ourselves to introducing ideas and presenting simple illustrative programs.

The process that we have described in this section is known as **linear interpolation** - linear because we have approximated our unknown function by a straight line and interpolation because the point at which the approximation is obtained lies between points at which function values are known and through which the approximating function passes.

7.1.2 Extrapolation

If the value of x for which the value of f(x) is required lies outside the interval defined by the points at which function values are known, the process of finding an approximation to f(x) is known as **extrapolation.** The idea of **linear extrapolation** is illustrated in Figure 7.3.

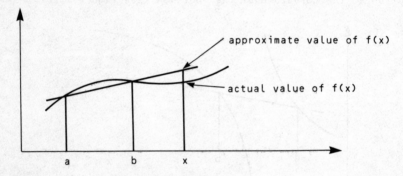

Figure 7.3. Linear extrapolation

The equation of the line between the points (a,f(a)) and (b,f(b)) is as before and Program 7.1 can be used exactly as it stands to perform linear extrapolation. Most texts on numerical analysis give the warning that extrapolation is much less reliable than interpolation and should be used only with great care.

One common situation in which extrapolation is the only course open occurs in economic planning where, for example, previous levels of consumption of a product have to be used to predict future trends.

7.1.3 Handling tables of function values

In this section, we illustrate how a table of known function values can be used in calculating linear approximations to required function values. Let us assume that a table of values for a function, f, has been obtained in some way and that this table is stored in a file in the form of a list of pairs of values:

162

$$x_0, f(x_0), \quad x_1, f(x_1), \quad \ldots, \quad x_n, f(x_n)$$

i.e., n+1 pairs of values altogether.

Initially, we assume that the x-values are **not** equally spaced but that they **are** arranged in increasing numerical order. For a given x-value, our program will find the two table-entries whose x-values lie on either side of the given value as illustrated in Figure 7.4.

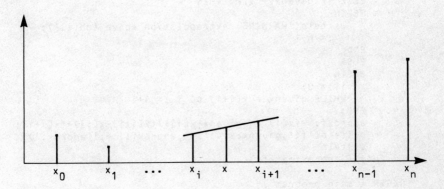

Figure 7.4   Selecting a pair of values for approximating f(x)

Program 7.2

This program accepts a sequence of given values for x and, for each value, prints an approximation to f(x) using linear interpolation between two of the values stored in the file.

```
PROGRAM TableInterp(input,output,functionfile);

CONST n = 20;

TYPE subs = 0..n;

VAR j : subs;
    x, fx : ARRAY[subs] OF real;
    givenx : real; nextchar : char;
    functionfile : text;
```

163

```
      PROCEDURE approximatef(givenx : real);
      VAR i : subs;
          approxf : real;
      BEGIN
         IF givenx < x[0] THEN
         BEGIN
            writeln('WARNING: extrapolation below table.');
            i := 0
         END
         ELSE IF givenx > x[n] THEN
         BEGIN
            writeln('WARNING: extrapolation above table.');
            i := n-1
         END
         ELSE
         BEGIN
            i := 0;
            WHILE givenx > x[i+1] DO i := i+1
         END;
         approxf:= fx[i] + (givenx-x[i])/(x[i+1]-x[i])*fx[i+1];
         writeln('f(',givenx:1:4,')=',approxf:1:6,' approx.');
         writeln
      END; { approximatef }

   BEGIN { main program }
      reset(functionfile);
      FOR j := 0 TO n DO read(functionfile, x[j], fx[j]);

      REPEAT
         write('x = ');  readln(givenx, nextchar);
         approximatef(givenx)
      UNTIL nextchar = '*'
   END.
```

Remember to read the main program block first - it is here that
you should find an outline description of what the program does.
The details of the approximation process for a single given
x-value have been written as a procedure "approximatef". If the
given value lies outside the range of x-values contained in the
file then extrapolation has to be used and a warning to that
effect is output. Otherwise the table is searched for the first
value of i such that x_{i+1} is greater than the given x-value. The
function values at x_i and x_{i+1} are then used for linear
interpolation.

Minor improvements in efficiency could be made by reducing the
number of times that the above program evaluates the expression
"i+1" but in the interests of clarity we have not done this.

If the stored x-values were **equally spaced,** and stored in
increasing order as before, then the program need not search for
the two values on either side of a given x-value. It can easily
calculate the position of these values in the table. Say we have

the sequence of x-values:

$$x_0, \quad x_1 = x_0+h, \quad x_2 = x_0+2h, \quad \ldots, \quad x_n = x_0+nh$$

For a given x-value such that

$$x_0+ih <= x < x_0+(i+1)h$$

we can calculate i as "trunc((x-x[0])/h)" and the compound statement that searches through the x-values in Program 7.2 can be replaced by the single statement

        i := trunc((x - x[0])/h)

7.1.4 Quadratic interpolation

A more accurate approximation to a value of an unknown function can be obtained by basing the approximation on more than two known values. Given two known function values, the simplest approximating function that passes through the two function points is a straight line. Given three known function values, we can approximate the unknown function by a quadratic that passes through the three known points. This is known as **quadratic interpolation** and is illustrated in Figure 7.5.

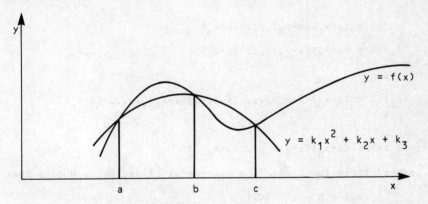

Figure 7.5 Approximation of a function by a quadratic

There is a unique polynomial of degree n that passes through n points. (We shall not prove this here - for further reading, see the Bibliography.) In particular, the quadratic function that passes through three points is unique. If we can write down the equation of any quadratic function that passes through the three points (a,f(a)), (b,f(b)) and (c,f(c)) then this will be the approximating function that we require. There are several different ways in which we could write such an equation, but our knowledge that the quadratic is unique tells us that they are all different ways of representing the same function. For example, the following function is a quadratic:

$$y = \frac{(x-b)(x-c)}{(a-b)(a-c)}f(a) + \frac{(x-a)(x-c)}{(b-a)(b-c)}f(b) + \frac{(x-a)(x-b)}{(c-a)(c-b)}f(c)$$

It is easy to see that it passes through the three points because, if x=a, then the right-hand side reduces to f(a). Similarly it passes through the points (b,f(b)) and (c,f(c)). It therefore represents the unique quadratic that passes through the given points.

We leave it as an exercise to the reader to write a program similar to Program 7.1, but which uses quadratic interpolation to calculate an approximation to f(x) for a value of x supplied as input.

7.1.5 Polynomial interpolation

Linear interpolation and quadratic interpolation are special cases of polynomial interpolation where we approximate an unknown function for which we know values at n+1 points by the unique polynomial of degree n that passes through these points. We shall construct one form of the equation for the polynomial passing through the points

$$(x_0, f(x_0)), \quad (x_1, f(x_1)), \quad \ldots \quad , \quad (x_n, f(x_n))$$

It is easier to write the equation if we first define functions:

$$l_0(x) = (x-x_1)(x-x_2) \ldots (x-x_n)$$

$$l_1(x) = (x-x_0)(x-x_2) \ldots (x-x_n)$$

$$\vdots$$

$$l_i(x) = (x-x_0)(x-x_1) \ldots (x-x_{i-1})(x-x_{i+1}) \ldots (x-x_n)$$

$$\vdots$$

$$l_n(x) = (x-x_0)(x-x_1) \ldots (x-x_{n-1})$$

Each of these functions is a polynomial of degree n. Notice that

$$l_i(x_j) = 0 \qquad i <> j$$

$$l_i(x_i) <> 0$$

We can use these functions to construct a polynomial of degree n that passes through our n+1 points as follows:

$$P(x) = \frac{l_0(x)}{l_0(x_0)}f(x_0) + \frac{l_1(x)}{l_1(x_1)}f(x_1) + \ldots + \frac{l_n(x)}{l_n(x_n)}f(x_n)$$

It should be obvious that

$$P(x_i) = f(x_i) \qquad i = 1, 2, \ldots, n$$

and that $P(x)$ is therefore one way of writing the unique polynomial passing through the given points. (Again, we have not proved the uniqueness of such a polynomial.) The above polynomial is called **Lagrange's interpolation polynomial**. The next program demonstrates how Lagrangian interpolation can be used to calculate an approximation to $f(x)$ for a single given value of x.

Program 7.3

Given a file containing values
$$x_0, f(x_0), \quad x_1, f(x_1), \quad \ldots \quad , \quad x_n, f(x_n)$$
this program reads a value x from the keyboard and evaluates Lagrange's interpolation polynomial to give an approximation to $f(x)$.

```
PROGRAM polynomialinterp(input, output, functionfile);

CONST n = 10;
VAR i, j : integer; p, termi, givenx : real;
    x, fx : ARRAY[0..n] OF real;
    functionfile : text;

BEGIN
    reset(functionfile);
    FOR i := 0 TO n DO readln(functionfile, x[i], fx[i]);

    write('x value:');  readln(givenx);

    p := 0;
    FOR i := 0 TO n DO
    BEGIN
        termi := 1;
        FOR j := 0 TO n DO
            IF j <> i THEN
                termi := termi*(givenx-x[j])/(x[i] - x[j]);
        p := p + termi*fx[i]
    END;

    writeln('Approximation to f(', givenx:1:3, ')=', p:1:6)
END.
```

If a program were required to evaluate approximations for several x-values, then it would be advantageous to express our approximating polynomial as
$$P(x) = a_0 \, l_0(x) + a_1 \, l_1(x) + \ldots + a_n \, l_n(x)$$

where $a_i = f(x_i)/l_i(x_i)$

Since the a-values are constant, they could be computed once at

167

the start of the program, thus reducing the amount of computing time subsequently required to evaluate P(x) for each given x-value. (See Exercise 6.)

Lagrange's form of the interpolation polynomial is easy to write down and is usually used to introduce the idea of polynomial interpolation. However, other forms of the interpolating polynomial are often computationally more convenient. For further reading, see the Bibliography.

Finally, if a table of function values has been obtained by experiment or measurement and these values are therefore subject to experimental error, it will often be more appropriate to use data fitting techniques to derive the polynomial of given degree that most closely approximates the given values without necessarily passing through all the points determined by the given values. An introduction to such techniques is given in Chapter 12.

7.2 Solving equations

In the remainder of this chapter, we introduce some simple numerical techniques for solving equations that do not lend themselves to straightforward analytic solution. A detailed mathematical analysis of these techniques is, of course, beyond the scope of this book, but the fundamental ideas will be described and illustrated using Pascal programs. We shall consider equations involving one variable of the form

$$f(x) = 0$$

where f(x) is a continuous function and we shall examine the problem of finding a value for x that satisfies the equation.

An equation such, as:

$$4x - 7 = 0$$

can be easily manipulated to give the required value for x. On the other hand, an equation such as:

$$\cos(x) - x/4 = 0$$

can not be manipulated to give a value for x and techniques for calculating an approximate solution must be used.

7.2.1 Searching for a root

One approach to solving an equation of the form:

$$f(x)=0$$

is to search systematically for a value of x that is sufficiently close to a root of the equation. The standard method of doing this is known as the **bisection algorithm**. We start by finding an interval in which the root of our equation must lie. For example,

Figure 7.6 is a sketch graph of the function

f(x) = cos(x) - x/4

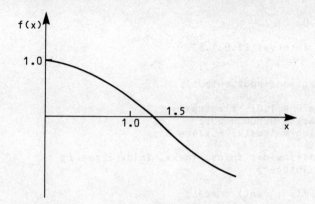

Figure 7.6 Sketch graph of the function f(x) = cos(x) - x/4

We can see from the graph that the equation has a root somewhere between x=1.0 and x=1.5, ie in the interval [1.0,1.5]. We can confirm this by calculating

f(1.0) = 0.290
f(1.5) = -0.304

Since f(x) is positive for one value of x and negative for the other, and since f(x) is a continuous function, there must be a value of x in the interval [1.0,1.5] for which f(x) = 0. A program can test whether a function changes sign over an interval [a,b] by testing whether

f(a)*f(b) < 0

To apply the bisection algorithm, we halve the initial interval by finding the midpoint x=1.25. By evaluating the function at the midpoint we can decide whether the root lies in the first half of the interval or the second half. In this case, we have

f(1.25) = 0.0028

The change of sign takes place in the interval [1.25,1.5] and the root therefore lies in this interval. The process can be repeated, and at each step we find a smaller interval within which the root must lie. The midpoint of our interval represents an approximation to the root. The process can be terminated when the interval is smaller than the accuracy to which we require to calculate the root.

Program 7.4

This program uses the bisection algorithm to find a root of the equation

cos(x) - x/4 = 0

using the initial interval [1.0,1.5].

```
PROGRAM bisection(input,output);

CONST firstmin = 1.0;  firstmax = 1.5;
      accuracy = 0.000000005;
      equation = 'cos(x) - x/4 = 0';

VAR minx, maxx, midx, fminx, fmaxx, fmidx : real;
    steps : integer;

   FUNCTION f(x : real) : real;
   BEGIN
      f := cos(x) - x/4
   END;

BEGIN
   minx := firstmin;  maxx := firstmax;
   fminx := f(minx);  fmaxx := f(maxx);
   steps := 0;

   REPEAT
      steps := steps + 1;
      midx := (minx + maxx)/2;
      fmidx := f(midx);
      IF fminx*fmidx > 0 THEN
         BEGIN  minx := midx;  fminx := fmidx  END
      ELSE
         BEGIN  maxx := midx;  fmaxx := fmidx  END
   UNTIL (maxx - minx) < accuracy;

   writeln('Root found for ', equation);  writeln;
   writeln('x = ', midx:10:8,
                   ' found after ', steps:1, ' steps.')
END.
```

The output produced by the program is

Root found for cos(x) - x/4 = 0

x = 1.25235323 found after 27 steps.

The accuracy to which such a program can work will be limited by the representation of real numbers in the Pascal system that we are using. On some small systems, you may only be able to work to seven significant digits.

The above program could be extended to find its own initial interval. The following program fragment considers a succession of intervals each of length "xstep" until an interval is found over which the sign of f(x) changes.

```
write('start search at:');  readln(minx);
write('search step:');  readln(xstep);
maxx := minx + xstep;

WHILE f(minx)*f(maxx) > 0 DO
BEGIN
   minx := maxx;
   maxx := maxx + xstep
END;
```

This fragment of program could be used in place of the initialization

```
minx := firstmin;
maxx := firstmax;
```

in Program 7.4. Of course, there is a possibility that this loop will never terminate if there is no root greater than the initial value of "minx". An additional test could be included to terminate execution of the WHILE statement if "minx" exceeds some specified value. Alternatively, we could rely on the use of the 'interrupt' key on our terminal to interrupt such an infinite loop.

Once an initial interval has been found, the bisection algorithm can be relied upon to approach as close to a root as is possible within the limits of the precision of our computer. However, a function with several roots can give rise to problems. For example, if there are an even number of roots within an interval, the sign of the function will be the same at both ends of the interval and the program will not recognize that the interval contains a root. Another disadvantage of the bisection algorithm is that it converges fairly slowly by comparison with other methods of finding roots. An alternative approach is introduced in the next section.

7.2.2 Iterative methods for finding roots

A widely used method for finding a root of an equation of the form

$$f(x) = 0$$

is to make an initial guess at the required root and to use this initial estimate to calculate a more accurate approximation to the root. This process is then repeated until a test indicates that the current approximation to the root is sufficiently accurate. If this happens, the process is said to **converge** to a root.

The method usually proceeds by repeatedly obeying a Pascal statement of the form

    x := g(x)

where the **iteration function** g(x) represents the calculation used to convert an approximate root into a more accurate approximation. One necessary condition for such a process to converge to a root, a, of the equation

    f(x) = 0

is that

    a = g(a)

In other words, a must be a root of the equation

    x = g(x)

There are many ways of rewriting a given equation in this form, but not all of these will result in a process that converges to a root. For example, one way of rewriting the equation

    cos(x) - x/4 = 0

is

    x = x + cos(x) - x/4

giving

    g(x) = x + cos(x) - x/4

Using this as an iteration function results in a sequence of values for x that **do** converge to a root of our equation.

Program 7.5

Uses the above iteration function to find a root of the equation

    cos(x) - x/4 = 0

The program lists the successive approximations to the root.

```
        PROGRAM iterate(input,output);

        CONST accuracy = 0.000000005;
             equation = 'cos(x) - x/4 = 0';

        VAR x, previousx : real;

           FUNCTION g(x : real) : real;
           BEGIN
             g := x + cos(x) - x/4
           END;

        BEGIN
           writeln('Solving the equation:  ', equation);
           writeln;
           write('Initial aproximation to root:');  readln(x);
           writeln;  writeln('Successive approximations are:');

           REPEAT
              previousx := x;
              x := g(x);
              writeln(x:15:10)
           UNTIL abs(x-previousx) < accuracy;

           writeln;
           writeln('Root found is  x = ', x:10:8);  writeln
        END.
```

Given an initial approximation of 1.5, execution of this program
produces the following display at the terminal:

```
   Solving the equation:  cos(x) - x/4 = 0

   Initial aproximation to root: 1.5

   Successive approximations are:
       1.1957372017
       1.2631304461
       1.2501827819
       1.2527859863
       1.2522667737
       1.2523705010
       1.2523497853
       1.2523539228
       1.2523530964
       1.2523532615
       1.2523532285
       1.2523532351
       1.2523532338

   Root found is  x = 1.25235323
```

If the above program had used the iteration function

173

```
g(x) = x - (cos(x) - x/4)
```

then the iterative process would **not** have converged.

A discussion of the conditions under which convergence occurs is beyond the scope of this text. In view of the possibility that a particular iterative process may not converge, we should perhaps have included a counter in our REPEAT-loop to keep a count of the number of iterations that have taken place. The process could then be automatically terminated if this count became excessive:

```
noofiterations := 0;
REPEAT
   noofiterations := noofiterations +1;
   .
   .
UNTIL ((abs(x-previousx) < accuracy)
      OR (noofiterations > 100);
```

We have instead relied on the use of the 'interrupt' key on our terminal to interrupt the execution of the program should it fail to converge.

7.2.3 The Newton-Raphson method

One well-known technique for deriving an iterative function g(x) gives rise to the **Newton-Raphson method**. The situation in the region around a root of an arbitrary equation:

```
f(x) = 0
```

is illustrated in Figure 7.7.

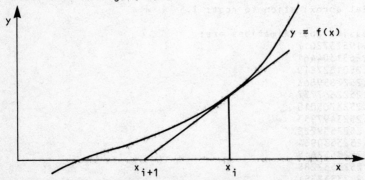

Figure 7.7   The region around a root of an equation f(x) = 0.

If we have obtained the value x_i as an approximation to our root, we can approximate our curve at the point $x=x_i$ by a straight line and use the point x_{i+1} at which this line crosses the x-axis as a better approximation to the root. An obvious line to use is the tangent to the curve at the point x_i. This line has gradient $f'(x_i)$ and passes through the point $(x_i, f(x_i))$. The equation of of this line is therefore

$$y = f(x_i) + f'(x_i)(x - x_i)$$

and our next approximation x_{i+1} is given by

$$f(x_i) + f'(x_i)(x_{i+1} - x_i) = 0$$

which gives

$$x_{i+1} = x_i - \frac{f(x_i)}{f'(x_i)}$$

Thus the iteration function is

$$g(x) = x - \frac{f(x)}{f'(x)}$$

Applying this to the problem of solving the equation

$$\cos(x) - x/4 = 0$$

we get the iteration function

$$g(x) = x + \frac{\cos(x) - x/4}{\sin(x) + 1/4}$$

If Program 7.5 is rewritten to use this function the display produced is:

    Solving the equation: cos(x) - x/4 = 0

    Initial aproximation to root: 1.5

    Successive approximations are:
        1.2561009851
        1.2523550511
        1.2523532340
        1.2523532340

    Root found is x = 1.25235323

As you can see, convergence is very rapid indeed and there is no further change in the first five decimal places after the second iteration.

We shall not present a detailed analysis of the conditions under which the Newton-Raphson method converges, but it should be obvious from the iteration function that problems can arise in regions where $f'(x)$ is close to zero.

7.2.4 The secant method

Occasionally we require to find a root of an equation

$$f(x) = 0$$

where the function $f(x)$ is difficult to differentiate. In this case, we can use an alternative to the Newton–Raphson method that does not require us to differentiate the function. Again, at each step, we obtain a new approximation to the root of our equation by approximating the function with a straight line. In this case, we use the straight line (the secant) that passes through the curve at the points corresponding to the **two** most recent approximations to the root. This is illustrated in Figure 7.8.

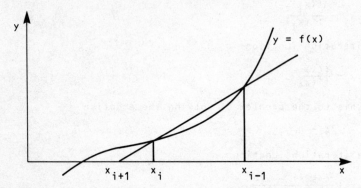

Figure 7.8   Illustration of the Secant method.

The equation of the line passing through the two points

$$(x_{i-1}, f(x_{i-1})) \quad \text{and} \quad (x_i, f(x_i))$$

is $y = f(x_i) + \dfrac{f(x_{i-1}) - f(x_i)}{x_{i-1} - x_i} (x - x_i)$

and this crosses the x-axis at the point

$$x_{i+1} = x_i - f(x_i) \frac{x_{i-1} - x_i}{f(x_{i-1}) - f(x_i)}$$

Note that the process described by the above equation is very similar to that used in the Newton–Raphson method. The gradient of the line passing through two points on the curve is used in place of the gradient of the tangent at x_n.

To start the process off, we need two initial guesses at the root. The following Pascal fragment would perform the required iteration.

176

```
      previousx := firstguess;  x := secondguess;
      REPEAT
         newx := x - f(x)*(previousx - x)/(f(previousx) - f(x));
         previousx := x;  x := newx;
         writeln(x :15:10)
      UNTIL abs(x-previousx) < accuracy
```

If this is applied to the equation

$\cos(x) - x/4 = 0$

using the values 1.5 and 1.4 as our two initial guesses, the
display produced might be

```
   Solving the equation:  cos(x) - x/4 = 0

   First approximation to root: 1.5
   Second approximation to the root: 1.4

   Successive approximations are:
   1.2550809448
   1.2523969772
   1.2523532495
   1.2523532340
   1.2523532340

   Root found is  x = 1.25235323
```

7.2.5 Finding roots of polynomials

As a final example, we illustrate the application of the Newton-
Raphson method to the important problem of finding roots of
polynomials.

Say $P(x) = a_n x^n + a_{n-1} x^{n-1} + \ldots + a_1 x + a_0$

To find a root of the equation

$P(x) = 0$

we can use the Newton-Raphson iteration function

$$g(x) = x - \frac{P(x)}{P'(x)}$$

where

$P'(x) = na_n x^{n-1} + (n-1)a_{n-1} x^{n-2} + \ldots + 2a_2 x + a_1$

Of course, a polynomial of degree n has n roots, some or all of
which may be imaginary. If there is more than one real root, the
initial approximation chosen will determine which root is found by
the process. If there are no real roots, the process will not

177

converge. As is always the case with the Newton-Raphson method, problems can arise in regions where P'(x) is close to zero (see Section 7.2.3).

Program 5.10 demonstrated the well-known nested multiplication technique for evaluating a polynomial. A function for evaluating a polynomial and a procedure for differentiating a polynomial were defined and used in Program 5.10. These procedures are used in Program 7.6 which requests the degree and coefficients of the polynomial to be input at the terminal. The user also has to supply an initial approximation to the root. Of course, if a lot of work is being done with a particular polynomial, it would be better to keep the degree and coefficients of the polynomial in a file and make the program read the specification of the polynomial from the file.

Program 7.6

Attempts to find a real root of a specified polynomial (of degree <=10) given the coefficients of the polynomial and an initial approximation to the required root. A given polynomial will have several roots and the root found by the program will depend on the initial approximation supplied.

```
PROGRAM PolynomialRoots(input, output);

CONST maxdegree = 10;   accuracy = 0.0000005;

TYPE   terms = 0..maxdegree;
       polynomials = ARRAY [terms] OF real;

VAR    i, degree : terms;   x, previousx : real;
       p, pdiff : polynomials;

    FUNCTION ValueOfPoly(VAR a : polynomials;
                              n : terms;  x : real): real;
    VAR total : real;   i : terms;

    BEGIN
       total := a[n];
       FOR i := n-1 DOWNTO 0 DO
          total := total*x + a[i];
       ValueOfPoly := total
    END;

    PROCEDURE DiffPoly(VAR coeff, diffcoeff : polynomials;
                              n : terms);
    VAR i : terms;

    BEGIN
       FOR i := n-1 DOWNTO 0 DO
          diffcoeff[i] := (i+1)*coeff[i+1]
    END;
```

```
BEGIN { main program }
    write('Degree of polynomial:');  readln(degree);
    write('Polynomial coefficients, highest order first:');
    FOR i := degree DOWNTO 0 DO read(p[i]);  readln;

    DiffPoly(p, pdiff, degree);

    write('Initial approximation to root:');  readln(x);
    writeln;  writeln('Successive approximations are:');

    REPEAT
        previousx := x;
        x := x - ValueOfPoly(p,degree,x)/
                 ValueOfPoly(pdiff,degree-1,x);
        writeln(x:12:8)
    UNTIL abs(x-previousx) < accuracy;

    writeln;  writeln('Root is x = ', x:1:6)
END.
```

The following display was produced as a result of executing this program:

```
Degree of polynomial: 3
Polynomial coefficients, highest order first: 1  12  17  -80
Initial approximation to root: 2.0

Successive approximations are:
 1.87012987
 1.86596544
 1.86596121
 1.86596121

Root is x = 1.865961
```

Note that there are many problems that can arise in finding roots of apparently innocuous polynomials. For further reading, see the Bibliography.

Exercises

(1) Modify Program 7.1 to output a warning if extrapolation has to be used.

(2) It was suggested in connection with program 7.2 that, if the x-values in the table are equally spaced, then the process of finding the values is considerably easier. Simplify the program as suggested to deal with a table of function values at equally spaced points.

(3) In the case where the entries in a table of function values are not equally spaced, but are in order, the process of finding the entries on either side of a given x-value can be speeded up by using the process known as 'binary search'. At each step, two subscript values ("bottom" and "top" say) indicate the area of the table in which the two required values are known to lie. The process starts with:

```
bottom := 1;
top := n;
```

At each step, this area of the table is halved by calculating a subscript in the centre of the current area:

```
mid := (bottom+top) DIV 2;
```

and replacing either "bottom" or "top" by the value of "mid". When "bottom" and "top" have adjacent values, these are the subscripts of the entries required.
  Modify Program 7.2 so that it uses binary search.

(4) Write a program similar to Program 7.1, but which uses quadratic interpolation to calculate an approximation to f(x).

(5) Write a program that generates a file of reals representing a table of values of sinh(x) at x-intervals of 0.01 for

$$0 <= x <= 3.5$$

and a similar file containing values of cosh(x).
  Now write a program that uses these values to calculate approximations to sinh(x) and cosh(x) for x-values typed at the keyboard. For a given x-value, the program should use quadratic interpolation with the three table entries whose x-values are closest to the given x-values.

(6) In the text, an alternative form for Lagrange's interpolation polynomial was suggested for use if approximations to f(x) were to be calculated for several values of x. Write a program that uses this alternative approach to evaluating the approximating polynomial.

(7) A sequence of values representing the population of a city (in hundreds of thousands) over a period of five years is as follows:

1977	1978	1979	1980	1981
2.38	2.41	2.45	2.50	2.57

Write a program that uses a polynomial approximation to predict what the population will be over the next three years. Do the values produced by your program appear reasonable? See the Bibliography for further reading on the use of polynomial approximations.

(8) Modify Program 7.4 so that it finds its own initial interval

in which to search for a root of the equation being solved.
Your program should accept input of two x-values indicating
the end-points of an interval in which a root is known to
lie. In case the area specified includes an even number of
roots (the signs of the function values at the end-points are
the same) your program should scan the interval repeatedly,
using smaller and smaller step lengths until an interval is
found over which the sign does change.

(9) Write programs that solve the equation

$$f(x) = x - \exp(1/x) = 0$$

using the bisection algorithm, the Newton-Raphson method and
the secant method. Compare the rates of convergence of the
three methods.

(10) A Pascal function can be supplied as a parameter to another
function or procedure. For example, the heading of a
procedure for applying the Newton-Raphson method to find a
zero of a specified function might be:

```
PROCEDURE Newton( FUNCTION f(x:real):real;
                  InitialGuess, Accuracy : real;
                  MaximumIterations : integer;
                  VAR RootFound : boolean;
                  VAR Root : real );
```

The first parameter supplied to this procedure when called
must be the name of a user-defined function. Write such a
procedure and test it by using it to solve the equation used
in Program 7.4.

(11) Write a program that uses the secant method to find a root of
a polynomial given two close initial approximations.

(12) Write a program that can be used to set up a file of real
numbers representing the coefficients of a polynomial of
fixed degree, the coefficients being input at the keyboard. A
second file should also be created containing the
coefficients of the derivative of the polynomial. Now write a
program that can be used to

(a) evaluate the polynomial and its derivative for a given
value of x,

or (b) use the Newton-Raphson method to find a root of the
polynomial given an initial approximation input at the
keyboard.

where the user indicates the operation to be carried out by
inputting a code letter 'a' or 'b'.

8 Calculus

The solution of a problem in the physical world often involves
differentiation or integration of functions that constitute part
of a mathematical model of the problem. When convenient analytic
methods of solution are not available for the functions involved,
or if only limited information about a function is available, as
output from an experiment say, then numerical approximation
techniques have to be used. In the same way, many differential
equations that arise from the analysis of scientific or
engineering problems can be solved only by numerical methods. In
this chapter, we introduce the commonly used methods for obtaining
approximate solutions to calculus problems and we present some
Pascal programs that apply these methods.

8.1 Numerical differentiation

Let us consider the problem of differentiating a function f(x) and
obtaining the value of the derivative f'(x) for a particular value
of x. Many functions that arise in scientific and engineering
applications can be differentiated analytically, and particular
values of x can be substituted into the expression obtained. For
this reason, numerical differentiation is not a widely used
technique. If, however, the function f(x) is complicated, symbolic
differentiation may be difficult and it may be more convenient to
use a numerical technique to obtain an approximate value of f'(x)
for a particular value of x. Similar techniques will be needed if
function values are known only at discrete points. Recall the
definition of the differential of f(x) with respect to x.

$$f'(x) = \lim_{h \to 0} \frac{f(x+h)-f(x)}{h}$$

This suggests that we can use the expression

$$\frac{f(x+h)-f(x)}{h}$$

as an approximation to f'(x) for small values of h. We shall
illustrate the process with a function that can be easily
differentiated symbolically so that we can compare the true value
of f'(x) with our approximations.

Program 8.1

For the function

$$f(x) = 1/(\sin(x) + 2)$$

182

this program tabulates values of the expression

$$\frac{f(x+h) - f(x)}{h}$$

for ten progressively smaller values of h. The value of x and the initial value of h are supplied as input. Each successive value of h is obtained by dividing the previous value by 10.

```
PROGRAM differentiate(input,output);

CONST functionstring = 'f(x) = 1/(sin(x)+2)';

VAR x, h : real;
    count : integer;

    FUNCTION f(x : real) : real;
    BEGIN
        f := 1/(sin(x) + 2)
    END;

BEGIN
    writeln('Differentiating ', functionstring);
    write('x = ');  readln(x);
    write('h = ');  readln(h);

    writeln;
    writeln('h':8, 'approximation to f''(x)':37);
    FOR count := 1 TO 10 DO
    BEGIN
        writeln(h:14:12, (f(x+h)-f(x))/h:25:8);
        h := h/10
    END;

    writeln;  writeln;
    writeln('True value of f''(x) = ',
                -1/sqr(sin(x) + 2) * cos(x) :1:8)
END.
```

Note that if we want a single prime to appear in an output message, a double prime must be inserted in the corresponding string in the program. A run of this program produced the following display:

```
Differentiating f(x) = 1/(sin(x)+2)
x = 1.5
h = 1.0

        h                    approximation to f'(x)
1.000000000000                  0.05122963
0.100000000000                 -0.00231183
0.010000000000                 -0.00731601
0.001000000000                 -0.00781714
0.000100000000                 -0.00786726
0.000010000000                 -0.00787227
0.000001000000                 -0.00787278
0.000000100000                 -0.00787281
0.000000010000                 -0.00787281
0.000000001000                 -0.00787281


True value of f'(x) = -0.00787283
```

Notice that we are approximating f'(x) by calculating the gradient
of the straight line that passes through two points on the curve.
A more accurate approximation can be obtained by using two points
on either side of the point at which we require an estimate of
f'(x). If we take the points on the curve at x-h and x+h, this
gives the expression:

$$\frac{f(x+h) - f(x-h)}{2h}$$

The two methods of approximation are illustrated graphically in
Figure 8.1.

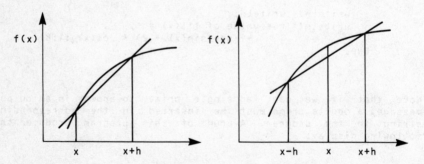

Figure 8.1   Approximation of f'(x) by the gradient
              of a straight line

We leave it as an exercise to modify Program 8.1 so as to use this
new approximation and compare the accuracy of the values obtained
with those output by the previous version of the program.

Users of the above techniques should be aware of difficulties that can arise as h gets smaller. In theory, the smaller the value of h, the more accurate our approximation to $f'(x)$, but in practice, the value obtained for $f(x+h)-f(x)$ may be unreliable because of rounding errors that take place during the evaluation of $f(x)$ and $f(x+h)$. The number of significant digits used to represent these two values will be fixed for a particular computer and if these values are large, or if the difference between them is relatively small, then the difference may be severely distorted. Division by a very small value of h further magnifies this distortion.

Finally, note that even if an analytic expression for our function is not available, but values of $f(x)$ are known at discrete points, techniques of interpolation (Chapter 7) or regression (Chapter 12) can be used to approximate the unknown function by a straight line. The gradient of the straight line can then be used as an approximation to the gradient of the unknown function. Approximation of an unknown function by a higher degree polynomial in order to estimate a derivative can give rise to problems, a discussion of which is beyond the scope of this book.

8.2 Numerical integration

The problem of finding an algebraic expression for the integral of a function $f(x)$ is in general more difficult than that of algebraic differentiation and is far more often impossible. For this reason, the techniques of numerical integration introduced in this section are more widely used than those of numerical differentiation described in Section 8.1. Fortunately, whereas numerical differentiation is fraught with problems, numerical integration tends to be comparatively trouble-free. Let us consider the problem of evaluating

$$y = \int_a^b f(x)\,dx$$

This is equivalent to finding the area under the curve

$$y = f(x)$$

between the points x=a and x=b as illustrated in Figure 8.2.

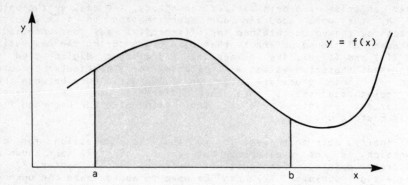

Figure 8.2 Graphical representation of integration

The methods that we shall consider proceed by approximating the given function by another function that is easily integrated. The simplest approximating function would be a straight line from the point (a, f(a)) to (b, f(b)), but since a and b are not necessarily close together, this could be very inaccurate.

We can retain the advantages of simple linear approximation, but with improved accuracy, by dividing the interval [a,b] into small sub-intervals and approximating the function by a straight line in each sub-interval. Figure 8.3 illustrates one simple way in which this could be done.

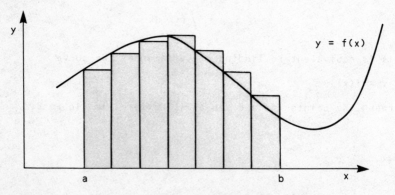

Figure 8.3 Illustration of the rectangle rule

The shaded area represents an approximation to our integral. This approximation is obtained by summing the areas of the small shaded

186

rectangles, where the height of each rectangle is given by the function value at the start of the corresponding sub-interval. The smaller the sub-intervals the more accurate will be the approximation. For obvious reasons, the method is known as the **rectangle rule.** We shall not program this method, but shall instead proceed to the next section where we present a program for the more accurate **trapezoidal rule.**

8.2.1 The trapezoidal rule

A more accurate approximation to

$$y = \int_a^b f(x)\,dx$$

can be obtained by using linear interpolation in each sub-interval of the the interval [a,b] as illustrated in Figure 8.4.

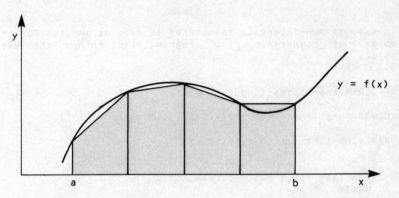

Figure 8.4 Illustration of the trapezoidal rule

The shaded area now consists of a number of trapezoids, one for each sub-interval. If there are n intervals, each of equal length, the length of each interval is given by

$$h = \frac{b - a}{n}$$

Let us name the endpoints of each interval as follows:

$$x_0 = a, \quad x_1 = a+h, \quad x_2 = a+2h, \quad \ldots \quad , x_n = b$$

The area of the i'th trapezoid is

$$\frac{h}{2}(f(x_{i-1}) + f(x_i))$$

and this is the trapezoidal rule in its simplest form. The total shaded area is

$$\frac{h}{2}(\ (f(x_0)+f(x_1)) + (f(x_1)+f(x_2)) + \ldots + (f(x_{n-1})+f(x_n)) \ )$$

$$= \frac{h}{2}(f(x_0) + 2f(x_1) + 2f(x_2) + \ldots + 2f(x_{n-1}) + f(x_n))$$

This expression therefore represents an approximation to our integral. It is the composite form of the trapezoidal rule, often referred to simply as the trapezoidal rule.

Program 8.2

This program uses the trapezoidal rule to calculate an approximation to

$$\int_a^b \sin(x)\cos^2(x)dx$$

The number of sub-intervals to be used is read as input. For the purposes of comparison, the program also prints the exact integral.

```
PROGRAM trapezoidal(input,output);

CONST functionstring = 'f(x) = sin(x)*sqr(cos(x))';

VAR a, b : real;   n : integer;

    FUNCTION f(x : real) : real;
    BEGIN
        f := sin(x)*sqr(cos(x))
    END;

    FUNCTION intf(x : real) : real;
    BEGIN  intf := -cos(x)*sqr(cos(x))/3  END;
```

```
      FUNCTION integral(a,b : real;  FUNCTION f : real;
                        n : integer) : real;
      VAR h, x, sum : real;  i : integer;

      BEGIN
         h := (b-a)/n;
         sum := f(a);  x := a;

         FOR i := 2 TO n-1 DO
         BEGIN
            x := x + h;
            sum := sum + 2*f(x)
         END;

         sum := sum + f(b);
         integral := sum*h/2
      END;


   BEGIN { main program }
      writeln('Integrating the function ', functionstring);
      write('FROM? ');  readln(a);
      write('  TO? ');  readln(b);
      write('Number of intervals = ');  readln(n);

      writeln('Approx integral is ', integral(a,b,f,n) :11:8);
      writeln('Exact integral is  ', intf(b) - intf(a) :11:8)
   END.
```

The following display was produced by a run of this program with
n=10.

```
   Integrating the function f(x) = sin(x)*sqr(cos(x))
   FROM? 0.0
     TO? 1.0
   Number of intervals = 10
   Approx integral is  0.24914806
   Exact integral is   0.28075713
```

Of course, smaller values of h would give rise to a more accurate
approximation at the cost of more work. For example, with n=100,
the program produced the following display:

```
   Integrating the function f(x) = sin(x)*sqr(cos(x))
   FROM? 0.0
     TO? 1.0
   Number of intervals = 100
   Approx integral is  0.27822679
   Exact integral is   0.28075713
```

8.2.2 Simpson's rule

We saw in Chapter 7 that a more accurate approximation to a function can be obtained if the approximation is based on three known function values, the approximating function being a quadratic. This suggests that a better approximation to

$$y = \int_a^b f(x)\,dx$$

could be obtained if we divided the interval [a,b] into an **even** number of sub-intervals and used a quadratic function to approximate the given function in each consecutive pair of sub-intervals. This is illustrated in Figure 8.5.

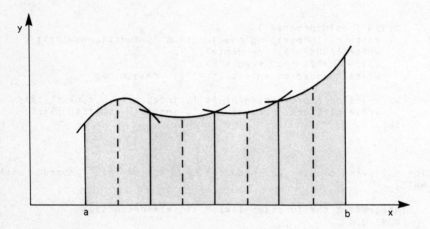

Figure 8.5 Illustration of Simpson's rule

The area under the approximating quadratic in the corresponding pair of sub-intervals is used as an approximation to the integral over these two sub-intervals, and the sum of these areas over all pairs of sub-intervals gives an approximation to the required integral. A considerable amount of algebraic manipulation is required to obtain the resulting formula. For this reason, we shall not derive the formula but shall simply state it. Using the same notation for the partition of the interval [a, b] as was used in section 8.2.1, but with the additional requirement that n is even, an approximation to

$$y = \int_a^b f(x)\,dx$$

is given by

$$\frac{h}{3}(f(x_0)+4f(x_1)+2f(x_2)+4f(x_3)+ \ldots +2f(x_{n-2})+4f(x_{n-1})+f(x_n))$$

This is the widely used **Simpson's rule** for integration, or, to be more precise, the composite form of Simpson's rule. It is more accurate than the trapezoidal rule and yet is still fairly straightforward to evaluate.

Program 8.3

This program uses Simpson's rule to evaluate an approximation to

$$\int_a^b \sin(x)\cos^2(x)dx$$

```
PROGRAM Simpson(input,output);

CONST functionstring = 'f(x) = sin(x)*sqr(cos(x))';

VAR a, b : real;   n : integer;

    FUNCTION f(x : real) : real;
    BEGIN
        f := sin(x)*sqr(cos(x))
    END;

    FUNCTION integral(a,b : real;  FUNCTION f : real;
                      n : integer) : real;
    VAR h, x, sum : real;  i : integer;
    BEGIN
        h := (b-a)/n;
        sum := f(a);  x := a;

        FOR i := 1 TO n-1 DO
        BEGIN
            x := x + h;
            IF odd(i) THEN sum := sum + 4*f(x)
                      ELSE sum := sum + 2*f(x)
        END;

        sum := sum + f(b);
        integral := sum*h/3
    END;
```

```
BEGIN
    write('Integrating ', functionstring);
    writeln(' using Simpsons rule.');
    write('FROM? ');  read(a);
    write('  TO? ');  read(b);
    write('Number of intervals, n = ');  readln(n);

    WHILE odd(n) DO
    BEGIN
        write('n must be even. Try again. n = ');
        readln(n)
    END;

    writeln('Approx integral is ', integral(a,b,f,n) :11:8)
END.
```

The following display was produced by a run of this program:

```
Integrating f(x) = sin(x)*sqr(cos(x)) using Simpsons rule.
FROM? 0.0
  TO? 1.0
Number of intervals, n = 10
Approx integral is  0.28076474
```

Use of Simpson's rule has given us a much more accurate approximation than did the trapezoidal rule with the same h-value.

8.3 First-order ordinary differential equations

Any attempt to create a mathematical model of a continuously changing system in science or engineering invariably results in one or more differential equations that describe the behaviour of the system. For example, the distance, y miles, covered in time x hours, by a vehicle travelling at a constant velocity of 50 mile/h is defined by the simple differential equation

$$\frac{dy}{dx} = 50$$

An analytic expression for y can of course be easily obtained:

$$y = 50x + d$$

where d is the constant of integration. The analytic solution in fact represents a whole family of curves (straight lines in this case) each of which satisfies the original differential equation. Different values for the constant of integration give rise to different members of this family of solutions. The constant of integration, d, can only be given a value if we know the value of y for some value of x. Such known values will usually represent the initial state of the system, and in this case we might have:

$$y = 0 \text{ when } x = 0.$$

Thus d = 0 giving the solution:

$$y = 50x$$

The right-hand side of such a differential equation might be a function of x, y or both. For example, the equation

$$\frac{dy}{dx} = y$$

has the analytic solution

$$y = ae^x$$

where a is an arbitrary constant determined by the initial conditions of the system represented by the differential equation. In general, an equation of the form

$$\frac{dy}{dx} = f(x,y) \qquad \text{or} \qquad y' = f(x,y)$$

is described as a 'first-order ordinary' differential equation (first-order because it does not involve derivatives of second or higher order, and ordinary because it involves no partial derivatives).

Many such equations can be solved analytically by classical methods, but there are also many others for which classical methods are not available, or for which the analytic solution is so complex that its evaluation is difficult. For example, the simple equation

$$y' = x^2 + y^2$$

has no convenient analytic solution. In these cases, numerical methods can be used to tabulate approximate values of y for various values of x.

In the following sections, we introduce some elementary techniques that can be used for obtaining approximate solutions for such equations. We shall assume that we are given an equation of the form

$$y' = f(x,y)$$

and that we are also given a value of y for an initial value of x, say

$$y = y_0 \quad \text{when} \quad x = x_0$$

An approximate solution to the equation will consist of a table of y-values for a sequence of equally spaced x-values:

$$x_0, \ x_1 = x_0 + h, \ x_2 = x_0 + 2h, \ \ldots \ , \ x_n = x_0 + nh$$

8.3.1 Euler's method

In this section, we describe the simplest approach to obtaining an approximate solution to the equation

$$y' = f(x,y)$$

Figure 8.6 illustrates the method.

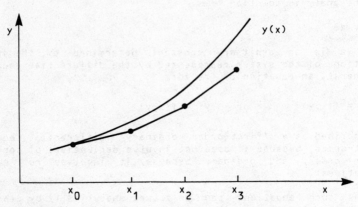

Figure 8.6   Illustration of Euler's method

The curve $y(x)$ represents the exact (but unknown) solution that we are seeking. We are given the value

$$y_0 = y(x_0)$$

and this value can be used to calculate the gradient of the curve at x_0. We can then approximate our curve over the interval $[x_0, x_1]$ by a straight line passing through the point x_0, y_0 and with gradient $f(x_0, y_0)$. The equation of this line gives us

$$y_1 = y_0 + hf(x_0, y_0)$$

The process can be continued:

$$y_2 = y_1 + hf(x_1, y_1)$$
$$\vdots$$
$$y_{i+1} = y_i + hf(x_i, y_i)$$

This simple technique is known as Euler's method and it is used in Program 8.4 in which we apply it to an equation for which an analytic solution is known. The approximate values obtained by

194

Euler's method can thus be compared with the exact solution.

Program 8.4

This program uses Euler's method to tabulate an approximate solution to the equation

$$y' = 2y$$

for initial values of x and y specified at the keyboard. The number of steps and the step length for which the solution is to be tabulated are specified from the keyboard. In addition, the program tabulates exact y-values obtained from the analytic solution:

$$y = ae^{2x}$$

where

$$a = y_0/\exp(2*x_0)$$

```pascal
PROGRAM Euler(input, output);

CONST equationstring = 'y'' = 2y';

VAR x, yapprox, h, a : real;  i, n : integer;

    FUNCTION f(x,y : real) : real;
    BEGIN  f := 2*y  END;

BEGIN
    writeln('Solving the equation ', equationstring,
            ' using Eulers method.');
    write('Initial values, x = ');  readln(x);
    write('                y = ');  readln(yapprox);
    write('      step length = ');  readln(h);
    write('  number of steps = ');  readln(n);
    writeln;

    a := yapprox/exp(2*x);  { constant of integration }
    writeln('x':6, 'approx y':16, 'exact y':16);
    writeln('-':6, '--------':16, '-------':16);

    FOR i := 1 TO n DO
    BEGIN
        yapprox := yapprox + h*f(x,yapprox);
        x := x + h;
        writeln(x :6:2, yapprox :16:10, a*exp(2*x):16:10)
    END
END.
```

The following display was produced by a run of this program:

195

```
        Solving the equation y' = 2y  using Eulers method.
        Initial values, x = 0.0
                        y = 1.0
               step length = 0.1
          number of steps = 10

              x         approx y              exact y
              -         --------              -------
            0.10     1.2000000000          1.2214027582
            0.20     1.4400000000          1.4918246976
            0.30     1.7280000000          1.8221188004
            0.40     2.0736000000          2.2255409285
            0.50     2.4883200000          2.7182818285
            0.60     2.9859840000          3.3201169227
            0.70     3.5831808000          4.0551999668
            0.80     4.2998169600          4.9530324244
            0.90     5.1597803520          6.0496474644
            1.00     6.1917364224          7.3890560989
```

The accuracy of the approximation obtained can of course be
improved by using a smaller h-value and calculating y-values at
more frequent intervals.

   Euler's method is one of the oldest and best known methods for
solving differential equations numerically. However, as can be
seen from the output of the above program, it can have a fairly
large 'truncation' error arising from the fact that a curve is
being approximated by a sequence of straight line segments. It may
be necessary to use a **very** small h-value to attain acceptable
accuracy. Also, the method often suffers from the problem of
'instability' - small errors in the initial values of y are
magnified as the method proceeds. A detailed discussion of the
different types of error that can occur, and their magnitude, is
beyond the scope of this book. For further reading, see the
Bibliography.

8.3.2 Runge-Kutta methods

Euler's method is in fact the simplest of a whole family of
methods for solving differential equations. These methods are
known as Runge-Kutta methods. The distinguishing features of these
methods are

(a) Only information at the point (x_i, y_i) is used to estimate
    y_{i+1}.

(b) No derivatives of f(x,y) need be evaluated.

We can develop other Runge-Kutta methods that are more accurate
than Euler's method by attempting to find a more accurate estimate
of the gradient of the line from (x_i, y_i) to (x_{i+1}, y_{i+1}). From
Figure 8.7, it is clear that the gradient of the curve y(x) at the
mid-point of the interval $[x_i, x_{i+1}]$ would be a more accurate
estimate of the gradient of this line. An observation similar to

this has already been made in connection with numerical differentiation in Section 8.1.

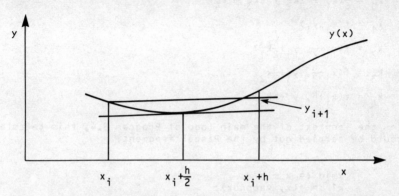

Figure 8.7   Illustration of the Modified Euler method

We can use Euler's method to calculate an approximate y-value at this point:

$$y(x_i + \frac{h}{2}) = y_i + \frac{h}{2} y_i'$$

and this value can be used in calculating an estimate of the gradient of the curve at this point:

$$k = f(x_i + \frac{h}{2}, \; y_i + \frac{h}{2} y_i')$$

This value, k, is used in calculating an estimate for y_{i+1}:

$$y_{i+1} = y_i + hk$$

This method is known as the 'modified Euler method'. Euler's method is a 'first-order Runge-Kutta method' (the error introduced at each step is roughly proportional to h^2). The modified Euler method is an example of a 'second-order Runge-Kutta method' (the error introduced at each step is roughly proportional to h^3).

One very popular Runge-Kutta method is a fourth-order method (with error roughly proportional to h^5). In fact this method is often referred to as 'The Runge-Kutta method'. We shall not present a derivation of this method, but simply define it as follows:

$$y_{i+1} = y_i + hk_0$$

where

$$k_0 = \frac{h}{6}(k_1 + 2k_2 + 2k_3 + k_4)$$

$$k_1 = f(x_i, y_i)$$

$$k_2 = f(x_i + \frac{h}{2}, y_i + \frac{h}{2}k_1)$$

$$k_3 = f(x_i + \frac{h}{2}, y_i + \frac{h}{2}k_2)$$

$$k_4 = f(x_i + h, y_i + hk_3)$$

In the context of the main loop of Program 8.4, this calculation could be carried out by the Pascal fragment:

```
xmid := x + h/2;
k1 := f(x, yapprox);
k2 := f(xmid, yapprox + h/2*k1);
k3 := f(xmid, yapprox + h/2*k2);
x := x + h;
k4 := f(x, yapprox + h*k3);
yapprox := yapprox + h/6*(k1 + 2*k2 + 2*k3 + k4)
```

We leave it as an exercise to reprogram the main loop in Program 8.4 so as to use the modified Euler method as well as the fourth-order Runge-Kutta method just described. The accuracy of the results obtained by the three methods should then be compared.

8.3.3 Predictor-corrector methods

In this section, we introduce an example of the family of methods known as **predictor-corrector methods**. In many practical applications a combination of Runge-Kutta and predictor-corrector techniques will be used.

We note first of all that the more accurate higher-order Runge-Kutta methods require evaluation of our function $f(x,y)$ for several combinations of x and y values. Once the solution process has started, and has passed step i, this function has already been evaluated for several points at steps 1, 2, 3, ..., i. We can use these prior values to 'predict' a value for y at step i+1. For example, we could use the modified Euler method over the interval $[x_{i-1}, x_{i+1}]$ with x_i as the mid-point, giving the formula:

$$y_{i+1} = y_{i-1} + 2hf(x_i, y_i)$$

Note that two previous y-values are needed in order to calculate the next y-value, and the solution process has to be started by using a different method such as a Runge-Kutta method to calculate y_1 from y_0.

Once an approximate value for y_{i+1} has been obtained, a more accurate estimate can be obtained as follows:

(a) Calculate $y'_{i+1} = f(x_{i+1}, y_{i+1})$

(b) Draw a line through the point (x_i, y_i) with a gradient that is the average of y'_i and y'_{i+1}

(c) Take the y-value on this line at x_{i+1} as a new estimate of y_{i+1}. The new value for y_{i+1} is given by:

$$y_i + \frac{h}{2}(f(x_i, y_i) + f(x_{i+1}, y_{i+1}))$$

This so-called 'corrector' process is in fact a variant of another Runge-Kutta method. The corrector stage can be repeated as often as we like until the value of y_{i+1} is no longer changing significantly, i.e. we can 'iterate to convergence'. It can be shown that for 'sufficiently small' h, repeated application of the above corrector process will converge.

Although both the predictor and corrector methods described above are variants of Runge-Kutta techniques, this does not imply that all predictor-corrector methods are variants of Runge-Kutta techniques.

Program 8.5

This program uses the predictor-corrector method described above to solve the differential equation

$$y' = x^2 + y^2$$

with initial conditions, step-length h, and the range of x-values to be considered all specified at the keyboard. The solution is started using the improved Euler method.

```
PROGRAM predictorcorrector(input,output);

CONST smallvalue = 0.0000000001;

VAR previousx, x, newx, finalx, h,
    previousy, y, newy,
    fxy, newfxy : real;
    correctionsneeded : integer;

    FUNCTION f(x, y : real) : real;
    BEGIN
        f := sqr(x) + sqr(y)
    END;
```

```
        PROCEDURE start;
        BEGIN
            fxy := f(x,y);
            newx := x + h;
            newy := y + h*f(x + h/2, y + h/2*fxy);
            newfxy := f(newx, newy)
        END;

        PROCEDURE predict;
        BEGIN
            newx := newx + h;
            newy := previousy + 2*h*fxy;
            newfxy := f(newx, newy)
        END;

        PROCEDURE correct;
        VAR lastnewy : real;
        BEGIN
            correctionsneeded := 0;
            REPEAT
                lastnewy := newy;
                newy := y + h/2*(fxy+newfxy);
                newfxy := f(newx, newy);
                correctionsneeded := correctionsneeded + 1
            UNTIL abs(newy - lastnewy) <= smallvalue
        END;


    BEGIN
        write('    Initial x = ');  readln(x);
        write('    Initial y = ');  readln(y);
        write('Step length h = ');  readln(h);
        write('      Final x = ');  readln(finalx);  writeln;

        writeln('x':6, 'approx y':16, 'corrections needed':22);
        writeln('-':6, '--------':16, '------------------':22);

        start;
        writeln(newx:6:2, newy:16:10);

        REPEAT
            previousx := x;   x := newx;
            previousy := y;   y := newy;
            fxy := newfxy;

            predict;
            correct;

            writeln(newx:6:2, newy:16:10, correctionsneeded:14)
        UNTIL newx >= finalx

    END.
```

The following display was produced by a run of this program:

```
       Initial x = 0.0
       Initial y = 0.0
Step length h = 0.1
         Final x = 1.0
```

x	approx y	corrections needed
0.10	0.0002500000	
0.20	0.0027503814	3
0.30	0.0092550424	4
0.40	0.0217830502	4
0.50	0.0423966491	4
0.60	0.0732548364	5
0.70	0.1167041428	5
0.80	0.1754238114	6
0.90	0.2526541941	6
1.00	0.3525608592	7
1.10	0.4808359791	7

When the above program was modified so as to apply it to the equation

$$y' = 2y$$

the following display was produced:

```
       Initial x = 0.0
       Initial y = 1.0
Step length h = 0.1
         Final x = 1.0
```

x	approx y	corrections needed
0.10	1.2200000000	
0.20	1.4911111111	9
0.30	1.8224691358	9
0.40	2.2274622771	9
0.50	2.7224538942	9
0.60	3.3274436484	9
0.70	4.0668755703	10
0.80	4.9706256971	10
0.90	6.0752091853	10
1.00	7.4252556709	10
1.10	9.0753124867	10

The accuracy of these results should be compared with the results obtained by previous methods for the same equation. (The exact solution was tabulated by Program 8.4.)

Exercises

(1) Write a program that tabulates the approximation to $f'(x)$ given by

$$\frac{f(x+h) - f(x-h)}{2h}$$

for progressively smaller values of h. Test the program on the same function as that used in Program 8.1 and compare the accuracy of your results with those of Program 8.1.

(2) A sequence of altimeter readings taken by an ascending weather balloon at half-second intervals is available for input to a Pascal program. Write a program that tabulates time, height and approximate velocity. Wherever possible, obtain velocity approximations by using the method of Exercise 1. The less accurate formula will have to be used for the initial and final points.

(3) Write a program that integrates a simple function such as

$$f(x) = x^3 + 2x - 1$$

using the rectangle rule, the trapezoidal rule and Simpson's rule, with different values of h. The program should tabulate the results together with the exact solution so that the accuracy of the three methods can be compared.

(4) At a particular position along its length, a river is 25 metres wide. Depth soundings have been taken at 0.5 metre intervals across the river and the approximate linear rate of flow (metres/second) of the river at this position has been measured. Write a Pascal program that uses the trapezoidal rule in calculating an approximation to the total volume of water flowing down the river in one day.

(5) Part of the inertial guidance system of a space probe transmits the forward acceleration (in m/s^2) at one second intervals to the onboard computer. Write a Pascal program that reads such a sequence of values and calculates the approximate change in forward velocity over a period of 10 seconds. Use the fact that the change in velocity is given by

$$\int_0^{10} a(t)\,dt$$

where $a(t)$ is the acceleration expressed as a function of time. Use Simpson's rule to obtain the approximation.

(6) Write a program that uses the trapezoidal rule to calculate an approximation to

$$\int_a^b f(x)\,dx$$

where f is a function that can be evaluated by the program. At each step, the program should adjust the length of the step according to the rate of change of the function. Experiment with different strategies for adjusting h. One simple possibility is as follows: at step i, if $f(x_i+h)$ differs from $f(x_i)$ by more than 10% say, then h should be halved. If the difference is less than 5% then h could be doubled. Note that because the value of h keeps changing, the program will have to calculate the area of each trapezoid separately. For further possible strategies, see the references in the Bibliography.

(7) The accuracy of the solution obtained by Program 8.4 can be improved by using smaller h-values, but this could result in excessive output from the program as it stands. Modify the program so that the user can specify the points at which the solution is to be tabulated.

(8) Write a program that uses Euler's method, the modified Euler method and the fourth-order Runge-Kutta method to solve the differential equation of Program 8.4. For the purpose of comparison, the program should tabulate the solutions obtained by the three methods alongside each other.

(9) Modify Program 8.5 so that the user can specify (as in Exercise 7) the number of points at which the solution is to be tabulated.

(10) The 'logistic equation':

$$\frac{dN}{dt} = rN(1 - \frac{N}{K}) \qquad r,K > 0$$

describes the density-dependent growth of a population N. r and K are parameters representing rate of growth and maximum sustainable population. Write a Pascal program that can be used to solve this equation for a given initial population and given values for r and K. Use the program output to sketch a graph that shows how the population grows.

(11) If a population, whose growth is described by the equation of Exercise 10, is harvested, the equation becomes:

$$\frac{dN}{dt} = rN(1 - \frac{N}{K}) - EN$$

where E is a parameter representing harvesting 'effort'. Use a Pascal program to solve this equation for different combinations of values of r, K and E. Use the results produced to sketch graphs indicating the behaviour of the population for each set of parameter values.

9 Linear equations

Matrices and two-dimensional tables of information crop up in many computer applications in science and engineering. Pascal programs to handle such information involve the extensive use of two-dimensional arrays. In this chapter, we shall further demonstrate the use of two-dimensional arrays by presenting techniques for solving simultaneous linear equations and by writing Pascal programs that implement these techniques.

A well-known practical context that produces sets of linear simultaneous equations is a linear electrical network:

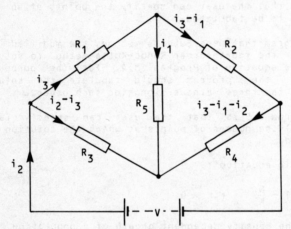

Given values for V and the resistors, Kirchoff's law applied to the above network results in a set of 3 equations in 3 unknowns, i_1, i_2, i_3:

$$-R_2 i_1 \qquad\qquad + (R_1+R_2) i_3 = V$$
$$R_5 i_1 - R_3 i_2 + (R_1+R_3) i_3 = 0$$
$$-(R_2+R_4+R_5) i_1 - R_4 i_2 + (R_2+R_4) i_3 = 0$$

Such equations could be solved manually, but it is considerably more convenient if a computer program can be used.

Nowadays there are applications that produce very large sets of equations that could not possibly be solved manually. A good example is **computer X-ray tomography**. Here a linear equation results from the intensity value of a narrow beam of X-rays after it has passed through part of the body.

The received intensity is an exponential function of the transmitted intensity I_0:

$$I = I_0 \exp\left(-\sum_i \alpha_i l_i\right)$$

$$\ln I - \ln I_0 = -\sum_i \alpha_i l_i$$

giving
$$\sum_i \alpha_i l_i = \ln I_0 - \ln I$$

The alpha-values are the set of absorbtion coefficients for each elemental area of tissue encountered by the beam and the l-values are the path lengths through each area.

Rotating and translating the beam so that it passes through the body in many different otientations in a single transverse plane produces a very large set of equations. The l-values are known from the geometry of the system. This large set of equations is solved for the alpha-values and a plane of absorption coefficients is constructed. This forms a two-dimensional tomographic image of the plane covered by the X-rays.

9.1 Simple elimination

9.1.1 A worked example

We present a worked example of the use of a simple **elimination** technique to solve three simultaneous linear equations in three variables. This will serve as a useful introduction to the method used by the program we develop in subsequent sections. It may seem that we present the solution process in rather tedious detail, but a clear understanding of each step involved is necessary to develop of a program to carry out the process. For the moment, we shall assume that nothing can go wrong in the course of solving the equations. This is certainly not the case, but we shall deal

Later with difficulties that can arise.

The problem that we consider is the following:

Find values for x, y and z that satisfy the equations:

$$3x + 2y + z = 12 \quad (1)$$
$$x + 3y + 2z = 13 \quad (2)$$
$$2x + 4y + 3z = 20 \quad (3)$$

The solution process takes place in two main stages.

Stage 1 - Elimination

We start by using equation (1) to eliminate the first variable, x, from each of the other equations. We could do this by using equation (1) to give us an expression for x involving y and z:

$$x = 4 - \frac{2}{3}y - \frac{1}{3}z$$

This expression for x could be substituted in equations (2) and (3) to give new forms for equations (2) and (3). It is well known that this process of substitution is exactly equivalent to subtracting a multiple of equation (1) from equation (2) and a different multiple from equation (3), the multiples being chosen so that the x term disappears from equations (2) and (3). To eliminate x from equation (2), the **multiplier** required for equation (1) is

$$\frac{\text{the coefficient of x in equation (2)}}{\text{the coefficient of x in equation (1)}} = \frac{1}{3}$$

To eliminate x from equation (3), the multiplier required for equation (1) is

$$\frac{\text{the coefficient of x in equation (3)}}{\text{the coefficient of x in equation (1)}} = \frac{2}{3}$$

We get

equation (1) as before:

$$3x + 2y + z = 12 \quad (1)$$

equation (2) $- \frac{1}{3}$*equation (1), giving a new equation (2):

$$\frac{7}{3}y + \frac{5}{3}z = 9 \quad (2)$$

equation (3) $- \frac{2}{3}$*equation (1), giving a new equation (3):

$$\frac{8}{3}y + \frac{7}{3}z = 12 \quad (3)$$

Note that we have replaced our set of three equations by a new, but **equivalent,** set of equations. We are no longer interested in the original form of the three equations and so we now use the numbers (2) and (3) to refer to the second and third equations in the new set. Such renumbering will be important when we come to store our equations in a Pascal program.

Equations (2) and (3) now constitute **two** simultaneous equations in **two** variables, y and z. We can use equation (2) to eliminate y from equation (3) in the same way as before. We multiply equation (2) by

$$\frac{\text{the coefficient of y in equation (3)}}{\text{the coefficient of y in equation (2)}} = \frac{\frac{8}{3}}{\frac{7}{3}} = \frac{8}{7}$$

and we subtract this multiple of equation (2) from equation (3) giving a new version of equation (3):

$$3x + 2y + z = 12 \qquad (1)$$

$$\frac{7}{3}y + \frac{5}{3}z = 9 \qquad (2)$$

$$\frac{3}{7}z = \frac{12}{7} \qquad (3)$$

The first of the two main stages in the solution process is now complete and the equations are said to be in **triangular form** because of their shape. We now proceed to

Stage 2 - Back substitution

Equation (3) can be easily solved for z. From (3)

$$z = \frac{\frac{12}{7}}{\frac{3}{7}} = \frac{12}{3} = 4$$

Substituting this value of z in equation (2) gives us

$$y = \frac{9 - \frac{5}{3}*4}{\frac{7}{3}} = 1$$

Values for y and z can now be substituted in equation (1) to give

$$x = \frac{12 - 2 - 4}{3} = 2$$

It should be clear that the above process is easily extended to deal with systems of n equations in n variables where n>3. For example, with 4 equations in 4 variables, x, y, z, t say, Stage 1 proceeds as follows:

(a) Use equation 1 to eliminate x from equations (2), (3) and (4).
(b) Use equation 2 to eliminate y from equations (3) and (4).
(c) Use equation 3 to eliminate z from equation (4).

Stage 2 is then straightforward:

(a) Solve equation (4) for t.
(b) Solve equation (3) for z.
(c) Solve equation (2) for y.
(d) Solve equation (1) for x.

Exercise 1 provides an example of a 4 variable system for you to solve by hand.

Before proceeding, we again draw attention to the fact that there are various things that can go wrong during the above process. For example, at step (b) in stage 1, the coefficient of y might be zero, in which case we could not calculate a multiplier for eliminating y from equations (3) and (4). It might even turn that there is no solution that satisfies our set of equations, or there might be an infinite set of solutions. Any program for solving simultaneous equations must eventually look out for and deal appropriately with such difficulties. It will simplify presentation of the first program if, for the time being, we continue to assume that nothing can go wrong.

9.1.2 Matrix notation

At this stage, we need to introduce a systematic way of referring to the coefficients and variables of our system of equations, so that we can describe the solution process more precisely and implement it as a computer program. For a system involving n variables, the variables are usually named

$$x_1, x_2, \ldots\ldots, x_n$$

and the coefficients are subscripted to indicate where they appear in the set of equations. For example, a system of 3 equations is usually written as

$$a_{11}x_1 + a_{12}x_2 + a_{13}x_3 = b_1$$
$$a_{21}x_1 + a_{22}x_2 + a_{23}x_3 = b_2$$
$$a_{31}x_1 + a_{32}x_2 + a_{33}x_3 = b_3$$

More generally, a system of n equations is written as

$$a_{11}x_1 + a_{12}x_2 + a_{13}x_3 + \cdots + a_{1n}x_n = b_1$$
$$a_{21}x_1 + a_{22}x_2 + a_{23}x_3 + \cdots + a_{2n}x_n = b_2$$
$$\vdots$$
$$a_{n1}x_1 + a_{n2}x_2 + a_{n3}x_3 + \cdots + a_{nn}x_n = b_n$$

This can be written in matrix notation as

$$A\underline{x} = \underline{b}$$

where

$$A = \begin{bmatrix} a_{11} & a_{12} & a_{13} & \cdots & a_{1n} \\ a_{21} & a_{22} & a_{23} & \cdots & a_{2n} \\ \vdots & & & & \\ a_{n1} & a_{n2} & a_{n3} & \cdots & a_{nn} \end{bmatrix} \quad \underline{x} = \begin{bmatrix} x_1 \\ x_2 \\ \vdots \\ x_n \end{bmatrix} \quad \underline{b} = \begin{bmatrix} b_1 \\ b_2 \\ \vdots \\ b_n \end{bmatrix}$$

It should be obvious that the only information needed to describe the set of equations is the matrix A and the vector $\underline{b}$ and that this is the information that has to be stored in a computer program that solves the system of equations.

The above notation suggests the use of the Pascal data types

```
TYPE   subscript = 1..n;
       coeffmatrix = ARRAY[subscript,subscript] OF real;
       vector = ARRAY[subscript] OF real;
```

with declarations

```
VAR  A : coeffmatrix;
     b : vector;
```

9.1.3 A simple elimination program

In Section 9.1, we saw that the solution process takes place in two main stages. This suggests the following outline Pascal program.

```
BEGIN
    readcoefficients;
    elimination;
    backsubstitution
END.
```

The procedure "readcoefficients" is straightforward and the details appear in Program 9.1. Note the way in which the loops have been organized so as to permit the most natural ordering of the input data - each complete row of A being followed by the corresponding value of $\underline{b}$.

Let us now consider the process of "elimination" in more detail:

First we use equation 1 to eliminate x_1
     from equation 2 to equation n.
Then we use equation 2 to eliminate x_2
     from equation 3 to equation n.

Then we use equation 3 to eliminate x_3
from equation 4 to equation n.
$$\vdots$$
and so on.

This can be outlined in Pascal as:

```
FOR i := 1 TO n-1 DO

    Use equation i to eliminate x_i
    from equations i+1 onwards.
```

Filling in more details, we get

```
FOR i := 1 TO n-1 DO
    FOR k := i+1 TO n DO

        Use equation i to eliminate x_i
        from equation k.
```

To eliminate x_i from equation k, we replace equation k by

(equation k) - a[k,i]/a[i,i] * (equation i)

In the context of our Pascal program, an equation is represented
by its coefficients, and subtracting equations means subtracting
corresponding coefficients. To subtract an appropriate multiple of
equation i from equation k, we require the following Pascal
program fragment:

```
BEGIN
    multiplier := a[k,i]/a[i,i];
    FOR j := i+1 TO n DO
        a[k,j] := a[k,j] - multiplier*a[i,j];
    b[k] := b[k] - multiplier*b[i];
    a[k,i] := 0
END
```

This is inserted in the previous outline to give the procedure
"elimination" in Program 9.1. Actually, the last statement in the
above fragment,

```
a[k,i] := 0
```

could be omitted. We have included it to emphasize that after
eliminating x_i from equation k, the coefficient a_{ki} is zero.
However, the value stored in location a[k,i] is never referred to
again by the program after this elimination step and it does not
matter what value is left there. In fact, some more sophisticated
methods take advantage of this and store other information in
locations of "a" that are no longer needed.

The procedure "backsubstitution" is used to calculate values
for

210

$$x_1, x_2, \ldots, x_n$$

and store these values in locations

$$x[1], x[2], \ldots, x[n].$$

This needs a loop of the form:

```
FOR i := n DOWNTO 1 DO
```

   calculate a value for x[i]

To see why the x-values have to be calculated in reverse order, refer back to the example that we solved manually. When the procedure is activated, our equations have the form

$$a_{11}x_1 + a_{12}x_2 + \cdots\cdots\cdots + a_{1n}x_n = b_1$$
$$a_{22}x_2 + \cdots\cdots\cdots + a_{2n}x_n = b_2$$
$$\cdot$$
$$\cdot \quad \cdot$$
$$a_{ii}x_i + \cdots + a_{in}x_n = b_i$$
$$\cdot$$
$$\cdot \quad \cdot$$
$$a_{nn}x_n = b_n$$

where the a_{ij} are of course completely new values.

Provided that values for

$$x_{i+1}, x_{i+2}, \ldots, x_n$$

have already been calculated, we can calculate x_i as follows:

$$x_i = \frac{b_i - a_{i,i+1}x_{i+1} - a_{i,i+2}x_{i+2} - \cdots - a_{in}x_n}{a_{ii}}$$

This is done by the Pascal fragment

```
BEGIN
    s := b[i];
    FOR j := i+1 TO n DO
        s := s - a[i,j]*x[j];
    x[i] := s/a[i,i]
END
```

Notice that x[n] is also evaluated by the above fragment. When i=n, the loop specified by

```
FOR j := i+1 TO n DO
```

is not executed at all and the above fragment is equivalent to

```
         x[n] := b[n]/a[n,n]
```

We now present the complete program whose construction has been
described in this section.

Program 9.1

A simple elimination program to solve a system of n simultaneous
linear equations in n variables. The program will be modified
later to deal with the various problems that can arise during the
solution process.

```
    PROGRAM solve(input,output);

    CONST n = 4;

    TYPE   subscript = 1..n;
           coeffmatrix = ARRAY [subscript, subscript] OF real;
               vector = ARRAY [subscript] OF real;

    VAR  a : coeffmatrix;
         b, x : vector;

       PROCEDURE readcoefficients;
       VAR i,j : subscript;
       BEGIN
          FOR i := 1 TO n DO
          BEGIN
             FOR j := 1 TO n DO read(a[i,j]);
             readln(b[i])
          END
       END;

       PROCEDURE elimination;
       VAR i,j,k : subscript;
           multiplier : real;
       BEGIN
          FOR i := 1 TO n-1 DO
             FOR k := i+1 TO n DO
             BEGIN
                multiplier := a[k,i]/a[i,i];
                FOR j := i+1 TO n DO
                   a[k,j] := a[k,j] - multiplier*a[i,j];
                b[k] := b[k] - multiplier*b[i];
                a[k,i] := 0
             END
       END;
```

```
PROCEDURE backsubstitution;
VAR i,j : subscript;
    s : real;
BEGIN
   FOR i := n DOWNTO 1 DO
   BEGIN
      s := b[i];
      FOR j := i+1 TO n DO
         s := s - a[i,j]*x[j];
      x[i] := s/a[i,i]
   END
END;

PROCEDURE writesolution;
VAR i : subscript;
BEGIN
   FOR i := 1 TO n DO
      writeln('x', i:1, ' = ', x[i]:8:3)
END;

BEGIN  { main program }
   readcoefficients;
   elimination;
   backsubstitution;
   writesolution
END.
```

The above program carries out a simplified version of the process
known as **Gaussian elimination**.

9.2 Singular equations

There are in fact three possible outcomes to an attempt to solve a
set of simultaneous equations of the type that we have been
discussing. An understanding of these possibilities will be useful
before we attempt to improve Program 9.1. For a given set of
equations, we shall find that one of the following holds:

   (1) There is a unique solution.
   (2) There is no solution.
   (3) There is an infinite number of solutions.

In cases (2) and (3) the set of equations is said to be **singular**.
We can illustrate these three possibilities graphically for
equations in two variables.

Case 1

The following pair of equations has a unique solution.

$$3x - 6y = 6$$
$$x + 4y = 8$$

The solution is of course x=4, y=1. A graphical representation of the equations appears in Figure 9.1.

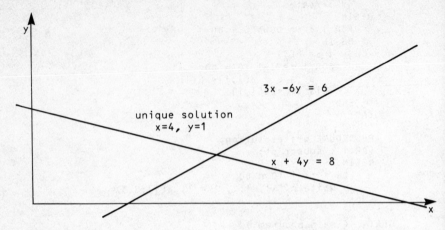

3x -6y = 6

unique solution
x=4, y=1

x + 4y = 8

Figure 9.1   Two equations with a unique solution

The two lines represented by the equations intersect at a point that represents the solution.

Case 2

The following pair of equations has no solution:

    x + 2y = 4
    3x + 6y = 6

These equations are represented graphically in Figure 9.2.

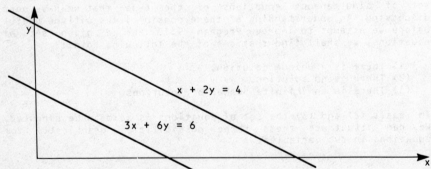

x + 2y = 4

3x + 6y = 6

Figure 9.2   Two equations with no solution

In this case, the two lines represented by the equations are parallel and they never meet. There is no point on the coordinate plane that lies on both lines.

Case 3

The following pair of equations has an infinite number of solutions.

$$x + 4y = 5$$
$$3x + 12y = 15$$

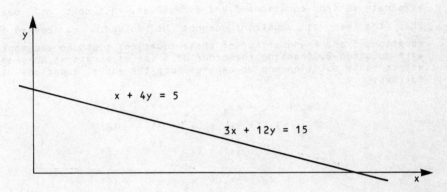

Figure 9.3   Two equations with an infinite number of solutions

In fact the second equation is a multiple of the first and they both represent the **same** line. **Any** point on this line satisfies both equations.

   This two-dimensional model of two variables can be extended to an n-dimensional model representing n variables. Each equation represents a hyperplane and the point of intersection of the hyperplanes is the solution.

9.3 An improved Gaussian elimination program

We now return to our simple elimination program (Program 9.1). The step in the solution process at which difficulties can arise is the step at which we wish to use equation i to eliminate the variable x_i from equations i+1, i+2, ..., n. If the variable x_i does not appear in equation i (i.e., it has a zero coefficient), then equation i can not be used to eliminate x_i from the other equations. As an example, consider the following set of equations in four variables.

$$2x_1 + 4x_2 + x_3 + 2x_4 = 17$$
$$x_1 + 2x_2 + 2x_3 + 3x_4 = 16$$
$$2x_1 + x_2 + 3x_3 + 3x_4 = 16$$
$$x_1 + 3x_2 + x_3 + 2x_4 = 14$$

After the first step in the elimination process, these become

$$2x_1 + 4x_2 + x_3 + 2x_4 = 17 \qquad (1)$$

$$\frac{3}{2}x_3 + 2x_4 = \frac{15}{2} \qquad (2)$$

$$-3x_2 + 2x_3 + x_4 = -1 \qquad (3)$$

$$x_2 + \frac{1}{2}x_3 + x_4 = \frac{11}{2} \qquad (4)$$

x_2 does not appear in equation 2 and equation 2 can not be used to eliminate x_2 from equations 3 and 4. However, this does not mean that the set of equations cannot be solved. x_2 appears in equations 3 and 4 and either of these equations could be exchanged with equation 2. Changing the order of a set of equations does not affect their solution and we can renumber the above equations as follows:

$$2x_1 + 4x_2 + x_3 + 2x_4 = 17 \qquad (1)$$

$$-3x_2 + 2x_3 + x_4 = -1 \qquad (2)$$

$$\frac{3}{2}x_3 + 2x_4 = \frac{15}{2} \qquad (3)$$

$$x_2 + \frac{1}{2}x_3 + x_4 = \frac{11}{2} \qquad (4)$$

The new equation 2 now has a non-zero coefficient for x_2 and we could proceed with the elimination process.

As the above discussion suggests, at each execution of the main loop in our procedure "elimination" we are going to make sure, by interchanging two rows of coefficients if necessary, that a[i,i] is non-zero. In fact we shall do rather more than this. Problems are just as likely to arise if a[i,i] is very small. We shall find the equation (from equation i onwards) that has the x_i coefficient of **largest** magnitude and we shall interchange this equation with equation i. This will have the effect of making the magnitude of a[i,i] as large as possible. It can be shown that this will reduce rounding errors that take place during subsequent calculations - a detailed discussion of why this is so is beyond the scope of this text.

When we are about to eliminate x_i from equations i+1, i+2, ..., n, there is a possibility that all of equations i, i+1, ..., n have zero coefficients for x_i. If this happens, it means that the system of equations being solved is singular and that either there is no solution or there is an infinite number of solutions. Our improved elimination program will detect a singularity, but it will not distinguish the two types of singularity.

We now consider in detail the modifications to Program 9.1 that will reorder the equations where necessary and possibly detect that they are singular. We shall use a boolean variable to indicate whether a singularity has been detected during the

216

elimination process:

```
    singularitydetected : boolean;
```

The main program block needs to be modified to test this variable immediately after the call of the procedure "elimination". If the equations are singular, then the program must terminate immediately with an appropriate message.

```
    readcoefficients;
    elimination;
    IF singularitydetected THEN
        writeln('The equations are singular.')
    ELSE
    BEGIN
        backsubstitution;
        writesolution
    END
```

We now need to change the procedure "elimination" so that, for each value of i, the equations are reordered if necessary and also checked for singularity. Because the process must terminate as soon as a singularity is detected, the main loop in this procedure must now be a REPEAT loop. The outline structure required is as follows:

```
    i := 1;
    REPEAT
        reorder equations if necessary
          (and check for singularity);

        IF NOT singularitydetected THEN

            eliminate x  from equations i+1 onwards;
                      i

        i := i+1
    UNTIL (i = n) OR singularitydetected;
```

In order to discover whether equation i has to be replaced, we must scan through rows i, $i+1$, ..., n of the coefficient matrix, examining the ith element in each row:

```
    l := i;
    FOR k := i+1 TO n DO
        IF abs(a[k,i]) > abs(a[l,i]) THEN l := k;
```

On exit from this loop, the value of "l" tells us which row had the x_i coefficient with the largest magnitude. If a[l,i] is zero, then all the x_i coefficients examined must be zero and this means that the equations are singular. In fact we should test whether a[l,i] is **close** to zero - it is always safer to do this when handling real numbers. If a singularity has not been discovered, then equation l must be exchanged with equation i (unless of course $i=l$ in which case the exchange is unnecessary).

217

```
    IF abs(a[l,i])<=assumedzero THEN
        singularitydetected := true
    ELSE  IF i<>l THEN
```

interchange equations i and l

To swap equations i and l, we must swap corresponding coefficients in rows i and l of array "a" and we must also swap $b[i]$ and $b[l]$. The first $i-1$ coefficients in these equations are all zeros and can be ignored. (At this stage, variables x_1, x_2, ..., x_{i-1} have all been eliminated from equations i, i+1, ..., n.) We require

```
    BEGIN
        FOR j := i TO n DO  swap(a[i,j], a[l,j]);
        swap(b[i], b[l])
    END
```

where the procedure "swap" exchanges the contents of the two variables supplied as parameters.

There is one further possibility to be covered. After the elimination process has been completed, the last equation has the form

$$a_{nn}x_n = b_n$$

It may be that we end up with $a_{nn}=0$ which again indicates that the system of equations is singular. This possibility has not yet been covered. It can be dealt with by inserting one final statement at the end of the procedure "elimination":

```
    IF NOT singularitydetected THEN
        singularitydetected := abs(a[n,n])<=assumedzero
```

Collecting all these details together gives us

Program 9.2

A complete Gaussian elimination program for solving a set of n simultaneous equations in n variables. We have omitted details of procedures that are identical to those in Program 9.1.

```
PROGRAM solve(input,output);

CONST n = 4;

TYPE    subscript = 1..n;
        coeffmatrix = ARRAY [subscript, subscript] OF real;
            vector = ARRAY [subscript] OF real;

VAR  a : coeffmatrix;
     b, x : vector;
     singularitydetected : boolean;

   PROCEDURE readcoefficients;

        { as before }

   PROCEDURE elimination;
   CONST assumedzero = 0.00001;
   VAR i,j,k : subscript;
       multiplier : real;

      PROCEDURE swap(VAR x,y : real);
      VAR t : real;
      BEGIN    t:=x;   x:=y;   y:=t END;

      PROCEDURE reorderequations;
      VAR k, l, j : subscript;
      BEGIN
         l := i;
         FOR k := i+1 TO n DO
            IF abs(a[k,i]) > abs(a[l,i]) THEN l := k;

         IF abs(a[l,i])<=assumedzero THEN
            singularitydetected := true
         ELSE  IF i<>l THEN
               BEGIN
                   FOR j := i TO n DO  swap(a[i,j], a[l,j]);
                   swap(b[i], b[l])
               END
      END  { reorderequations };
```

```
        BEGIN  { elimination }
           singularitydetected := false;
           i := 1;
           REPEAT
              reorderequations;
              IF NOT singularitydetected THEN
                 FOR k := i+1 TO n DO
                 BEGIN
                    multiplier := a[k,i]/a[i,i];
                    FOR j := i+1 TO n DO
                       a[k,j] := a[k,j] - multiplier*a[i,j];
                    b[k] := b[k] - multiplier*b[i];
                    a[k,i] := 0
                 END;
              i := i+1
           UNTIL (i = n) OR singularitydetected;
           IF NOT singularitydetected THEN
              singularitydetected := abs(a[n,n])<=assumedzero
        END  { elimination };

        PROCEDURE backsubstitution;

              { as before }

        PROCEDURE writesolution;

              { as before }

     BEGIN
        readcoefficients;
        elimination;
        IF singularitydetected THEN
           writeln('The equations are singular.')
        ELSE
        BEGIN
           backsubstitution;
           writesolution
        END
     END.
```

We mention one further possible modification to the program. As it stands, the value of n is written into the program. If we want to solve a system of 10 equations in 10 variables, the second line of the program must be changed to

        CONST n = 10;

If instead, we wish the program to work for any value of n without the program having to be edited, we could declare arrays that are much bigger than we are ever likely to need and make "n" a variable whose value is read by the program. The new declarations might be:

        CONST maxn = 50;

```
TYPE subscript = 1..maxn;

VAR n : subscript;
```

and at the start of the main block, we require

```
read(n);
```

The rest of the program would remain the same. Note that if, for example, the value 10 is given for the variable n, then the program allocates space for a 50x50 array of coefficients, but uses only a 10x10 subset of the locations of this array, the remaining locations being ignored by the program. Similarily, only part of the arrays "b" and "x" are used.

9.4 Iterative methods

An interesting alternative approach to the solution of a set of simultaneous linear equations is the use of an iterative technique. Iterative techniques for solving equations in one variable were introduced in Chapter 7. We start with an initial guess at a solution and at each step we calculate a new (hopefully better) estimate of the solution from the previous one. This approach can be generalized to solving a set of simultaneous equations in several variables.

9.4.1 The Gauss-Seidel method

One iterative technique for use in the case of linear equations is known as the Gauss-Seidel method. We illustrate the basic idea with a set of 3 equations in 3 variables:

$$a_{11}x_1 + a_{12}x_2 + a_{13}x_3 = b_1$$
$$a_{21}x_1 + a_{22}x_2 + a_{23}x_3 = b_2$$
$$a_{31}x_1 + a_{32}x_2 + a_{33}x_3 = b_3$$

These equations can be rewritten in the form:

$$x_1 = \frac{b_1 - a_{12}x_2 - a_{13}x_3}{a_{11}}$$

$$x_2 = \frac{b_2 - a_{21}x_1 - a_{23}x_3}{a_{22}}$$

$$x_3 = \frac{b_3 - a_{31}x_1 - a_{32}x_2}{a_{33}}$$

and it is from this form of the equations that our iterative technique is developed.

We assume that the a-values and the b-values are stored in two Pascal arrays "a" and "b" exactly as before. We start with an

221

initial set of guesses at the values x_1, x_2, x_3 stored in the locations x[1], x[2], x[3]. New estimates for x_1, x_2, x_3 are then calculated by repeatedly obeying:

```
x[1] := (b[1] - a[1,2]*x[2] - a[1,3]*x[3]) / a[1,1];
x[2] := (b[2] - a[2,1]*x[1] - a[2,3]*x[3]) / a[2,2];
x[3] := (b[3] - a[3,1]*x[1] - a[3,2]*x[2]) / a[3,3];
```

Notice that each time a new value is assigned to x[i], the most up-to-date values for the other variables are used in calculating the new value. **Under certain conditions** that we shall state later, the values x[1], x[2] and x[3] will get closer and closer to a set of values that represent the solution to the equations. Let us illustrate this for a simple example:

$$4x_1 + x_2 + 2x_3 = 18$$
$$x_1 + 2x_2 + x_3 = 13$$
$$3x_1 + 2x_2 + 6x_3 = 32$$

We start with x[1]=x[2]=x[3]=1. (Actually, the initial value of x[1] is irrelevant.) The following table gives the values contained in these three locations after each application of the above three assignment statements.

	x[1]	x[2]	x[3]
	1.00000000	1.00000000	1.00000000
1	3.75000000	4.12500000	2.08333333
2	2.42708333	4.24479167	2.70486111
3	2.08637153	4.10438368	2.92201968
4	2.01289424	4.03254304	2.98270520
5	2.00051164	4.00839158	2.99694699
6	1.99942861	4.00181220	2.99968163
7	1.99970614	4.00030612	3.00004489
8	1.99990102	4.00002704	3.00004047
9	1.99997300	3.99999326	3.00001574

The values are getting closer and closer to the exact solution

$$x_1 = 2, \quad x_2 = 4, \quad x_3 = 3$$

A commonly used alternative initial solution is given by:

```
x[1] := b[1]/a[1,1];
x[2] := b[2]/a[2,2];
x[3] := b[3]/a[3,3]
```

We must now decide when to stop the process. The normal procedure in implementing an iterative method for solving equations is to stop when the solution is no longer changing, or is changing by only a very small amount. In this case, we have three values that change each time the above three assignments are obeyed. We shall stop the process when all three values have changed by less than some small quantity that represents the accuracy to which we are working. In the above example, we might stop when all the x-values have changed by less than 0.001, ie after step 8. Note that stopping when **all** x-values have changed by less than the required accuracy is equivalent to stopping when the **largest** change in x-value is less than the required accuracy.

In the more general case of a system of n equations in n variables, we express the equations in the form

$$x_1 = \frac{b_1 - a_{12}x_2 - a_{13}x_3 - \cdots - a_{1n}x_n}{a_{11}}$$

$$x_2 = \frac{b_2 - a_{21}x_1 - a_{23}x_3 - \cdots - a_{2n}x_n}{a_{22}}$$

$$\vdots$$

$$x_i = \frac{b_i - \sum_{k=1}^{i-1} a_{ik}x_k - \sum_{k=i+1}^{n} a_{ik}x_k}{a_{ii}}$$

$$\vdots$$

and the iteration formulae are derived directly from this form of the equations.

9.4.2 A Gauss-Seidel iteration program

In this section, we develop a program to apply the Gauss-Seidel method to a system of n equations in n variables. The overall program structure will be as follows:

readcoefficients;

make a first guess at the solution;

REPEAT

calculate a new set of x-values;
(and take note of the maximum change in x-value);

UNTIL maxchange < accuracy;

writesolution;

As our first guess at the solution, we shall simply set all the x-values to 1.

The process of changing the x-values can be outlined as follows:

```
    maxchange := 0;
    FOR i := 1 TO n DO
    BEGIN

        calculate a "newxi" value;

        change := abs(x[i] - newxi);
        IF change>maxchange THEN maxchange := change;
        x[i] := newxi
    END
```

To calculate the new x_i value, we need to evaluate the expression for x_i given at the end of the last section:

$$x_i = \frac{b_i - \sum_{k=1}^{i-1} a_{ik} x_k - \sum_{k=i+1}^{n} a_{ik} x_k}{a_{ii}}$$

which becomes in Pascal:

```
    s := b[i];
    FOR k := 1 TO i-1 DO s := s - a[i,k]*x[k];
    FOR k := i+1 TO n DO s := s - a[i,k]*x[k];
    newxi := s/a[i,i];
```

Putting the details together, we get the complete program.

Program 9.3

Uses the Gauss-Seidel iteration method to solve a system of n simultaneous equations in n variables. The program makes the assumption that the Gauss-Seidel method will converge.

```
    PROGRAM GaussSeidel(input,output);

    CONST n = 3;
          accuracy = 0.0001;

    TYPE   subscript = 1..n;
           coeffmatrix = ARRAY [subscript, subscript] OF real;
              vector = ARRAY [subscript] OF real;

    VAR a : coeffmatrix;
        b, x : vector;
        maxchange : real;
        i : subscript;
```

```
      PROCEDURE readcoefficients;
      VAR i,j : subscript;
      BEGIN
         FOR i := 1 TO n DO
         BEGIN
            FOR j := 1 TO n DO read(a[i,j]);
            readln(b[i])
         END
      END;

      PROCEDURE changexvalues;
      VAR i,k : subscript;
          s, change, newxi : real;
      BEGIN
         maxchange := 0;
         FOR i := 1 TO n DO
         BEGIN
            s := b[i];
            FOR k := 1 TO i-1 DO s := s - a[i,k]*x[k];
            FOR k := i+1 TO n DO s := s - a[i,k]*x[k];
            newxi := s/a[i,i];
            change := abs(x[i] - newxi);
            IF change>maxchange THEN maxchange := change;
            x[i] := newxi
         END
      END;

      PROCEDURE writesolution;
      VAR i : subscript;
      BEGIN
         FOR i := 1 TO n DO
            writeln('x', i:1, ' = ', x[i]:8:3)
      END;

   BEGIN   { main program }
      readcoefficients;
      FOR i := 1 TO n DO x[i] := 1;

      REPEAT
         changexvalues
      UNTIL maxchange < accuracy;

      writesolution;
   END.
```

9.5 Final remarks

Gaussian elimination is one of the most widely used methods for
solving simultaneous linear equations. **In theory** it is an exact
method that will solve any set of equations, unless the equations
are singular in which case the method will discover that they are
singular. In practice, the values involved in calculating the
solution can not be stored exactly and rounding errors usually
take place at each step in the solution process. In most

applications, the rounding errors will not be significant, but occasionally, cases crop up where the accumulation of rounding errors does become significant. There are other techniques that can be used for improving a solution that contains errors, but such techniques are beyond the scope of this text. As a general rule, Gaussian elimination is used when the coefficient matrix is 'big and full'.

As we mentioned earlier, the Gauss-Seidel method can be applied only under certain conditions. A **sufficient** condition for the Gauss-Seidel method to converge for a given set of equations is that, for all values of i,

$$|a_{ii}| >= |a_{i1}| + |a_{i2}| + \ldots + |a_{i,i-1}| + |a_{i,i+1}| + \ldots + |a_{in}|$$

and for at least one value of i, strict inequality holds. Note that this is not a **necessary** condition – there are many sets of equations that do not satisfy this condition but which still converge under the Gauss-Seidel method.

Although the above condition may appear rather strict, there are many practical applications in which the equations to be solved are rather **sparse** and **diagonally dominant.** In other words, most of the coefficients off the leading diagonal are zero. In such cases, it can often be shown from the way in which the equations are generated that the above condition does hold. In general, Gauss-Seidel is used for sets of equations with sparse coefficient matrices.

Exercises

(1) Use the elimination technique presented in Section 9.1.1 to solve, by hand, the following system of equations:

```
 x +  y +  z +  t = 12
3x + 2y +  z +  t = 17
2x +  y + 2z + 2t = 23
 x + 3y + 3z +  t = 22
```

(2) Modify Program 9.1 so that it outputs the coefficient matrix at each step during the solution process. Use the modified program to solve the equations of Exercise 1 and check your hand-solution.

(3) Give values to the resistances and the voltage V in the electrical network presented in the introduction to this chapter and use a Pascal program to solve the network.

(4) It is required to determine the member forces in the 13-member plane truss shown below:

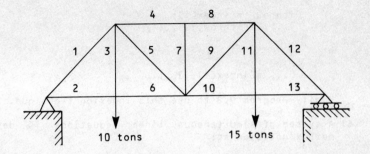

10 tons   15 tons

An analysis of this truss gives rise to the set of equations:

$$A\underline{x} = \underline{b}$$

where

$$
A =
\begin{bmatrix}
r & 0 & 0 & 1 & r & 0 & 0 & 0 & 0 & 0 & 0 & 0 & 0 \\
r & 0 & 1 & 0 & -r & 0 & 0 & 0 & 0 & 0 & 0 & 0 & 0 \\
0 & 1 & 0 & 0 & 0 & 1 & 0 & 0 & 0 & 0 & 0 & 0 & 0 \\
0 & 0 & 1 & 0 & 0 & 0 & 0 & 0 & 0 & 0 & 0 & 0 & 0 \\
0 & 0 & 0 & 1 & 0 & 0 & 0 & 1 & 0 & 0 & 0 & 0 & 0 \\
0 & 0 & 0 & 0 & 0 & 0 & 1 & 0 & 0 & 0 & 0 & 0 & 0 \\
0 & 0 & 0 & 0 & r & 1 & 0 & 0 & r & 1 & 0 & 0 & 0 \\
0 & 0 & 0 & 0 & -r & 0 & 1 & 0 & r & 0 & 0 & 0 & 0 \\
0 & 0 & 0 & 0 & 0 & 0 & 0 & 1 & r & 0 & 0 & r & 0 \\
0 & 0 & 0 & 0 & 0 & 0 & 0 & 0 & r & 0 & 1 & -r & 0 \\
0 & 0 & 0 & 0 & 0 & 0 & 0 & 0 & 0 & 1 & 0 & 0 & 1 \\
0 & 0 & 0 & 0 & 0 & 0 & 0 & 0 & 0 & 0 & 1 & 0 & 0 \\
0 & 0 & 0 & 0 & 0 & 0 & 0 & 0 & 0 & 0 & 0 & r & 1 \\
\end{bmatrix}
$$

where $r = \sin 45° = \cos 45°$

and

$$\underline{b} = (0, 0, 0, 10, 0, 0, 0, 0, 0, 0, 0, 15, 0)^{T}.$$

Use a Pascal program to solve the system.

(5) During the Gaussian elimination process used in Program 9.2, we frequently interchanged rows of the coefficient matrix A. We can make this process more efficient by setting up a one-dimensional 'index array' which contains a list of row numbers. The index array will be initialised by:

        FOR i := 1 TO n DO index[i] := i;

The first entry in the index array tells us which is currently the first row of A, the second entry tells us which is currently the second row of A and so on. Where previously we would have swapped all the contents of rows i and l of A, we now simply swap the contents of locations i and l in the index array. Row i of A must be accessed by something like:

```
        ithrow := index[i];
        ... a[ithrow,j] ...
```

or

```
        ... a[index[i],j] ...
```

Modify Program 9.2 to use this indexing technique.

(6) A system of simultaneous linear equations is described in matrix notation as:

$$A\underline{x} = \underline{b}.$$

Solving the system involves finding a set of x-values that satisfy the above equation. The x-values can also be obtained by forming:

$$\underline{x} = A^{-1}\underline{b}$$

If we use I to refer to the unit matrix, then the above equations can be rewritten as:

$$A\underline{x} = I\underline{b}$$
$$I\underline{x} = A^{-1}\underline{b}$$

The elimination stage in Program 9.2 involved a sequence of 'row-operations'. Any sequence of row-operations that converts the matrix A into I will also convert the matrix I into the matrix A^{-1}.

Write a Pascal program that uses this approach to invert a matrix.

10 Character graphics

The treatment in the next two chapters is device oriented. It assumes the reader will have access to character 'printers' (VDU's, line and matrix printers), high resolution microcomputer graphics such as the APPLE (hereinafter referred to as HRMC graphics) and incremental plotters. Most if not all readers will have access to character printers and this chapter describes simple techniques that can be employed to effect on such devices. The next chapter concentrates on line graphics using incremental plotters and HRMC graphics.

User designed character graphics programs are a little more tedious to write than their equivalent using line graphics. However, the techniques are still worthy of study because even though a HRMC graphics display is probably the commonest graphics device, character printers are the commonest hard copy device.

10.1 About programs in the graphics chapters

In general the programs below are written to be as short as possible. They are programs which illustrate technique and although they have been fully tested they mostly do not contain data validation and other error checks. Also for the sake of brevity in the programs, statements to produce legendry on the graphic displays are omitted. Somtimes empty procedures, or procedures with no text body have been included in programs. Again this is for the sake of brevity and clarity and such procedures will have been defined in a previous program.

Program results for the incremental plotter are unique both to the device used and the particular package used. Programs in the HRMC graphics section are for the APPLE. In both these cases the programs will transport to other systems with minor changes in detail. Wherever possible, use has been made of similar mathematical functions in different programs to illustrate different display modes. The reader thus has a basis for comparison of different methods.

10.2 Plotting f(x) on a character device

Character VDU's, matrix printers and line printers can be used to give approximate representations of functions of one and two variables. Thus a VDU capable of displaying m characters horizontally by n rows of characters vertically, where n is not necessarily limited to the screen height, can be visualized as a grid of mxn elements. A grid element can be 'on' or 'off' by printing a character in that position, or leaving it blank. Thus

printing a character in that position, or leaving it blank. Thus we can draw a graph, points of which consist of a character. The drawback with this scheme is twofold - coarse resolution and distortion due to the aspect ratio of characters. (The vertical dimension is 'stretched' by a ratio of approximately 7 to 5 over the horizontal.)

Program 10.1 plots a graph of the function:

$$y = \sin(x)/(x+1)$$

using this technique. The graph is plotted sideways with the x axis running down the centre of the screen. The program does not use any array storage and would be eminently suitable in a context such as a micro system where data storage is limited.

The program decides the status of each point to be plotted, i.e. whether the point lies in the LHS of the screen, on the x axis (centre of the screen) or in the RHS of the screen. It is selecting one out of three plotting sequences each time a point is to be plotted. The price paid for not using any buffer store is an increase in program complexity and program length. Also in this context the complexity has nothing to do with drawing graphs, but is a function of the technology of the device being used as a plotter. Yet another disadvantage of this program is that it cannot cope, without further modification with a multivalued function. The output shown in Figure 10.1 is for 3 periods at a period width of 10 points.

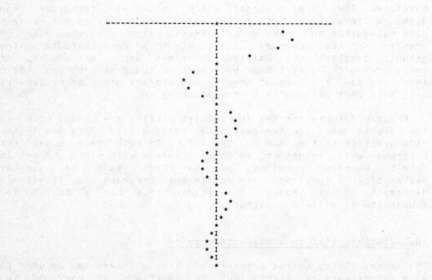

Figure 10.1   The graph of a harmonic function plotted using
              a character device. The output was generated
              by Program 10.1

Program 10.1

This program plots a graph of the function:

$$y = \sin(x)/(x+1).$$

```
PROGRAM plot (input,output);
   VAR noofperiods, periodwidth : integer;

   PROCEDURE plot(noofperiods, periodwidth : integer);

      CONST pi = 3.14159; xaxisch = 'I'; yaxisch = '-';
         space = ' '; screenwidth = 60; point = '*';

      VAR centre, width, period, row, fvalue, scale : integer;
         x , interval : real;

      FUNCTION  f(x : real) : real;
      BEGIN
         f := sin(x)/(x+1)
      END;

      PROCEDURE drawaxis;
         VAR  zerovalue, col : integer;
      BEGIN { of drawaxis }
         zerovalue := round(scale*f(0)) + centre;
         FOR col := 1 TO zerovalue-1  DO
            write(yaxisch);
         write(point);
         FOR col := zerovalue+1 TO width  DO
            write(yaxisch);
         writeln
      END { of drawaxis } ;
```

```
          BEGIN { of plot }
            width := screenwidth;
            IF odd(width) THEN centre :=  width DIV 2 + 1
            ELSE   BEGIN
               centre := width DIV 2;
               width  := width - 1
            END;
            scale := centre -1;
            drawaxis;  interval := 2*pi/periodwidth;  x := 0;
            FOR period := 1 TO noofperiods DO
              FOR row := 1 TO periodwidth DO
                BEGIN
                  x := x+ interval;
                  fvalue := round(scale * f(x) + centre);

                  IF fvalue < centre THEN
                     writeln(point:fvalue, xaxisch:centre-fvalue)
                  ELSE  IF fvalue > centre THEN
                     writeln(xaxisch:centre, point:fvalue-centre)
                  ELSE
                     writeln(point : centre)
              END;
          END { of plot };

        BEGIN { of program }
          write( 'Type  periods and  points per period :');
          read( noofperiods,periodwidth);
          plot(noofperiods, periodwidth)
        END.
```

Having seen how to plot a particular graph on a character
device we should now look at some of the general problems that are
always encountered when using computer graphics in mathematics.
The main problem encountered when plotting mathematical functions,
and this is device independent, is the transformation from
mathematical space to plotting space. For example the function:

$$y = \sin(x)$$

has a range of values:

$$-1 <= y <= 1$$
$$0 <= x <= 2*pi$$

These values must be converted or scaled into a plotting grid
which in this case is:

$$1 <= y <= 60$$
$$1 <= x <= \text{no. of periods} * \text{period width}$$

In Program 10.1 the values are explicitly scaled by multiplying by
half the screen width. The x values are implicitly scaled by
calculating, then adding, each time through the plotting loop, an
appropriate radian interval. This means that a jump of one line in
plotting space is related to the radian interval in mathematical

space. In standard graphics packages the transformation from mathematical space to plotting space is usually handled by the package.

10.3 Plotting f(x) on a character device using buffer store

If storage economy is not a prime consideration the tiresome selection of one out of three plotting sequences can be overcome by using a two dimensional array "screen" as a buffer store, representing the two dimensional plotting space of the character device.

This method is adopted in Program 10.2 which will produce almost exactly the same output as Program 10.1. The array "screen" is initialized to contain blanks, then each elaboration of the main plot loop loads a character into the appropriate column position in one row of the buffer array. When the loop is exhausted the buffer array will contain blanks overwritten at the appropriate points with axis and function points. One restriction contained in Program 10.2 is that "noofperiods" can no longer be sensibly input as data because the vertical (x axis) extent of the graph is fixed by the "screenheight" dimension of the buffer array "screen". The graph is plotted simply by printing out the contents of "screen". Another advantage of this approach is that it would be easy to arrange to draw the graph the right way up. Note that the transformation from mathematical space to plotting space is usually easier if the screen coordinates run from 0 upwards.

Program 10.2

This program plots the same harmonic function as Program 10.1 and will produce almost exactly the same output. However, this time a two-dimensional buffer is used.

```
PROGRAM screenplot (input,output);
   VAR periodwidth : integer;

   PROCEDURE plot(periodwidth : integer);

      CONST  pi = 3.14159; point = '*'; xaxisch = 'I';
         yaxisch = '-';   space = ' '; screenheight =  22;
         screenwidth = 60; ycentre = 30; yscale = 30;

      VAR
       screen:ARRAY[0..screenheight,0..screenwidth] OF char;
       x, interval        : real;
       period, row, fvalue  : integer;

      FUNCTION f(x:real):real;
      BEGIN
          f := sin(x)/(x+1)
      END  { of f(unction) };
```

```
PROCEDURE drawaxes;
   VAR row,col : integer;
BEGIN { of drawaxes }
   FOR col := 0 TO screenwidth DO
      screen[0,col] := yaxisch;

   FOR row:= 0 TO screenheight     DO
      screen[row,ycentre] := xaxisch
END   { of drawaxes};

PROCEDURE insertspaces;
   VAR row,col : integer;
BEGIN { of insertspaces }
   FOR col := 0 TO screenwidth DO
      FOR row := 0 TO screenheight  DO
         screen[row,col] := space
END   { of insertspaces };

PROCEDURE drawgraph;
   VAR row,col : integer;
BEGIN { of drawgraph }
   FOR row := 0 TO screenheight     DO
   BEGIN
      FOR col := 0 TO screenwidth DO
         write(screen[row,col]);
      writeln
   END
END   { of draw graph};

BEGIN { start of plot}
   insertspaces;   drawaxes;
   interval := 2*pi/periodwidth;  x := 0;
   FOR row := 0 TO screenheight DO
   BEGIN
      fvalue := round(yscale * f(x) + ycentre);
      x := x + interval;
      screen[row,fvalue] := point
   END;
   drawgraph
END { of plot};

BEGIN   { of program }
   write('type in period width');
   read(periodwidth);
   plot(periodwidth)
END.
```

In Chapter 4, and in Program 10.2, we pictured our two-dimensional
arrays as being organized into rows and columns, the first
subscript selecting a row and the second selecting a column. This
corresponded to the usual mathematical conventions for matrices.
In graphics, it is often more natural to think of the first
subscript as corresponding to the x-coordinate and the second as
corresponding to the y-coordinate, and picture our array the other
way round. This convention is adopted in subsequent programs. Note
the need to redefine "drawgraph" to produce the plots the right

way up.

10.4 Handling polar coordinates on a character device

The techniques used in Program 10.2 are easily extended to cope
with multivalued functions and polar coordinates. Trivial
alterations to program 10.2 produces 10.3 which plots the
function:

$$r = f(theta) = k * theta \quad (a\ spiral)$$

This time we use a WHILE loop as the main program structure.
Whereas we can easily define the maximum and minimum extent of
harmonic functions, in the case of polar coordinates it is
generally easier to let the program determine when f(theta) 'hits'
the border of the plot. You can see from Figure 10.2 that one of
the effects of using "round" to obtain an (x,y) coordinate is a
thickening of the line in the display. Note that we have used a
scale of 1 in both the x and y directions.

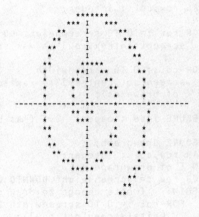

Figure 10.2   A spiral function plotted on a character printer.
The output was produced by Program 10.3

235

Program 10.3

This program plots a spiral function on a character printer by
evaluating a 'real' coordinate and rounding to the nearest
available coordinate on the character grid.

```
PROGRAM PolarPlot(input,output);
   VAR r,theta, interval,k : real;
       x,y,angleinterval : integer;

   PROCEDURE plot(angleinterval:integer; k:real);
   CONST  pi = 3.14159; point = '*'; xaxisch = '-';
       space = ' '; yaxisch = 'I'; screenheight = 22;
       screenwidth = 60; centrex = 30; centrey = 11;

   VAR screen :
          ARRAY[0..screenwidth, 0..screenheight] OF char;
       period, row,fvalue  : integer;

   FUNCTION f(theta:real):real;
   BEGIN
      f := k * theta;
   END  { of f(unction) };

   PROCEDURE drawaxes;
      VAR row,col : integer;
   BEGIN
      FOR row := 0 TO screenheight DO
         screen[centrex,row] := yaxisch;

      FOR col:= 0 TO screenwidth      DO
         screen[col,centrey] := xaxisch
   END  { of drawaxes};

   PROCEDURE insertspaces;  ... { as before }

   PROCEDURE drawgraph;
      VAR row,col : integer;
   BEGIN { of drawgraph }
      FOR row := screenheight DOWNTO 0 DO
      BEGIN      { note change to draw graph right way up }
         FOR col := 0 TO screenwidth DO
            write(screen[col,row]);
         writeln
      END
   END  { of draw graph};
```

```
      BEGIN  { plot }
        insertspaces;  drawaxes;
        theta := 0; interval :=  pi * angleinterval /180;
        y := 0;    x:= 0;
        WHILE (abs(y) <= centrey) AND ( abs(x) <= centrex) DO
        BEGIN
           screen[ x+centrex, y+ centrey ] := point;
           r := f(theta);  theta := theta + interval;
           x:= round( r* cos(theta));
           y:= round( r* sin(theta))
        END;
        drawgraph
      END { of plot};

   BEGIN  { of program }
      write('type in ang. int and k');
      read(angleinterval,k);
      plot(angleinterval,k)
   END.
```

10.5 Vector plotting on a character device

Plotting on an incremental plotter or a HRMC graphics device is
handled at the atomic level (the lowest level that a high level
programmer has access to) by a vector plotting routine. Thus to
plot a straight line

        lineto(x,y)

is used. In the APPLE system the same effect is achieved by a
procedure moveto(x,y) used in conjunction with a single procedure
pencolor(color); where "color" can be "none".

Now a coarse line drawing procedure apeing "lineto" can be used
to drive a character VDU. The principal defect is that sloping
lines are mapped into rather crude steps. (Incidentally exactly
the same process takes place in HRMC graphics but in this case the
increase in resolution makes the steps either barely visible or
tolerable.)

Program 10.4 plots a square spiral using a "lineto" method to
set up "lines" of characters between two points. Items of interest
are firstly the algorithm in "lineby". This is an elaboration of
"lineto" and operates on the difference between the previous and
current coordinates, rather than absolute values. The algorithm
works out how to draw a sloping line between two coordinates in
the form of a series of generally irregular steps. (Again such an
algorithm will be incoporated in HRMC graphics software where it
is of course transparent to the user). For a line of any slope the
algorithm will distribute the steps reasonably evenly along the
lines. This effect is shown in Figure 10.3. Secondly note the use
of the CASE statement in the main program which continuously
changes the current direction so that the 'curve' is always moving
counter-clockwise - thus plotting a counter-clockwise square

spiral. In this program, because the user specifies absolute coordinates, checking is absolutely critical, and error detection facilities have been included. The main program loop has been set up to deliberately cause the error detecting procedure to be invoked. Also in this respect note that even if an error is detected the output generated up to the error point can be printed and would undoubtedly help in debugging. A general principle in error detection is to feedback as much information as possible. The next program is long and somewhat complex in parts. It is, however, an example of a complete miniture graphics system using characters. The behaviour of the GOTO statement in the fail procedure should be obvious. This is an example of one of the rare situations in which this statment is used in Pascal.

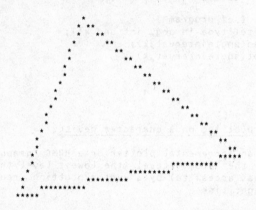

Figure 10.3   Demonstrating the way in which the line drawing algorithm breaks up a line into equally distributed plateaus or steps

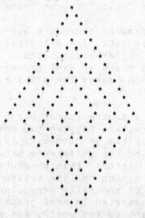

Figure 10.4   The output from Program 10.4 - a square spiral rotated through 45 degrees

238

Program 10.4

This program incoporates a line drawing algorithm suitable for a
character device. The demonstration is a square spiral rotated
through 45 degrees.

```
PROGRAM graphics (input,output);
  LABEL   999;
  CONST screenwidth = 60; screenht = 26;
  VAR curserx, cursery : integer;
      screen : ARRAY [0..screenwidth,0..screenht] OF char;
      x,y,length,dn : integer; forever : boolean;

  PROCEDURE fail (x,y : integer);
  BEGIN {fail}
    writeln (x, ', ', y, ' is off the screen');
    GOTO 999
  END; {fail}

  PROCEDURE lineby (xdif,ydif:integer);
    CONST   star = '*';
    VAR xmax : boolean; slope, sum : real;
        xsign, ysign, i, maxval, finalx, finaly : integer;
  BEGIN {lineby}
    finalx := xdif+curserx;
    IF  (finalx>screenwidth) OR (finalx<0)
        THEN fail(finalx, finaly);
    finaly := ydif+cursery;
    IF  (finaly>screenht) OR (finaly<0)
        THEN  fail(finalx, finaly);
    screen [curserx,cursery] := star;
    IF  (xdif<>0) OR (ydif<>0)   THEN
    BEGIN
       xmax := abs(xdif) > abs(ydif);
       IF  xmax  THEN  slope := abs(ydif/xdif)
       ELSE  slope := abs(xdif/ydif);
       IF  xdif > 0  THEN  xsign:=1  ELSE  xsign:=-1;
       IF  ydif > 0  THEN  ysign:=1  ELSE  ysign:=-1;
       sum := 0.5;
       IF  xmax  THEN  maxval:=abs(xdif)
          ELSE maxval := abs(ydif);
       FOR  i:=1 TO maxval  DO
       BEGIN
          sum := sum+slope;
          IF  sum > 1.0  THEN
          BEGIN
             IF  xmax  THEN  cursery:=cursery+ysign
             ELSE  curserx := curserx+xsign;
             sum := sum-1
          END;
          IF  xmax  THEN cursery:=curserx+xsign
          ELSE  cursery := cursery+ysign;
          screen [curserx,cursery] := star;
       END
    END
  END {lineby};
```

```
PROCEDURE lineto (u,v:integer);

    VAR xdif, ydif : integer;

BEGIN {lineto}
    xdif := u-curserx;
    ydif := v-cursery;
    lineby (xdif, ydif)
END; {lineto}

PROCEDURE moveby (a,b : integer);
    VAR error : boolean;
BEGIN {moveby}
    IF a < 0 THEN  error := -a > curserx
    ELSE   error := screenwidth-a <curserx;
    IF  NOT error THEN
        IF  b < 0  THEN  error := -b > cursery
        ELSE   error := screenht-b <cursery;
    IF  error  THEN  fail (curserx+a, cursery+b);
    curserx := curserx+a;
    cursery := cursery+b
END; {moveby}

PROCEDURE moveto (x,y:integer);
BEGIN {moveto}
    IF  (x>screenwidth) OR (y>screenht) OR (x<0) OR (y<0)
        THEN fail (x,y);
    curserx := x;
    cursery := y
END; {moveto}


PROCEDURE insertspaces; ... { as before }
PROCEDURE drawgraph; ... { as before }
BEGIN {program}
    insertspaces;   moveto(screenwidth DIV 2,screenht DIV 2);
    x := screenwidth DIV 2;  y :=  screenht DIV 2;  dn := 1;
    forever := true;   length := 0;
    WHILE forever DO
    BEGIN
        CASE dn OF
            1: BEGIN dn := 2; x := x+length;  y := y+length  END;
            2: BEGIN dn := 3; x := x-length;  y := y+length  END;
            3: BEGIN dn := 4; x := x-length;  y := y-length  END;
            4: BEGIN dn := 1; x := x+length;  y := y-length  END
        END;
        lineto(x,y); length := length + 1
    END;
    999: drawgraph
END.
```

240

10.6 Plotting f(x,y) on a character device

Approximate representations of functions of two variables can be achieved on a character VDU by using different characters to represent different values of the function f. Now variations in f are represented by different characters rather than by variations in the two-dimensional position of a character. Program 10.5 is a representation of the function:

$$f(x,y) = \cos(x) + \cos(y)$$

There are two mappings involved, the (x,y) coordinate values that have to be converted to a plotting grid of 70x60 say and the values of f that have to be mapped into a range defined in this case by the main program CASE statement of:

$$0 <= f <= 10.$$

These are performed for emphasis in "scale" and "transform" although in practice they are of course trivial and need not be separate modules. Note that logically we are really doing things the wrong way round. We should be calculating our function irrespective of the plotter device in use and then map the results onto the character, VDU. In practice, however, the constraints of the VDU are so severe that it is easier to proceed as below.

Figure 10.5   The output from Program 10.5 - using characters to represent two-dimensional functions

241

Program 10.5

Using characters to represent the function:

$$f(x,y) = \cos(x) + \cos(y)$$

```pascal
PROGRAM cosplot     (input,output);

  PROCEDURE plot;
    CONST space = ' ';     screenheight = 60;  ycentre = 30;
          screenwidth = 70; xcentre = 35;
          xscale = 7; yscale = 7;

    VAR screen :
          ARRAY[0..screenwidth,0..screenheight] OF char;
        interval, xs, ys, fvalue  : real;
        period, row,ft, x, y, startx,starty,
        stopx, stopy : integer;
        point : char;

    FUNCTION f(x,y:real):real ;
    BEGIN
      f := cos(x) + cos(y)
    END  { of f(unction) };


    PROCEDURE scale(x,y : integer; VAR xs, ys : real);
    BEGIN
      xs := x/xscale;   ys := y/yscale
    END;

    PROCEDURE transform( fvalue : real; VAR ft : integer);
    BEGIN
      ft := round((fvalue  + 2) * 2.5)
    END;

    PROCEDURE insertspaces;  ... { as before }
    PROCEDURE drawgraph; ... { as before }
```

```
BEGIN { start of plot}
   insertspaces;
   startx := -xcentre;  stopx := xcentre;
   starty := -ycentre;  stopy := ycentre;
   FOR y := starty TO stopy DO
      FOR x := startx TO stopx DO
      BEGIN
         scale(x, y, xs, ys);
         fvalue := f(xs, ys);
         transform(fvalue, ft);
         CASE ft OF

             0: point:= 'A';  1: point:= ' ';
             2: point:= 'B';  3: point:= ' ';
             4: point:= 'C';  5: point:= ' ';
             6: point:= 'D';  7: point:= ' ';
             8: point:= 'E';  9: point:= ' ';
            10: point:= 'F'

         END;
         screen[x+xcentre, y+ycentre] := point
      END;

      drawgraph
   END { of plot};

BEGIN  { of program }
   plot
END.
```

A practical trick used in this program is to represent every
second value in the range of possible values by a blank. This
results in the skeletal plot shown that almost mimics a contour
plot and is more easily interpreted than a plot without blanks.

10.7 Plotting f(x,y) on a line printer

If a line printer is available f(x,y) can be plotted using overprinting. This is a commonly used technique and examples are usually seen adorning walls and featuring anything from the Mona Lisa downwards (in taste). Although the particular mechanism to get your line printer to overprint will be unique to your system, the programming technique is universal and the use of overprinting is now so common that it is worthy of inclusion here.

In overprinting programs the value of f is represented by varying degrees of blackness, achieved by printing different characters on top of each other. The kernel of the scheme is an overprinting table. The one used in Program 10.6 is incorporated in the procedure "initialize". Each 8-character string is a specification of the set of characters to be printed all in the same position, to achieve the desired degree of blackness. Each point in f(x,y) is mapped into one of the strings depending on the value of f. When a point is printed, overprinting will occur to a degree depending on the number of non blank characters in the string. In Program 10.6 buffering is limited to one line to save on data stored. Each line can be viewed as a two-dimensional array of 8 rows coming out of the paper. As a line is printed the problem is to make the line printer print out the 8 lines on top of each other. To save space the (x,y) and function value scalings are incorporated in the definition of the function "f".

Figure 10.6   The output from Program 10.6 – using overprinting
to represent two-dimensional functions

244

Program 10.6

Plots an overprinted representation of the function:

$$f(x,y) = \cos(x) + \cos(y)$$

```
PROGRAM overcosplot (input,printplot);
VAR printplot : text;

  PROCEDURE overplot;
    CONST screenwidth=70;  xcentre=35;
          screenheight=60; ycentre=30;
    TYPE overcol =  PACKED ARRAY [1..8] OF char;
    VAR x, y, starty, stopy, startx, stopx  : integer;
        table : ARRAY [ 0..20 ] OF overcol;
        buffer: ARRAY [ 0..screenwidth] OF overcol;
        screen: ARRAY [ 0..screenwidth,0..screenheight]
                OF integer;

    FUNCTION f(x,y:integer):real;
    BEGIN
        f  := (cos(x/7) + cos(y/7) + 2) * 5
    END { of f(unction)};

    PROCEDURE initialize;
    BEGIN
        table[0]  := '        ';
        table[1]  := '-       ';
        table[2]  := '=       ';
        table[3]  := '+       ';
        table[4]  := ')       ';
        table[5]  := '1       ';
        table[6]  := 'Z       ';
        table[7]  := 'X       ';
        table[8]  := 'A       ';
        table[9]  := 'M       ';
        table[10] := 'O-      ';
        table[11] := 'O=      ';
        table[12] := 'O+      ';
        table[13] := 'O+,     ';
        table[14] := 'O+,.    ';
        table[15] := 'O+,.=   ';
        table[16] := 'OX,.-   ';
        table[17] := 'OX,.HC  ';
        table[18] := 'OX,.HB  ';
        table[19] := 'OX,.HBV ';
        table[20] := 'OX,.HBVA'
      END { of initialize };
```

```
            PROCEDURE overprint;
                VAR row,col,level : integer;
            BEGIN
                FOR row := screenheight DOWNTO 0 DO
                BEGIN
                    FOR col:= 0 TO screenwidth DO
                        buffer[col] := table[screen[col,row]];

                    FOR level := 1 TO 8 DO
                    BEGIN
                        IF level = 1 THEN
                            BEGIN
                                writeln(printplot); write(printplot,' ')
                            END
                        ELSE
                            BEGIN
                                writeln(printplot); write(printplot,'+')
                            END;
                            FOR col := 0 TO screenwidth DO
                                write(printplot,buffer[col] [level])
                    END
                END
            END  { of overprint };

        BEGIN { start of overplot }
            initialize;
            startx := -xcentre;  stopx := xcentre;
            starty := -ycentre;  stopy := ycentre;

            FOR y := starty TO  stopy DO
                FOR x := startx TO stopx DO

                    screen[x+xcentre, y+ycentre] := round(f(x,y));

            overprint

        END { of overplot };

    BEGIN
        rewrite(printplot);
        overplot
    END.
```

Note the use of the type PACKED ARRAY in the above program. A
string enclosed in single quotation marks represents a value of
type PACKED ARRAY. Until now this has not been relevant, but in
the above program, it is convenient to declare variables of this
type so that strings can be assigned in their entirety. Further
details concerning PACKED ARRAYS are beyond the scope of this
text.

It is usually possible to arrange for overprinting to take
place by sending the program output to a file with FORTRAN
carriage control characters at the start of every line. In the
FORTRAN programming language, the first character of a line of

246

text sent to a printing device is treated as a code that controls the flow of paper through the device. The control character is not printed. The character ' ' at the start of a line causes the line to be printed on the next line of the paper, (the normal requirement), whereas the character '+' causes the line to be overprinted on top of the previous line (no paper advance). In the above program, the first line of each group of 8 is preceded by a ' ', and the 7 following lines are each preceded by a '+'. The file was printed by sending it to a printer and telling the operating system that the file originated from a FORTRAN program.

Exercises

(1) Develop program 10.2 to:

   (a) Enable f(x) to be plotted with the x axis horizontal.

   (b) Provide a facility to enable legendry to be inserted along the x and y axis.

   (c) Provide an error checking facility that checks when an attempt is made to access a point outside the 'plotting area'. (See Program 10.4.)

   Test the program on a function of your choice.

(2) Write a program to generate an ellipse on a character printer using polar coordinates. (this is covered for an incremental plotter in Chapter 11.)

(3) Write and test a procedure to be inserted in Program 10.4 that will enable a legendry facility. The procedure should have as parameters a positional coordinate and a character variable.

11 Line graphics

In the case of incremental plotters and HRMC graphics, programming techniques are simplified by the availability of graphics packages. A graphics package provides a function not dissimilar to a compiler. It buffers the user from having to write in the machine code of the display processor. Another aim of standard graphics packages is universality or machine independence. For most people the choice of a graphics device is usually a matter of availability.

The programming techniques for both the incremental plotter and the HRMC graphics device overlap and are identical in most respects. Certain applications that require greater accuracy are best left to the incremental plotter, e.g. isometric projections of functions of two variables. Applications such as real time animation are unique to the HRMC graphics device. There are many different types of graphics devices but at the time of writing these two types are undoubtedly the most popular. They form the device foundation for this chapter.

Programming techniques covered here are designed to enable a user to write programs to plot functions of one or two variables on such devices. This covers a large proportion of the mainstream use of computer graphics in science and engineering. Other more exotic topics, such as clipping, representation of three-dimensional space, stereo views, hidden line removal and animation are outside the scope of this text. Unless the application is particularly specialized, a scientist or engineer usually has access to such facilities through mathematical graphics packages. Such facilities are now becoming as common as numerical analysis packages.

Generally scientific use of graphics devices takes place at one of three levels. These are, in increasing order of problem orientation:

(1) User designed graphics

   Most programs or software used in computer graphics is necessarily written by specialists. Graphics devices are complex as is the driving software required to plot say the orthogonal projection of a building and cause it to rotate about any axis. However sometimes a user does not have access to a graphics device, or it may be that the particular user application is not catered for by any of the available graphics software. In this case the user may design his own facilities, using the 'atomic' or lowest level facilities from a scientific graphics package (below). An example of this was

Program 10.1 - using a character VDU to display an approximate representation of a function of a single variable.

(2) Use of general purpose scientific graphics packages:

Such packages or libraries are usually mathematically based and will contain vector plotting procedures such as:

            moveto(x,y)
and
            lineto(x,y)

i.e. move from the current position, (CP), to a given point, (x,y), with the pen up, (in the case of HRMC graphics the pen is of course a high energy electron beam 'painting' a bright spot on the screen), and draw a line from the current position to (x,y). At the complex end a procedure which plots a function of two variables complete with hidden line removal is usually available. A user accesses such facilities by writing a program incorporating as **external** procedures, the required procedures selected from the package. (See for example Program 11.1.)

(3) Special purpose graphics packages:

Here a user will not be involved in producing a graphics program but in using one. For example an architect may input elevations of a building to a program which then produces an orthogonal projection. The program may then rotate this around any axis so that it can be viewed from any angle. Other elaborations, such as the effect of natural light on the interior of the building may also be available. Such packages or systems are problem oriented and may be used by laymen (in the programming sense). They may well include interaction via graphics input devices such as a light pen or graphics tablet.

This chapter deals with the rudimentary aspects of levels (1) and (2).

11.1 Incremental plotters

Incremental plotters are electromechanical devices of the cylinder or flatbed type. In the cylinder type a pen can move backwards or forwards along a fixed carriage, positioned on the surface of the cylinder and parallel to its long axis (Figure 11.1). Paper is secured to the cylinder surface which can move clockwise or counter-clockwise. Combination of the pen and cylinder movement give plotting in one out of 8 directions.

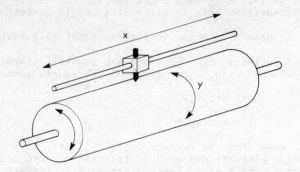

Figure 11.1 A schematic diagram of an incremental plotter,
            cylinder type

In the flatbed type, the paper is stationary and flat. The pen
can move over the paper in either the x or the y direction. Again
combination of these movements gives movement in one out of 8
directions (Figure 11.2).

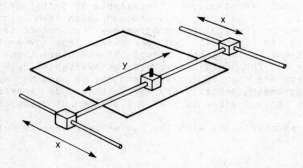

Figure 11.2 A schematic diagram of an incremental plotter,
            flatbed type

The movement in both devices is incremental with very small
increments. The illustrations below were produced on a Calcomp
1036 with increments of 0.0125mm.

The characteristics of both devices are extreme accuracy and
the production of a permanent accurate record. Curves are plotted
in a piecewise linear manner but because of the small steps the
piecewise linear effect is practically invisible. The high level
programming of both devices will be identical through the graphics
package although details such as paper size will differ.

250

These devices are true vector plotting or random scan devices. Their electronic equivalent is the random scan display, not dealt with in this text, because it is now far less common than the raster scan display.

One of the major engineering uses of a flatbed plotter is in the production of large scale maps of etching patterns in integrated circuit manufacture. These are then reduced photographically and used as etching masks.

Incidentally there are sometimes 3 or 4 pens on a device to give a colour choice.

Graphics packages are always available with such devices. As already mentioned graphics packages act in the same way as a compiler. They are to a greater or lesser extent universal, enabling device independence and they buffer the programmer from low level device code, enabling him to write programs using high level facilities. Packages themselves contain a hierarchy of facilities. Atomic facilities are the lowest level facilities available to the programmer along with various higher level facilities prewritten in terms of the atomic facilities. A programmer will write his program either entirely in atomic facilities or a mixture of atomic and higher level routines. The following is a list of atomic facilities for a typical incremental plotter:

Graphic Procedure	effect
moveto(x,y)	move from CP to (x,y)
moveby(x,y)	move to (x' + x, y' + y) where (x',y') is the CP
lineto(x,y)	draw a line from CP to (x,y)
lineby(x,y)	draw a line from CP to (x' + x, y' + y)
pointat(x,y)	draw a point at (x,y)
pointby(x,y)	draw a point at (x' + x, y' + y)
text(string)	draw a string of characters starting at CP

These facilities deal with graphic output or so called graphic primitives. Other atomic facilities included in such a system would be routines handling attributes such as pen colour and line thickness. Higher level facilities would also be included. A common example is "drawabox" which would be pre-written in terms of "moveby" and "lineby".

Finally it should be pointed out that characters for legendry are drawn on an incremental plotter in a piecewise linear manner and systems usually provide facilities for drawing strings of characters of a selected scale in a selected position. Details differ so much between systems that no information can usefully be incorporated in this text.

11.2 Plotting f(x) on an incremental plotter

In this section we have used a graphics package available on the authors' Pascal system. The precise details vary from system to system, but the facilities illustrated are fairly typical. Program 11.1 plots the function:

$$f(x) = \sin(x)/(x+1)$$

Coordinates of successive points on the graph are evaluated and straight lines connecting these points are drawn using the procedure 'Lineto'. The physical area of paper to be used by the program is determined by the statement:

    plottingspaceis(0.0, 0.5, 0.0, 0.5);

which says that we want to use half the length and half the width of the paper, the accessible area being 1x1 notional units.

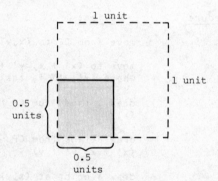

The other library procedure "map" is used to specify what range of x-values and y-values are to be mapped onto the plotter space selected. 'Map' divides this space up into a grid that is problem oriented. in this case:

    0 <= x <= noofperiods*2*pi   and

    -1 <= y <= 1

252

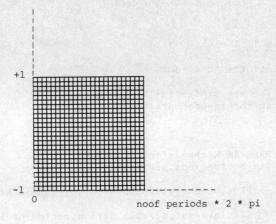

This is determined by the statement:

        map(0, noofperiods*2*pi, -1, 1);

which divides the plotting space into a grid system system having
a horizontal and vertical range specified in the parameter list of
"map". The maximum resolution of this grid is determined by the
plotter increment. The user program can now specify any two points
using his mathematical space system and the program will select
the equivalent two points on this grid. Thus a horizontal line
representing the x-axis is drawn by "drawaxis" which uses:

        moveto(0,0);
and
        lineto(noofperiods*2*pi, 0);

"Lineto" will join any two points using as straight a line as
possible. Thus 6 periods at a periodwidth of 50 will coarsen this
grid to a horizontal resolution of 300. Figure 11.3 is the output
from Program 11.1 using 6 periods and a period width of 50.

Program 11.1

A plot of the function:

    y = sin(x)/(x+1)
using an incremental plotter.

```
PROGRAM Harmonic(input,output);
VAR noofperiods,periodwidth : integer;

    PROCEDURE plot(noofperiods,periodwidth:integer);
    CONST pi = 3.14159;
    VAR interval,x:real; period,periodinc : integer;

    FUNCTION f(x:real):real;
    BEGIN
      f := sin(x)/(x + 1)
    END;

    PROCEDURE plottingspaceis(xmin,xmax,ymin,ymax:real);
                                  EXTERNAL;
    PROCEDURE border; EXTERNAL;

    PROCEDURE lineto(x,y:real); EXTERNAL;

    PROCEDURE map(xmin,xmax,ymin,ymax:real); EXTERNAL;

    PROCEDURE moveto(x,y:real); EXTERNAL;

    PROCEDURE drawaxis;
     BEGIN
       moveto(0,0);  border;
       lineto(noofperiods * 2 * pi,0)
     END;

    BEGIN { plot }
       plottingspaceis(0,0.5,0,0.0.25);
       interval := 2*pi/periodwidth; x := 0;
       map(0,noofperiods * 2 * pi,-1,1);
       moveto(0,0);
       FOR period := 1 TO noofperiods DO
          FOR periodinc := 1 TO periodwidth DO
            BEGIN
                lineto(x,f(x));   x:= x+interval
            END;
       drawaxis
    END; { plot }

BEGIN { main program }
    writeln('type no of periods, period width ');
    read(noofperiods,periodwidth);
    plot(noofperiods,periodwidth)
END.
```

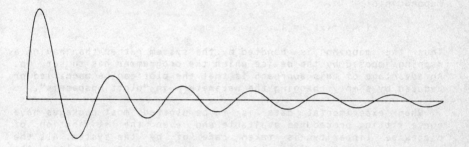

Figure 11.3 Output from Program 11.1

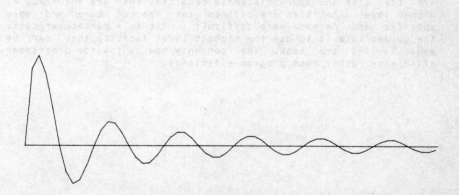

Figure 11.4 Output from the same program but with the
resolution coarsened to demonstrate the
emergence of the piecewise linear effect

Figure 11.4 is the output from the same program, this time using a period width of only 10, coarsening the grid horizontally to 60 units. There is no point in having program increments that are smaller than the plotter increment, but clearly the increments must be small enough to eliminate unecessary linearity if the plot is to represent a curve. The actual intervals between points on the plotter grid are determined along the x axis by the program loop increments

x plotting space / no. of periods * period width

and the y intervals by the evaluation of f(x) which is linearly mapped into:

-1 <= f(x) <= 1.

Thus the mapping is handled by the system rather than having a mapping imposed by the device which the programmer has to set up. An advantage of this approach is that the plot can be magnified or reduced by simply changing the parameters in "plottingspaceis".

When experimental data is to be plotted, most packages have curve fitting procedures available and even the elimination of piecewise linearity is taken care of by the system. All the programmer does here is to evaluate the function and load the results into a array referring to, say:

fitandplot(data)

to control the plotting of the values in array "data". The procedure will fit a curve to the data points. Options are usually available for curve fitting procedures that are to do with the technical details of various curve fitting methods. As with all software systems the higher the level of the facility the greater are the time and appropriateness penalties that are incurred. As higher level facilities are defined they become more and more specific and perhaps more difficult to fit to a particular task. The golden rule is to use the highest level facility that can be made to fit the task. The tendency now is towards programmer efficiency rather than program efficiency.

11.3 Basic shape generation

We shall start this section by illustrating some points concerning
the generation of probably the most common shape - the circle - by
plotting a regular polygon of 360 sides.

Program 11.2

Plots a circle given a centre coordinate and radius.


```
PROGRAM circle(input, output);

CONST pi = 3.14159;
VAR    xc, yc, r : real;

PROCEDURE plottingspaceis(xmin,xmax,ymin,ymax : real);
                          EXTERNAL;
PROCEDURE map(xmin, xmax, ymin, ymax : real); EXTERNAL;
PROCEDURE moveto(x, y : real); EXTERNAL;
PROCEDURE lineto(x, y : real); EXTERNAL;
PROCEDURE plotacircle(xc, yc, r : real );
  VAR x, y : real;
      theta : integer;
  BEGIN
    moveto(xc + r, yc);
    FOR theta := 10 TO 360 DO
      BEGIN
        x := r*cos(theta*pi/180);
        y := r*sin(theta*pi/180);
        lineto(xc + x, yc + y)
      END
  END;

BEGIN
  plottingspaceis(0, 0.25, 0, 0.25);
  read(xc, yc, r);
  map(0, 4*r, 0, 4*r);
  plotacircle(xc, yc, r)
END.
```


Here we are using polar coordinates to generate the polygon,
sweeping a radius through 360 degrees in 1 degree increments. The
polar coordinates are converted to cartesian coordinates and
straight lines are drawn from vertex to vertex on the polygon.

The next program uses the procedure developed above 7 times.

Program 11.3

This program generates a circle and then 6 more circles using as centres 60 degree intervals on the circumference of the first.

```
PROGRAM circle(input, output);

CONST pi = 3.14159;
VAR sx, sy,  xc, yc, r : real;
    circle, i : integer;
    .
    .
    .
BEGIN
    plottingspaceis(0, 0.25, 0, 0.25);
    read(sx, sy, r);
    map(0, 4*r, 0, 4*r);
    plotacircle(sx, sy, r);
    circle :=0;
    FOR i := 1 TO 6 DO
        BEGIN
            xc := sx + r*cos(circle/(2*pi));
            yc := sy + r*sin(circle/(2*pi));
            plotacircle(xc, yc, r);
            circle := circle + 60
        END
END.
```

Figure 11.5 The output from Program 11.3

Now if we take the above procedure and add two parameters that constrain the radial sweep of each of the 6 subsidiary circles such that they only appear when they are contained by the first — we get a petal diagram.

Program 11.4

Generates 'petals' by constraining the radial sweep of the plotted
circle to within 2 thresholds.

```
PROGRAM petals(input, output);

CONST pi = 3.14159;
VAR sx, sy,  xc, yc, r : real;
    circle, t1, t2, i : integer;

PROCEDURE plotacircle(xc, yc, r : real; t1, t2 : integer );
  VAR x, y : real;  theta : integer;
  BEGIN
    moveto(xc+r*cos(t1*pi/180, yc+r*sin(t1*pi/180));
    FOR theta := t1 TO t2 DO
      BEGIN
        x := r*cos(theta*pi/180);
        y := r*sin(theta*pi/180);
        lineto(xc + x, yc + y)
      END
  END;

BEGIN { main program }
  plottingspaceis(0, 0.25, 0, 0.25);
  read(sx, sy, r);
  map(0, 4*r, 0, 4*r);
  moveto(sx, sy);
  circle := 0;  t1 := 120;  t2 := 240;
  FOR i := 1 TO 6 DO
    BEGIN
      xc := sx + r*cos(circle*pi/180);
      yc := sy + r*sin(circle*pi/180);
      plotacircle(xc, yc, r,  t1, t2);
      circle := circle + 60;
      t1 := t1 + 60;  t2 := t2 + 60
    END
END.
```

Figure 11.6   The output from program 11.4

The technique of constraining a plot to a visible region that is mathematically determined is an important tool in advanced computer graphics. A more 'complex' shape than a circle is an ellipse. The equation for an ellipse is:

$$\frac{x^2}{a^2} + \frac{y^2}{b^2} = 1$$

where a and b are the semi-major and semi-minor axes. In polar coordinates this gives:

r=1/sqrt(cos(theta)*cos(theta)/(a*a)+sin(theta)*sin(theta)/(b*b))

The program is just that for the circle with the polar coordinate equation changed and the theta-increments changed to 10.

Program 11.5

This program generates an ellipse.

```
PROGRAM ellipse(input, output);

CONST pi = 3.14159;
VAR    xc, yc, a, b : real;

PROCEDURE plotanellipse(xc, yc, a, b : real );
  VAR x, y, r, sine, cosine : real;
      theta, t : integer;
  BEGIN
    moveto(xc + a, yc);
    theta := 0;
    FOR t := 1 TO 36 DO
      BEGIN
        theta := theta + 10;
        cosine := cos(theta*pi/180);
        sine   := sin(theta*pi/180);
        r := 1/sqrt(cosine*cosine/(a*a) + sine*sine/(b*b));
        x := r* cosine;  y := r * sine;
        lineto(xc + x, yc + y)
      END
  END;

BEGIN
  plottingspaceis(0, 0.25, 0, 0.25);
  read(xc, yc, a, b);
  map(0, 4*a, 0, 4*a);
  plotanellipse(xc, yc, a, b)
END.
```

Figure 11.7 The ellipse generated by Program 11.5

Now the point to notice from this figure is that the degree of piecewise linearity changes. This is because unlike the circle, the curvature in an ellipse is not constant. We are, however, generating the ellipse with constant increments in "theta". This means that where the curvature is high an increment in "theta" results in a large change in x or y. You can design your program to reduce the "theta" increment when the change in x or y rises above a certain threshold, until the change just dips below the threshold. After each line segment is drawn theta is adjusted. The idea is that the "theta" increment is controlled by the change in x or y that it produces. This approach is only really feasible on powerful processors because the extra processing to continually vary the "theta" increment will take longer than reducing the "theta" increment over the whole of the figure. Another approach is to have angular increments tailored to a specific figure. Thus for an ellipse that is elongated horizontally, we might have:

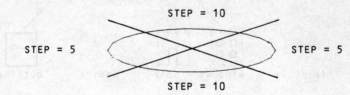

STEP = 10

STEP = 5   STEP = 5

STEP = 10

11.4 Object hierarchy

A large set of line drawings exhibit a hierarchy that can be usefully and profitably reflected in programs that produce line drawings. An electronic diagram for example is made up of resistors, capacitors and transistors. A resistor is made up of a line plus a rectangle plus a line:

A rectangle is made up of 4 lines. This may seem a rather trivial
statement of the obvious but such an approach can lead to powerful
programming techniques. Let's look at another simple example that
may demonstrate the point. A children's stylization of a house
(which is after all a simple reflection of an adult's
stylization), can be structured hierarchically as follows:

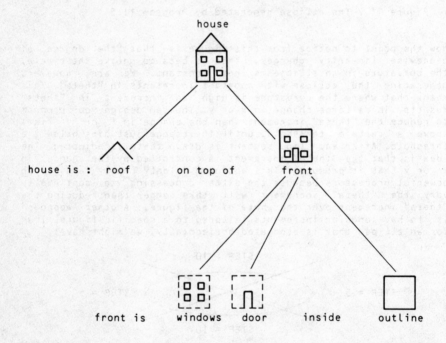

You can perhaps see from this that windows, doors and outlines are
all rectangles of different sizes bearing certain spatial
relationships to each other and can all use the same program
module or procedure. The object hierarchy in the above tree is
reflected in the procedure hierarchy in the next program.

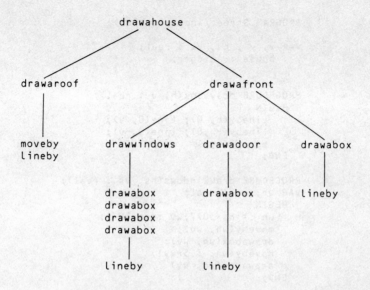

Thus the procedure "drawahouse" contains 2 procedure calls -
"drawaroof" and "drawafront". "Drawaroof" does not need any
further definition and contains only references to "lineby" and
"moveby". "Drawafront" contains 3 procedure calls - "drawindows",
"drawadoor" and "drawabox". "Drawindows" itself contains 4 calls
of "drawabox". "Drawabox" contains only "lineby". Technically
"moveby" and "lineby" are primitives or procedures that cannot be
further defined and are the leaves of the tree. The program builds
a hierarchy on "moveby" and "lineby" that reflects the hierarchy
in the picture. We can only scratch at the surface of this
particular topic and the power of the approach. This particular
program will generate a street of 6 houses; the user types 6 pairs
of data: the horizontal and vertical scale for each house. (To
keep the program length down we have missed out 2 windows and the
door.)

Program 11.6

This program draws a street of houses in the same style given a
horizontal and vertical scaling factor for each.

```
PROGRAM Street(input, output);

VAR x, y , hs, vs : real;
    house : integer;


PROCEDURE drawabox(h, v : real);
  BEGIN
     lineby(h, 0); line(0, v);
     lineby(-h,0); line(0,-v);
     moveto(x,y)
  END;

PROCEDURE drawwindows(hs, vs : real);
VAR wh, wv : real;
  BEGIN
    wh := hs*30/7;wv :=vs*30/5;
    moveby(wh, wv);
    drawabox(wh, wv);
    moveby(wh, 3.5*wv);
    drawabox(wh, wv)
  END;

PROCEDURE drawaroof(hs, vs :real);
  BEGIN
     moveby(hs*30, vs*30);
     lineby(-hs*15, vs*15);
     lineby(-hs*15, -vs*15);
     moveto(x,y)
  END;

PROCEDURE drawafront(hs, vs : real);
  BEGIN
     drawabox(hs*30, vs*30);
     drawwindows(hs, vs)
  END;

PROCEDURE drawahouse(hs, vs : real);
  BEGIN
     drawaroof(hs,vs);
     drawafront(hs, vs)
  END;

BEGIN
  plottingspaceis(0, 1, 0, 1);
  map(0,1800,0,300);
  x := 0; y := 0;
  FOR house := 1 TO 6 DO
   BEGIN
     moveto(x, y);
     read(hs, vs);
     drawahouse(hs, vs);
     x := x + hs*30
   END
END.
```

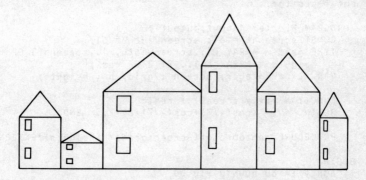

Figure 11.8   The output from Program 11.6

Note in this program the use of the differential procedures "moveby" and "lineby". Finally although advanced techniques exist to handle the spatial relationships (windows are a set of 4 boxes **inside** another box for example), these are outside the scope of this text and have been handled in an empirical or ad hoc manner, by controlling the start coordinate of each house.

11.5 Plotting f(x,y) on an incremental plotter

The next two examples demonstrate how easy it is to use high level plotting facilities to effect a task that would be difficult to program using atomic facilities. The ability to display f(x,y) as either a series of contours or as an isometric projection is almost certain to be incorporated in your mathematical graphics package. Program 11.7 plots a contour representation of the same function that was used in Programs 10.5 and 10.6, i.e:

$$f(x,y) = \cos(x) + \cos(y)$$

Here it is plotted firstly as a set of contours and then as an isometric projection. Again details will vary among systems. The contour plotting routine takes as input information two arrays. It is supplied with a two dimensional array containing values of f(x,y) and a one-dimensional array containing the f-values (heights) at which the contours are to be drawn. Space and mapping details are omitted for the sake of clarity.

265

Program 11.7

A plot of the function:
         f(x,y) = cos(x) + cos(y)
using a high level library procedure 'contourplot' driving an
incremental plotter.

```
PROGRAM Plotter (input,output);
  CONST screenht = 61; screenwidth = 61;
  TYPE grid = ARRAY [1..screenwidth, 1..screenht] OF real;
     heights = ARRAY [ 1.. 21 ] OF real;
  VAR x,y : integer; screen : grid; h : heights;

  FUNCTION f(x,y : real) : real;
  BEGIN   f := (cos(x/7)+cos(y/7)+2)*2.5   END;

  PROCEDURE contourplot(screen:grid; h:heights);EXTERNAL;

BEGIN
  FOR y := 30 DOWNTO -30 DO
     FOR x := -30 TO 30  DO
        screen[ x+31,y +31] := (f(x,y)+1);
  FOR x := 0 TO 20 DO
     h[x+1] := x/2;
  contourplot(screen,h)
END.
```

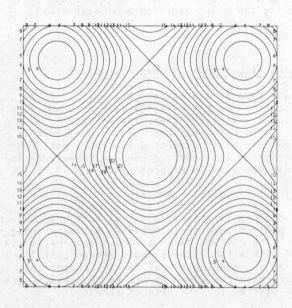

Figure 11.9 The output from Program 11.7 - a contour plot
               of a two-dimensional function using an inc-
               remental plotter

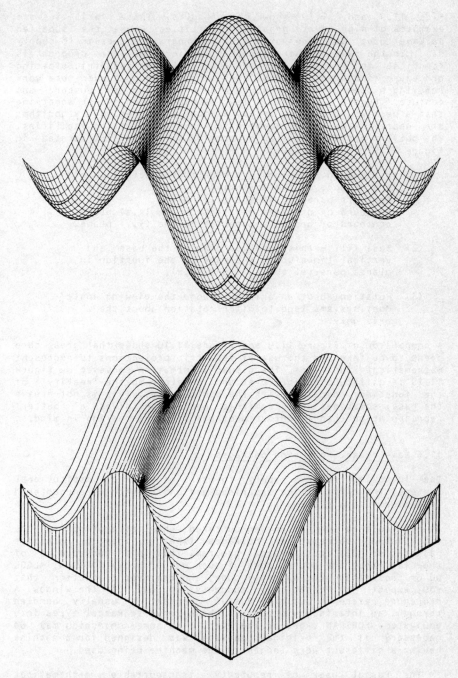

Figure 11.10 An isometric projection plot of the same
two-dimensional cosine function

Figs 11.9 and 11.10 show the results. These facilities are examples of high level graphics facilities where the supplied package does all the work. All the programmer does is to supply data. In the case of the isometric projections the program is identical to Program 11.7 except that an isometric plotting procedure is called. Here the system procedure does even more work removing hidden lines that would otherwise tend to obscure and confuse. Such a procedure is fairly involved and is not something that a user would want to write. Hidden line removal algorithms are nearly always incorporated in isometric plotting facilities. The options normally available, some of which are illustrated in Figure 11.9 are as follows:

(1) Filling in - options are usually the selection of
     one or more of the following:
     contours parallel to the (x,y) plane
     contours or profiles parallel to the (x,z) plane
     contours or profiles parallel to the (y,z) plane.

(2) Base fill - this involves drawing the base and
     vertical lines up to the edge of the function in
     planes parallel to (x,z) and (y,z).

(3) Rotation about an axis to change the viewing angle.
     Most systems tend to offer rotation about the z
     axis only.

A comparison of Figure 11.9 and Figure 11.10 shows that great care needs to be taken in the use of isometric projections to represent mathematical functions. The visual information conveyed by Figure 11.10 is difficult to interpret and to relate to the 'reality' of the function compared with the contour plot. This is not always the case; sometimes an isometric projection gives a 'better' representation than a contour plot but it needs bearing in mind.

11.6 Some remarks on using packages

The following remarks apply to users of large or institutional systems. The difficulties described are unlikely to be encountered in a micro based system.

Difficulties are often encountered when attempting to use established mathematics packages (whether they be graphics packages or not) from a Pascal program. This is a consequence of the fact that the source code of such was probably FORTRAN, ALGOL 60 or cross-assembled assembly code, and the type protection that you expect in Pascal may suddenly go out of the window. A procedure reference out of a Pascal program is usually handled through an interfacing procedure which converts Pascal types into equivalent FORTRAN types or whatever. Also some conversion may be necessary if the original package was designed for a machine having a different word length to the machine being used.

The Pascal user of reputedly transportable mathematical packages can encounter at least four difficulties. Firstly non simple Pascal types such as records may not be allowed. Secondly

passing an array of integers into a FORTRAN sub-routine when it
expects a real array may cause the integer array to be converted
as if it were real - with ensuing disaster. Thirdly all your
arrays may have to have a lower bound of unity. Finally all two
dimensional arrays are mapped into one-dimensional vectors, The
FORTRAN mapping is columnwise (1st subscript varies more rapidly
in the one-dimensional vector), in Pascal row wise (2nd subscript
varies more rapidly). A conversion may have to precede any
procedure call as for example:


```
        pascaldata : ARRAY[ 1..10, 1..20] OF real;
        fortrandata: ARRAY[ 1..20, 1..10] OF real;

        FOR i := 1 TO 10 DO
          FOR j := 1 TO 20 DO
            fortrandata[j,i] := pascaldata[i,j];

        process(fortrandata);
```


Such details should be carefully checked before any serious
program developement takes place; either by reading the
appropriate manuals or by writing test programs.

11.7 HRMC graphics

At the time of writing, a television monitor driven by HRMC
graphics hardware is now the most common graphics device. It has
overtaken the expensive devices such as the incremental plotter
and the storage tube normally found in institutional systems and
has made computer graphics accessible to virtually anyone who
possesses a microcomputer.

The HRMC graphics device can be categorized as a pseudo-vector
plotter. The screen can be considered as a grid of points. The
high resolution APPLE facility, for example, gives a maximum grid
resolution of 280 horizontally by 193 vertically, i.e. 54,040
points. Associated with this grid is a memory. The details of
memory organization are beyond the scope of this text and we can
simply say that the memory has 54,040 locations, one for each
point on the screen. The memory stores whether a point is on or
off (i.e. bright or dark) together with colour information.

At the atomic programming level the programmer plots single
points or vectors as with the incremental plotter. A combination
of software and hardware make up a line by filling in or brighting
up points on the screen grid, lying between the two line end
points, (in much the same way as Program 10.4 does, but at much
higher resolution), and loading these into the device memory. The
display is produced by causing the memory to output its contents
on to the screen one row at a time , via a digital to analogue
converter and the conventional TV scanning electronics.

The whole system is not unlike the procedure we developed for plotting on the character VDU The character is now a point and the buffering is now taken care of by memory hardware. Thus all the work of organizing the display into a series of lines is completely transparent to the user, who simply uses the device as if it were a vector plotter such as the incremental plotter.

HRMC graphics displays have developed very quickly for two reasons. Firstly the device itself can be a standard domestic TV and, secondly, the time taken to 'plot' a picture is independent of its complexity. Cheap implementation of quite complex games is therefore possible.

11.8 Plotting f(x) on HRMC graphics

Although the HRMC display is a vector plotting device, the main difference between it and the incremental plotter is resolution. Program 11.8 plots the sine function on an APPLE machine. Figure 11.11 shows output from Program 11.8. The first sine wave is plotted so that a single period occupies the screen-width of 280 points. This is the maximum resolution at which the function can be plotted. Plotting more then one period reduces the number of available pixells per period and piecewise linearity emerges.

Program 11.8

The function:
$$y = \sin(x)$$
on a HRMC graphics display.

```
PROGRAM Harmonic(input, output);
USES turtle graphics,transcend;
VAR noofperiods, periodwidth : integer;

    PROCEDURE plot(noofperiods, periodwidth : integer);
    CONST pi = 3.14159;
    VAR interval, xmath, ymath, xmathmin, xmathmax,
        ymathmax, ymathmin : real;
        xmin, xmax, ymin, ymax, x, y,
                    period, periodinc : integer;

        PROCEDURE space (x1, x2, y1, y2 : integer);
        BEGIN
            xmin := x1;   xmax := x2;
            ymin := y1;   ymax := y2
        END { of space };

        PROCEDURE map (x1, x2, y1, y2 : real);
        BEGIN
            xmathmin := x1; xmathmax := x2;
            ymathmin := y1; ymathmax := y2
        END { of map };
```

```
            PROCEDURE transform(xmath, ymath : real;
                               VAR x, y : integer);
       BEGIN
           x := xmin + round((xmath - xmathmin)/
                (xmathmax-xmathmin)*(xmax - xmin));

           y := ymin + round((ymath - ymathmin)/
                (ymathmax-ymathmin)*(ymax - ymin))
       END { of transform };

       FUNCTION f(x : real) : real;
       BEGIN
           f := sin(x)
       END { of f(unction) };


   BEGIN
       initturtle;
       space(0, 280, 0, 190);
       ymath := 0;  xmath := 0;
       interval := 2 * pi/periodwidth;
       map(0, noofperiods * 2 * pi, -1, 1);
       pencolor( none );
       transform(xmath, ymath, x, y);
       moveto(x, y);  pencolor ( white );

       FOR period := 1 TO noofperiods DO
        FOR periodinc := 1 TO periodwidth DO
          BEGIN
             xmath := xmath + interval;
             ymath := f(xmath);
             transform(xmath, ymath, x, y);
             moveto(x, y)
          END
   END { of plot };

BEGIN
   writeln( 'type no. of periods and period width');
   read(noofperiods, periodwidth);
   plot(noofperiods, periodwidth)
END.
```

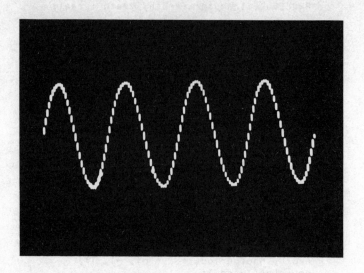

Figure 11.11   Display produced by Program 11.8

Unless you have access to a microcomputer graphics package you will inevitably have to do more work in your programs. Currently the graphics packages suplied by micro manufacturers contain only a very few atomic facilities and do not contain the volume and variety of high level facilities you would expect to find on a larger machine. Program 11.8 uses the basic APPLE utilities "moveto", "pencolor" etc. and performs the necessary conversion from mathematical space to plotting space itself. "Space" sets up the physical plotting space limits – a subset of the APPLE high resolution grid. "Map" assigns the mathematical limits to these and "transform" effects the conversion from mathematical space to plotting space. This of course was carried out by the system in Program 11.1 for the incremental plotter; in the APPLE system it is the programmer's responsibility. "Transform" is a completely general procedure and will work for any conversion.

Another consideration that has to be taken into account with most HRMC graphics systems, is clipping. In the APPLE system for example an attempt to plot to a coordinate such as (400,300) will produce an error message. Now plotting 'off the screen' deliberately, can be a useful technique. Some systems provide such a facility. In the APPLE system you must provide your own clipping procedure and if an off screen coordinate is specified, then the intersect with the screen boundary must be calculated and supplied to the APPLE utility instead of the off screen coordinate.

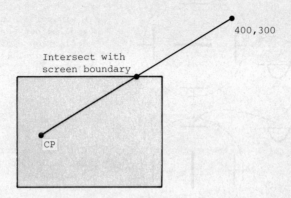

Figure 11.12   Clipping a line segment

Clipping is usually provided in mathematical packages that go with incremental plotters.

   The particular way of writing these procedures was chosen to keep Program 11.8 similar to Program 11.1. Clearly the assignments in "space" and "map" could be implemented as constant declarations and all three procedures merged into one; however, it is good program practice to keep these important logically distinct processes explicit and separate.

   The next program simulates Lissajous figures. These are produced when sinusoidal functions are applied to the X and Y deflection plates of an oscilloscope. If a sine wave (Figure 11.13) is applied between the X plates of an oscilloscope at a sufficiently high frequency, a horizontal line will be displayed. The sine wave 'pulls' the beam backwards and forwards from its central position causing it to 'paint' a line on the screen. Similarly a cosine wave applied to the Y plates will produce a vertical straight line. The effect of applying both simultaneously is to generate a circle. Increasing the frequency of say the sine wave over the cosine wave generates progressively more complex patterns. The series of patterns are known as Lissajous figures.

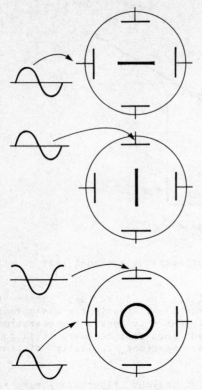

A sinusoidal function applied between the X deflection plates causes a horizontal line to be displayed

Similarly a vertical line can be produced by applying a sinusoidal function to the Y deflection plate

The simultaneous application of a sine and cosine function to both deflection plate pairs causes a circle to be produced

Figure 11.13   The production of Lissajous figures on an oscilloscope

Program 11.9 simulates these figures by evaluating two separate functions of a single variable and using the results as an (x,y) coordinate pair. Note in Program 11.9 the benefit of writing the general   procedures   'space',   'map',   and   'transform',   which transport from program to program, leaving the programmer free to concentrate on the mathematical aspects of the graphics.

Program 11.9

This program simulates the production of Lissajous figures on a HRMC graphics device.

```
PROGRAM Lissajous(input,output);
USES turtlegraphics, transcend;
VAR order, width : integer;

    PROCEDURE plot (order, width : integer);
    CONST pi = 3.14159;

    VAR interval, xmath, ymath, xmathmin, ymathmin,
        xmathmax, ymathmax,t : real;
        xmin, xmax, ymin, ymax, x, y, periodinc : integer;

        PROCEDURE space (x1, x2, y1, y2 : integer);

        PROCEDURE map (x1, x2, y1, y2 : real);

        PROCEDURE transform(xmath, ymath : real;
                                    VAR x, y : integer);

    BEGIN
       initturtle;
       space (0, 180, 0, 180);
       map( -1, 1, -1, 1);
       interval := 2 * pi/width;
       transform (xmath, ymath, x, y);
       pencolor (none);  moveto (x,y);
       pencolor (white);

       FOR periodinc := 1 TO width DO
          BEGIN
            t := t + interval;
            xmath := sin( order * t);
            ymath := cos( t );
            transform(xmath, ymath, x, y);
            moveto (x,y)
          END
    END { of plot };

BEGIN
  writeln( 'lissajous figs - type order and width');
  read(order, width);
  plot(order, width)
END.
```

Exercises

(1) Write a procedure to draw a square. Call this procedure from within a loop that decreases the size of the square and increases its rotation or orientation. You will find that this produces a pattern that appears to consist of interacting spirals, providing that you plot a sufficiently large number of squares.

(2) Develop Program 11.1 to plot a series of sine waves on the same axis. The sine waves are to have frequencies f, 2f, 3f etc. The amplitude of each harmonic is to be a, a*exp(-1), a*exp(-2) etc.

(3) Write a program to plot a simple diagram or stylization of a suspension bridge:

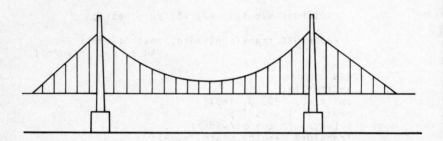

The span between piers is to be an input variable and the pier height proportional to span. The chain curve is a loaded catenary that can be approximated by a parabola.

(4) Develop Program 11.4 to produce a series of 10 'frames' where the 'petals' or 'spokes' would rotate if the 'frames' formed part of an animated sequence.

(5) Develop a program hierarchical in structure, that enables electrical circuit diagrams to be plotted. The diagrams are to consist of resistors and capacitors.

(6) Write a clipping procedure that guards an APPLE "moveto" and provides an intersect 'on' screen coordinate if an attempt is made to access an 'off' screen coordinate.

(7) Test the above procedure by incorporating it in a program that draws 'concentric' triangles of increasing size. Note that your procedure must take care of the eventuality that plotting from an 'off' screen coordinate to an 'off' screen coordinate, may produce no visible portion and thus no intersect 'on' screen coordinates.

12 Data analysis

In this chapter the most commonly used tools in data analysis are explored. First-order statistics of frequency distributions are possibly the most used tools in data analysis and these are dealt with in some detail, together with the errors that can occur when computing with very large data sets.

Fourier transforms are explained and a practical introduction to the use of a Fast Fourier Transform (FFT) algorithm is given. Finally the fundamental aspects of data aquisition are explained.

Throughout the chapter there is an emphasis on practical programming and the bias is always towards the use of the technique rather than the mathematical theory.

12.1 Frequency distributions

Analysis of data always involves reduction of the amount of information in the data set. We attempt to categorize the nature of the data by making measurements on them, or extracting parameters from them. The mean of a set of numbers reflects a data characteristic, and, in a single unit of information imparts a useful conceptual label that may have been deduced from thousands of numbers.

A frequency distribution is a description of data again involving considerable data reduction, but instead of being a single unit of information, it is a function. The following data are the number of children in a sample of Transylvanian families.

Number of children	Frequency
0	202
1	188
2	220
3	135
4	171
5	49
6	35

A frequency distribution is just the information in the table or more usually a graphical reflection of it.

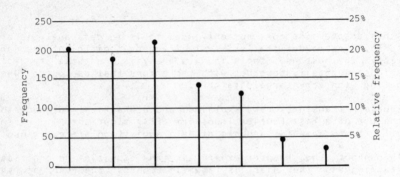

Figure 12.1   Frequency distribution of the number of children in a sample of 1000 families

The vertical scale can either be frequency or relative frequency. (where relative frequency is frequency divided by population or sample size, in this case 1000). The data may be presented as a list of a thousand unordered numbers, e.g:

    1,2,2,0,3,5,2,2,1,0 ...1,2.

If we are handling such data in a computer program, either to display a frequency distribution, or, to extract descriptive parameters from the distribution, it is usual to store the distribution as an array. We then use the data stream as a set of element addresses to accumulate the distribution in the array:

```
freqdist : ARRAY[0..6] OF integer;
relfreqdist : ARRAY[0..6] OF real;

initialize freqdist to zero;

FOR sample := 1 TO 1000 DO
  BEGIN
    read(noofchildren);
    freqdist[noofchildren] := freqdist[noofchildren] + 1
  END;

FOR noofchildren := 0 TO 6 DO
  relfreqdist[noofchildren] :=
                    freqdist[noofchildren]/1000
```

The values in our data are values of a discrete random variable -
it can only take on a finite number of values. In our computer
program we can use the value of this random variable directly as a
subscript to access a particular element of "freqdist". When using
raw data to access array elements it is, of course, vital to check
that the data sample falls into the subscript range:

```
FOR sampleno := 1 TO 1000 DO
  BEGIN
    read(datasample);
    datacheck := datasample IN [llimit .. ulimit];
    IF datacheck THEN
      freqdist [datasample] := freqdist[datasample] + 1
    ELSE writeln('Data sample no ', sampleno,
                 ' has erroneous value of ', datasample)
  END
```

otherwise an array subscript execution error can occur.

In practice, just as many data sets consist of real numbers or
continuous random variables. A common example is the heights of
individuals in a population. Raw data in the form of a set of,
say, 1000 heights in metres have to be processed into intervals.
Our original data could be as follows:

1.730, 1.840, 1.620, 1.910, 1.720, 1.750, etc.

Assuming a minimum height of 1.6 metres and a maximum of 2.0
metres we may decide as far as a simple demonstration is concerned
on 4-centimetre intervals and construct a table as follows:

Interval no.	Interval	Frequency
1	1.60 - 1.64	12
2	1.64 - 1.68	40
3	1.68 - 1.72	51
.	.	.
.	.	.
.	.	.
10	1.96 - 2.00	7

This information is represented graphically by a histogram in
Figure 12.2 where bars replace the lines.

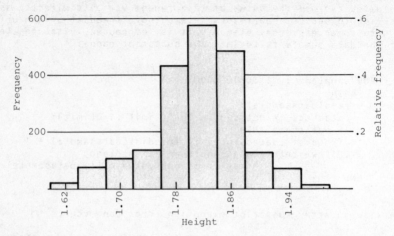

Figure 12.2 A histogram of 10 intervals : the heights of a
population of 1000 men

The bars indicate that a sample could have occurred anywhere
within the limits delineated by the bar edges and the histogram is
an approximation to a continuous distribution. Such a
representation is used by statisticians because they do not want
to collect too much detail, or for other practical reasons such as
the accuracy of the physical measurements, etc. In a computer the
representation of a continuous random variable must be discrete -
there is always a practical limit to array size. Therefore our
accumulating statement will have the general form:

```
        discretedata := transform(datasample);
        freqdist[discretedata] := freqdist[discretedata] + 1
```

In the case of the height data the function "transform" is:

```
        FUNCTION  transform(datasample : real) : integer;
           CONST   intervals = 40;
                   minht    = 1.60;
                   range    = 0.40;

           BEGIN
             IF datasample < 2.00 THEN
               transform :=
                       trunc((datasample-minht)/range*intervals)+1
             ELSE transform := 10
           END;
```

Note that if we decide to put 1.64 into the second interval and
1.68 into the third interval then we have to treat 2.00 as a
special case and put it into the 10th interval.

12.1.1 Example: use of frequency distributions in image processing

We shall now introduce a practical example in which a frequency
distribution is accumulated, analyzed, and information extracted
from the frequency distribution is used to process the original
data.

 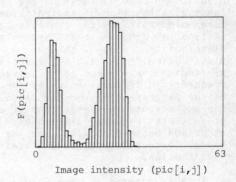

Image intensity (pic[i,j])

Figure 12.3   A simple image exhibiting two predominant
              grey levels

Figure 12.3 shows a simple image that was digitized using a CCTV
camera interfaced to a small computer. The image was deliberately
chosen to exhibit a bimodal frequency distribution. The image
could be represented in a program (ignoring memory constraints) by
a two-dimensional array:

        pic : array [1..512, 1..512] of integer;

and each element in "pic" takes values in the range 0 - 63, where
0 represents black and 63 white. Thus the value of pic[i,j]
represents the brightness of the corresponding point (a very small
area) in the original image. Now we can transform "pic" into a
binary valued image, where a point now has the value 0 or 1 by
thresholding:

```
FOR i := 1 TO 512 DO
   FOR j := 1 TO 512 DO
   IF pic[i,j] > threshold THEN pic[i,j] := 1
                           ELSE pic[i,j] := 0
```

281

Such an operation is used to segment images. For example we may wish to program a robot to pick up and orientate a machine part. Binarizing the image labels the areas of the image that belong to the machine part. Another common processing operation that succeeds binarization is area measurement. Consider a satellite image showing cloud (light) against ground or sea (dark). We assume that all the 1's represent cloud and the 0's background. A count of the number of 1's in the binary image will yield a value which, when multiplied by a constant, will equal the cloud area. The only problem in binarization is determining the threshold. A fixed threshold like 32, say, may not be good enough to dichotomize all the images successfully. The lightness of the clouds and the darkness of the background may vary from image to image as a function of ambient light level. We have to find a threshold that suits a particular image. This can be deduced by writing a program that accumulates a grey level frequency distribution and, with the a priori information that this distribution should exhibit 2 peaks, a threshold can be determined by finding the minimum point between the two peaks. A grey level frequency distribution gives the frequency of occurrence of each of the 64 grey levels in the image. The distibution should exhibit 2 peaks because the image consist of cloud and background only. A grey level frequency distribution of a satellite image comprising cloud and background will not be unlike the toy illustration above. Program 12.1 accumulates and processes the frequency distribution.

In this program we have used a text file as our image data structure. All the operations that we perform on the image consist of a calculation on one point followed by the same calculation on the neighbouring point. The access to the data is always sequential. It is extremely inefficient in such a context to use a two-dimensional array as a data structure, with lengthy and independent address calculations involved for each element access.

Program 12.1

An automatic thresholding program.

```
PROGRAM ImageProcessor(output, imagefile);
CONST filesize = 262144;
VAR imagefile : text;
    freqdist : ARRAY[0..63] OF integer;  threshold : real;

PROCEDURE initializefreqdist; ...

PROCEDURE getfreqdist;
   VAR i : integer;  picvalue : real;
   BEGIN
     reset(imagefile);
     FOR i := 1 TO filesize DO
      BEGIN
        read(imagefile, picvalue);
        freqdist[picvalue] := freqdist[picvalue] + 1
      END
   END;

PROCEDURE findthreshold; ...

PROCEDURE binarizefindarea;
   VAR i, area : integer;  picvalue : real;
   BEGIN
     reset(imagefile);
     FOR i := 1 TO filesize DO
      BEGIN
        read(imagefile, picvalue);
        IF picvalue >= threshold THEN BEGIN
                                      area := area + 1;
                                      picvalue := 1
                                    END
                                ELSE picvalue := 0
      END;
     writeln('Area of cloud cover is ', area)
   END;

BEGIN
   initialize; getfreqdist; findthreshold;
   binarizefindarea
END.
```

The bones of "findthreshold" have been omitted for the sake of
brevity and because the techniques involved have nothing to do
with frequency distributions. However it is not a difficult task
to find the minimum point provided it is known that only one such
point exists. Local irregularities can be removed by smoothing
(e.g., make a value equal to the average of its two neighbours).
After smoothing, the minimum point can be found by looking for the
occurrence of:

```
(freqdist[i] < freqdist[i-1] AND
          freqdist[i] < freqdist[i+1])
```

If we wanted to retain a binarized image then we would write the digitized "picvalues" to another file.

12.2 Frequency distribution parameters

Frequency distribution parameters are single numbers that reflect some attribute of the distribution. They enable us to quantify such observations as 'this distribution is thin', 'that distribution is fat', etc. The first three parameters are called centres because they categorize, according to a particular criterion, the centre of a distribution.

12.2.1 Mean

The mean of a distribution is the most commonly used central measure and is simply the average of all observations or samples in the data set:

$$x = \frac{1}{n}\sum_{i=1}^{n}x_i$$

In a program this can either be calculated from the raw data:

```
sum = 0;
FOR sample = 1 TO n DO
  BEGIN
    read(x);  sum := sum + x
  END;
mean := sum/n
```

or, if the data is already ordered into a frequency distribution we can use the following approximation:

$$\bar{x} = \sum_{j=1}^{m}x_j\,\frac{f_j}{n}$$

where:
  j is the interval no.
  m is the no. of intervals
  x_j is the (centre) value of the jth interval
  f_j/n is the relative frequency for the jth interval.

In Pascal this would be:

```
mean := 0;  xj := firstvalue;
FOR j := 1 TO m DO
  BEGIN
    mean := mean + xj*relfreqdist[j];
    xj   := xj + interval
  END
```

284

Note that this reduces the number of loop executions from n to m.

Figure 12.4 shows a frequency distribution of the grey levels in a chest X-ray image. Each point in the digitized image is represented by an integer in the range 0 (black) to 63 (white). In this example the first value is 0, the interval is 1 and m is 64. Using the above Pascal fragment the mean is calculated as 13.5.

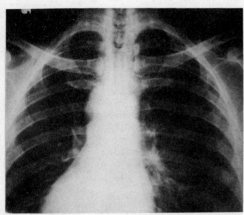 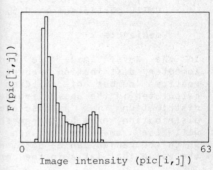

Figure 12.4   An example of a skewed distribution : the
               frequency of grey levels in an X-ray image

12.2.2 Mode

The mode is simply the most frequently occurring value. In a program we would proceed as follows:

```
maxsofar := 0;  xj := firstvalue;
FOR j := 1 TO m DO
  BEGIN
    IF relfreqdist[j] > maxsofar THEN
          BEGIN
              maxsofar := relfreqdist[j];
              mode := xj
          END;
      xj := xj + interval
  END
```

In the X-ray image the mode is calculated as 9.

12.2.3 Median

The median is that value below which 50% of the values in the sample fall. In a continuous distribution it would be given by the line dividing the area under the curve into 2 equal parts. In Pascal we would proceed as follows:

```
partialsum := 0;
j := 0;  xj := firstvalue;

REPEAT
  partialsum := partialsum + relfreqdist[j];
  xj := xj + interval;  j := j+1
UNTIL partialsum >= 0.5;

median := xj
```

In the X-ray image the median is calculated as 11. Now if our computer distribution represents a discrete distribution in reality (number of children for example), then the median as calculated in the above fragment is correct. If the computer distribution is a discrete representation of a continuous distribution, or a histogram then strictly speaking the median will lie somewhere between xj-interval and xj. Another way in which the median can be obtained is to sort the raw data and take the value that falls in the centre:

```
sort(rawdata, sortedata);
IF odd(n) THEN median := sortedata[n div 2 +1]
          ELSE median := sortedata[n div 2]
```

Finally consideration of the mean, mode and median as a set characterizes the shape of the distribution. In a single peak symmetric distribution:

```
mode = median = mean
```

The practical reality in the X-ray image is that the distribution is skewed because most of the information in the image is concentrated in variations at the dark end of the grey scale - the image is dark.

12.2.4 Variance and standard deviation

Mean, mode and median are measurements that give information on the centre of a distribution; the centre is defined according to one of these three criteria. Variance and standard deviation are measurements that characterize the shape of a distribution. Both are defined with respect to the mean. An intuitive feel for variance is best given by considering three extreme cases. Figure 12.5 shows three distributions. The number of samples, n, is the same in each case, which means that the area under each curve should be the same.

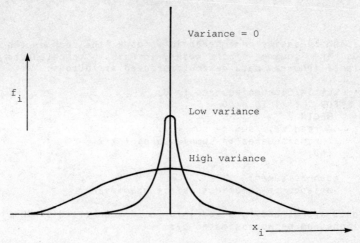

Figure 12.5 Three frequency distributions with the same mean
and zero, high and low variance

If all the samples had the same value, the distribution would be a
single line. If the samples exhibited a slight variation about
this value the distribution would be tall and narrow - low
variance. The more diverse the samples are - the shorter and wider
the distibution becomes. A short fat distribution exhibits a high
variance. Thus variance and standard deviation quantify the spread
of a distribution. Variance is defined as:

$$\text{variance} = s^2 = \frac{1}{n}\sum_{i=1}^{n}(x_i - \overline{x})^2$$

or the average of the squares of the deviations from the mean. S
is called the standard deviation. Strictly a divisor of (n-1)
should be used (see Bibliography) but n will suffice for our
purposes. An important computational point is that mean and
variance can be calculated simultaneously, from raw data in a
single loop, rather than two loops and a rescan of the data - the
first to calculate mean, the second variance. This follows from an
expansion of the above equation:

$$s^2 = \frac{1}{n}\sum(x_i^2 - 2x_i\overline{x} + \overline{x}^2)$$

$$= \frac{1}{n}\sum x_i^2 - 2\overline{x}\frac{1}{n}\sum x_i + \overline{x}^2$$

$$= \frac{1}{n}\sum x_i^2 - 2\overline{x}^2 + \overline{x}^2$$

$$= \frac{1}{n}\sum x_i^2 - \overline{x}^2$$

287

This can be easily remembered in words - 'the mean of the squares minus the square of the mean'. In Pascal, to calculate mean and variance from raw data we could proceed as follows:

```
sum := 0; sumofsquares := 0;
FOR i := 1 TO n DO
 BEGIN
   read(x);  sum := sum + x;
   sumofsquares := sumofsquares + x*x
 END;

mean := sum/n;
variance := sumofsquares/n - mean*mean
```

If data are already ordered into a frequency distribution then variance can be approximated by:

$$s^2 = \frac{1}{n}\sum_{j=1}^{m}(x_j - \overline{x})^2 f_j$$

and the following would be combined with the fragment in Section 12.2.1 that calculates the mean from a relative frequency distribution:

```
sum := 0;   xj := firstvalue;
FOR j := 1 TO m DO
 BEGIN
   sum := sum + (xj - mean)*(xj - mean)*relfreqdist[j];
   xj := xj + interval
 END;

variance := sum/n
```

Again, the two separate loops could be combined into one, allowing us to calculate mean and variance simultaneously.

12.3 Errors in dealing with large data sets

Quite often the consideration of errors is extremely important when using a computer. This can be a serious consideration in the practical analysis of time series or in any context where the data set is very large, particularly in obtaining statistical descriptions such as mean. In calculating a mean we could proceed as follows:

```
REPEAT
  read(newvalue);
  no := no + 1;
  sum := sum + newvalue
UNTIL endofdata;
mean := sum/no
```

and this is perfectly acceptable unless the number of samples is

288

very large. If this is the case, a point will be reached where the value of each individual sample will be insignificant with respect to the magnitude of the sum and may be lost. This effect is a consequence of the real number representation used inside a computer and can be illustrated with an example.

The table below shows the effect of accumulating random numbers in the range 1 - 199 on a computer using a real number representation that allows 13 significant decimal digits. Four different initial values for the sum are used:

$$10^{12}, 10^{13}, 10^{14}, 10^{15}$$

Inaccuracies in the value of the sum start to occur in this case between 10^{12} and 10^{13}. At this stage the individual values are no longer significant in relation to the sum that has been accumulated so far. This effect may also need to be taken into account in the calculation of variance.

Random number	Accumulating sum
112	1.000000000112 E12
43	1.000000000155 E12
168	1.000000000323 E12
.	.
.	.
84	1.000000000008 E13
64	1.000000000014 E13
151	1.000000000029 E13
.	.
.	.
53	1.000000000001 E14
99	1.000000000002 E14
36	1.000000000002 E14
.	.
.	.
98	1.000000000000 E15
141	1.000000000000 E15
80	1.000000000000 E15
129	1.000000000000 E15

It has to be emphasized that this effect depends on the accuracy with which your computer represents real numbers and the number of values that you are handling. If it is a problem then the calculation of mean should be tackled as follows:

```
totalsum := 0;
FOR i := 1 TO noofpartialsums DO
  BEGIN
    sum := 0;
    FOR j := 1 TO safelimit DO
    BEGIN
      read(x);  sum := sum + x
    END;
    totalsum := totalsum + sum
  END
```

A sub-total is added to the total sum only when it is large enough
for this to be done safely.

12.4 Relationship between frequency distribution and probability density function

The probability density function (PDF) is the limiting form of a
frequency distribution. As the sample size is increased and the
sampling interval decreased the frequency distribution approaches
more and more closely the PDF. A particular physical experiment,
if repeated, may produce slightly different frequency
distributions. This is due to the limitations and approximations
of sampling and the random element involved in the variations
exhibited by the experiment. However, it possesses only one PDF
which is inferred from the results. The shape of frequency
distributions is also influenced by the sampling interval and
range. This is illustrated in Figure 12.6 produced by Program 12.2
which samples a mathematical function - a sine wave. The first
histogram was produced by using 100 sample points equally spaced
along the x-axis. The y-range was divided into 10 equally spaced
pockets and the number of sampled function values in each pocket
were counted.

Program 12.2

This program samples a sine wave at regular intervals and accumulates a histogram.

```
PROGRAM Histo(input,output);
CONST pi = 3.141592;
VAR histogram : ARRAY[1..100] OF integer;
    noofsamples, noofintervals,i,j,pocket,d : integer;
    periodinc,x,y,r : real;
BEGIN
    writeln('type no. of samples(even no.)');
    Writeln('and no. of intervals');
    read(noofsamples, noofintervals);
    periodinc := 2*pi/noofsamples;
    x:= 0;
    FOR i := 1 TO noofintervals DO histogram[i] := 0;

    FOR i := 1 TO noofsamples DO
      BEGIN
        y := sin(x); x := x + periodinc;
        pocket := trunc((1+ y) * noofintervals/2 + 1);
        histogram[pocket] := histogram[pocket] + 1
      END;

    FOR i := 1 TO noofintervals DO
      BEGIN
       FOR j := 1 TO histogram[i] DO
          write('+');
       writeln
      END
END.
```

```
++++++++++++++++++++++
++++++++
++++++++
++++++
++++++
++++++++
++++++
++++++++
++++++++
++++++++++++++++++++++
```

Figure 12.6(a) Output from Program 12.2 for an input of 100,10

The resulting histogram exhibits two defects: it can only approximate the PDF because of the limited number of samples, and, the expression that maps a particular sample into a histogram pocket is biased in one direction for samples that lie on a borderline between ranges. Increasing the number of samples improves the approximation to the PDF shape but misallocations still occur.

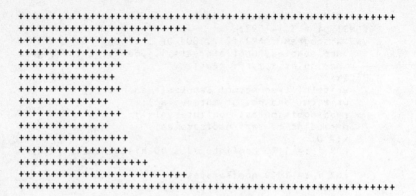

Figure 12.6(b) Output from Program 12.2 for an input of 500,15

We could never actually measure a PDF because we cannot consider an infinite number of samples or infinitely small range intervals. PDF's are useful, however, because they allow us an analytical basis on which to model the behaviour of a particular physical reality. This allows us to predict future behaviour amongst other things.

12.5 Simple linear regression - least squares

This section is concerned with fitting a straight line to data. Regression analysis in general is the study of the relationship between two variables, the dependent variable and the independent variable.

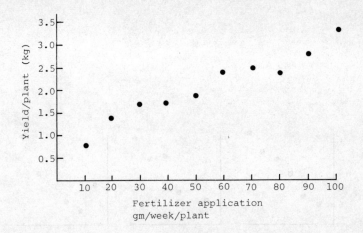

Figure 12.7   Showing the effect of fertilizer application on
             tomato plant yield

Figure 12.7 is a graph showing the effect of fertilizer
application on fruit yield in tomato plants. The x-variable is
called the independent variable because it is determined by the
experimenter, the y-variable the dependent variable because it
depends on fertilizer application. Scatter always occurs in such
contexts because other factors influence yield but if the
predominant influence is fertilizer application, the experimenter
will want to make some inferences on the relationship between the
two variables. This means reducing the data to a more manageable
and informative form, and if we fit a straight line to the data we
reduce all the points to two units of information - the value of a
and b, where the straight line is:

    y = a + bx

Now the commonest and simplest method of fitting a straight line
to such data is by eye. However, just how well we can do this
depends on the scatter of the data points. In Figure 12.8a we
could draw a line that would fit well; in Figure 12.8b we could
draw a reasonable line, but in Figure 12.8c we would not do very
well at all. The method of least squares introduces a mathematical
criterion to line fitting. The best fit is that achieved by
minimizing this criterion.

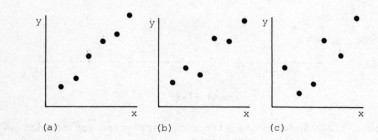

Figure 12.8   The difficulty of fitting a line by eye is a
              function of the degree of scatter

Refer to Figure 12.9. This shows a single data point (x_i, y_i).
The error between this data point and the fitted line is defined
as shown.

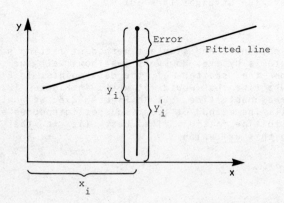

Figure 12.9   Definitions

The least squares criterion minimizes the sum of the squares of errors between each point and the fitted line, i.e.

$$\sum_{i=1}^{n}(y_i - y_i')^2$$

is minimized. Now:

$$y'_i = a + bx$$

where a and b are the constants of the fitted line, so we minimize:

$$s(a,b) = \sum_{i=1}^{n}(y_i - a - bx_i)^2$$

Partially differentiating the expression with respect to a and b and setting equal to zero yields:

$$a = \overline{y} - b\overline{x}$$

$$b = \frac{\sum(x_i - \overline{x})y_i}{\sum(x_i - \overline{x})^2}$$

For computational purposes these are more conveniently expressed as:

$$a = \frac{1}{n}\left(\sum y_i - b\sum x_i\right)$$

$$b = \frac{n\sum x_i y_i - \sum x_i \sum y_i}{n\sum x_i^2 - \left(\sum x_i\right)^2}$$

and of course this expression applies to a data set where there are n x and y values.

Program 12.3

The data reproduced in Figure 12.7 showing a set of yield values in the tomato crop example, is input to this program. Linear regression is used to fit a straight line to the data. The data

295

and line are reproduced in Figure 12.10

```
PROGRAM TomatoYield(input, output);
CONST n = 10;
VAR i : integer;
    xi, yi, xsum, ysum, xysum, xxsum, a, b : real;
BEGIN
    xsum := 0; ysum := 0; xysum := 0; xxsum := 0;
    FOR i := 1 TO n DO
     BEGIN
       read(xi, yi);
       xsum := xsum + xi;  ysum := ysum + yi;
       xysum := xysum + xi*yi;
       xxsum := xxsum + xi*xi
     END;
    b := (n*xysum - xsum*ysum)/(n*xxsum - xsum*xsum);
    a := (ysum - b*xsum)/n;

    writeln('values of a and b are',a,b)
END.
```

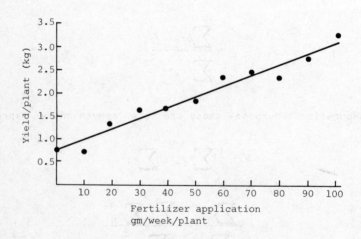

Figure 12.10   Data of Figure 12.7 input to Program 12.3 produces
              the fitted line shown

12.5.1 Use of linear regression, experimental errors and a practical example

Simple linear regression is a technique that elicits a relationship between a dependent and an independent variable.

Consider again the fertilizer-yield example (Figure 12.7). The layout of data on the graph implies that the experimenter has assumed that there is no error in the independent variable. Because of the nature of biological experiments and measurement errors, he knows that errors will occur in yield measurement; so the experiment is repeated for a particular fertilizer value many times. This results in a set of yield values for each fertilizer value and simple linear regression could then be used to fit a straight line relationship among the yield errors. Of course, there will be errors in the independent variable and these are ignored in this example. In the next example we change the role of the dependent and independent variable making the variable with less errors the independent one.

The lower yield stress δ_y for mild steel is related to grain size, d, by:

$$\delta_y = \delta_i + k_y \frac{1}{\sqrt{d}}$$

Given a set of values as shown in Table 12.1 relating yield stress to grain size, we wish to use linear regression to find values for δ_i and k_y. Now in reality grain size d is the independent variable being a function of a controlled manufacturing process, and lower yield stress is a factor consequential on the choice of d, and so is the dependent variable. However it so happens that errors in the measurement of grain diameter are very much greater than those involved in the measurement of lower yield stress (because of the relative difficulty in making these two measurements). We therefore regard yield stress as free from error and invert the equation, making δ_y the independent variable:

$$\sqrt{d} = \frac{-\delta_i}{k_y} + \frac{1}{k_y}\delta_y$$

and fit to the data:

$$y = a + bx$$

where:

$$y = \sqrt{d}, \qquad x = \delta_y$$

$$a = \frac{-\delta_i}{k_y}, \qquad b = \frac{1}{k_y}$$

The Pascal program would be the same as before with the addition of:

```
read(d, deltay);
yi := 1/sqrt(d);   xi := deltay;
```

inside the loop, and

```
ky := 1/b;   deltai := -a/b;
```

outside the loop after the calculation of a and b. For the data in Table 12.1 the complete program gives the following results:

```
a =        -5.721
b =        0.4956 E-01
ky =       20.176
deltai = 115.42
```

This is plotted together with the original data in Figure 12.11

Table 12.1

Grain size and yield point for mild steel

d(mm)	1/sqrt(d) (yi)	deltay (xi)	d(mm)	1/sqrt(d) (continued)	deltay
0.0096	10.21	315.1	0.0314	5.64	228.5
0.0097	10.15	321.3	0.0363	5.25	219.7
0.0109	9.58	312.0	0.0389	5.07	214.8
0.0109	9.58	305.8	0.0409	4.96	212.1
0.0114	9.37	305.9	0.0418	4.89	214.8
0.0114	9.37	304.3	0.0424	4.86	214.8
0.0135	8.61	284.2	0.0433	4.81	207.0
0.0148	8.22	278.5	0.0549	4.27	208.5
0.0151	8.14	285.8	0.0551	4.26	196.1
0.0151	8.14	271.8	0.0574	4.17	208.5
0.0152	8.11	291.9	0.0609	4.05	200.7
0.0195	7.16	258.9	0.0624	4.00	193.2
0.0206	6.97	256.9	0.0630	3.98	196.1
0.0210	6.90	253.0	0.0656	3.90	198.1
0.0219	6.76	250.1	0.0660	3.89	191.2
0.0237	6.50	247.1	0.0660	3.89	195.1
0.0284	5.93	236.3	0.0735	3.69	191.2

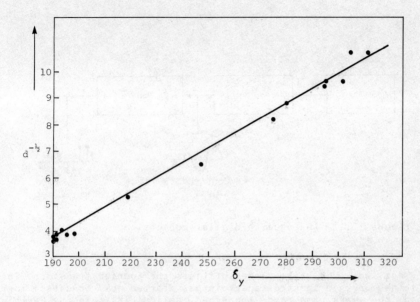

Figure 12.11   The reciprocal of the square root of grain size
as a function of yield point for mild steel.
The fitted line was produced by Program 12.3
supplied with the data in Table 12.1

Techniques   exist   where errors in both x and y are considered but
these are outside the scope of this text.

12.6 Time series - spectral analysis

A time series is the name   given   to   a   set   of   data   where   the
independent variable is time. Sometimes referred to as a signal it
is   usually   the electrical output of a transducer that converts a
quantity which   varies   as   a   function   of   time - temperature,
pressure   or   velocity   for   example,   into a continuously varying
current or signal.

A discrete form is obtained for analysis in a computer by using
an analogue to digital converter. Some data is originally discrete
and this is either man made (economic   data   for   example)   or   is
sampled discretely as in the example below.

In   practice,   to   this   may   be added such devices as an anti-
aliasing filter (below) and   a   multiplexor   if   the   computer   is
analyzing data from more than one source.

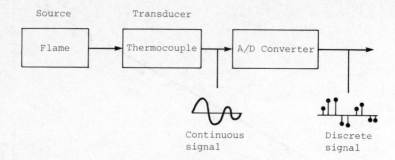

Figure 12.12 Analogue to digital conversion

Most work on time series utilizes the Fourier transform. The original work on spectral analysis was started by Schuster more than 80 years ago and concerned periodicities in the Earth's magnetic field. Spectral analysis has been applied in metreolgical, engineering, communication and electronic systems and also to physiological data.

The next section introduces the use of the Fourier transform in spectral analysis, although this is only a small part of the total application areas of the Fourier transform. The Fourier transform is the foundation stone of covariance and convolution calculations, measurement of power spectral density and digital filtering or signal processing. Fourier transform theory is a fairly advanced mathematical topic, but there is no good reason why it cannot be used as a tool in data analysis without reference to advanced mathematics. Here the treatment is completely informal and uses only sufficient "hard" mathematics to enable application of the technique to straightforward problems. The major practical problems are all dealt with below. First of all we introduce a practical example of spectral analysis.

Figure 12.13 shows a discrete time series that is derived from radar reflections of individual meteor trails. The meteor trails are a function of upper atmospheric wind velocity and provide a means of measuring such winds. The graph represents wind velocity in m/s as a function of time in hours. You can see from the original data that the function is periodic with a predominant 12-hour period due in fact to tidal activity. A 20-day series of this data produced the transform shown. Transforming such time series into the Fourier domain means that the function is 'decomposed' into a series of sine waves of different frequencies whose sum is equivalent to the original function. A plot of the relative amplitude of each sinusoid is a so-called frequency spectrum.

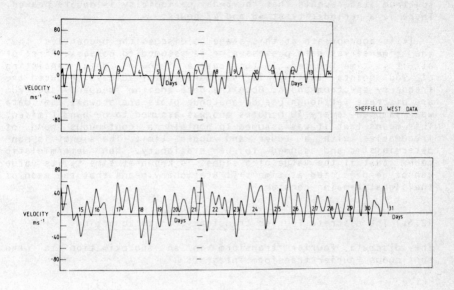

SHEFFIELD WEST DATA

Figure 12.13(a)   A section of a discrete time series - the upper
                   atmosphere wind velocity as measured from radar
                   reflections of meteor trails

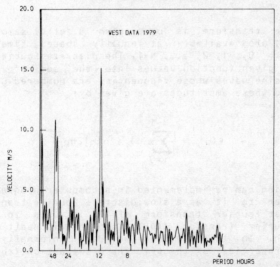

Figure 12.13(b)   Amplitude spectrum of part of the above data
                   showing periodicities at 12, 42 and 48 hours

The point about this particular example is that although the predominant periodicity is readily apparent in the original data, the 48-hour periodicity is more difficut to see and the frequency spectrum also reveals that the 2-day periodicity is double peaked. There is a periodicity at 48 and 42 hours.

It is appropriate at this stage to discuss the properties that the time series data possesses or is assumed to possess. First of all it is time limited. In this case a window of data consisting of 960 points lasting for a duration of 20 days produced the frequency spectrum shown. Both the data and the frequency spectrum are discrete (although pseudo analogue plots are shown). The data was sampled every 30 minutes and was assumed to be band limited. This means that it was assumed to contain a continuous band of frequencies with a lower and upper limit. The signal is non-deterministic and assumed to be stationary. Non deterministic means that if the value of a signal is known at time t, its value cannot be predicted at time t+T. Stationary means that the mean of the signal remains constant .

12.6.1 The discrete Fourier transform : an introduction

The discrete Fourier transform is an approximation to the continuous Fourier transform integral:

$$F(w) = \int_{-\infty}^{\infty} x(t) \exp(-j2\pi wt) dt$$

The discrete transform is used when a set of sample function values, $x(i)$, are available at equally spaced time intervals numbered $i = 0, 1, 2, ..., N-1$. The discrete Fourier transform converts the given function values into the sum of a discrete number of sine waves whose frequencies are numbered $u = 0, 1, 2, ..., N-1$, and whose amplitudes are given by:

$$F(u) = \frac{1}{N} \sum_{i=0}^{N-1} x(i) \exp(-j2\pi u \frac{i}{N})$$

This expression can be implemented in a computer program directly and we refer to it as a slow discrete Fourier transform. More usually a fast Fourier transform (FFT) is used to compute a Discrete Fourier transform (DFT) and this is dealt with in the next section. In this section we deal informally with the important properties of the DFT. The DFT equation (above) can be expressed as:

$$F(u) = \frac{1}{N}\sum_{i=0}^{N-1}x(i)\cos 2\pi u\frac{i}{N} - \frac{j}{N}\sum_{i=0}^{N-1}x(i)\sin 2\pi u\frac{i}{N}$$

and this form is used in the next program, Program 12.4, with incidentally no concession to numerical efficiency. The data function x(i) is a time limited cosine wave. This is the simplest possible input function we can use. In reality, data will consist of a band limited, time limited time series that can be considered as the summation of a number of sinusoids of different amplitudes and phase. The decomposition of such a time series into its constituent harmonics and their phase and amplitude relationships is of course the basis of Fourier analysis. The single cosine wave is expressed as:

$$x(i) = \cos(2\pi i f + phi)$$

and for phi = 0 and f = 0.25 the results are as shown immediately following the program. For the purpose of this example, we take one sample interval as our time unit so that a frequency of 0.25 means that one cycle will occur over four sample intervals.

Program 12.4

A 'slow' Fourier transform program.

```
PROGRAM SlowFT(input,output);

    CONST pi = 3.14159265;
    VAR   i,u : integer; ang,freq,phi,cossum,sinsum : real;
          x : ARRAY [0..15] OF real;

    BEGIN
        writeln('type frequency and phase');
        read(freq, phi);

        FOR i := 0 TO 15 DO
          x[i] := cos(2 * pi * i * freq + phi);

        FOR u := 0 TO 15 DO
        BEGIN
            cossum := 0;  sinsum := 0;
            FOR i := 0 TO 15 DO
            BEGIN
                ang := 2 * pi * i * u/16;
                cossum := cossum + x[i] * cos(ang);
                sinsum := sinsum - x[i] * sin(ang)
            END;
            writeln(u:4,cossum/16:14:8,sinsum/16:14:8)
        END
    END.
```

```
 0   -0.00000000    0.00000000
 1   -0.00000000   -0.00000000
 2   -0.00000000   -0.00000000
 3   -0.00000000    0.00000000
 4    0.50000000   -0.00000000
 5   -0.00000000   -0.00000000
 6   -0.00000000   -0.00000000
 7    0.00000000   -0.00000000
 8    0.00000000   -0.00000000
 9    0.00000000   -0.00000000
10    0.00000000   -0.00000000
11    0.00000001   -0.00000000
12    0.50000000    0.00000003
13   -0.00000001   -0.00000000
14   -0.00000000   -0.00000000
15   -0.00000000   -0.00000000
```

The two columns represent the cosine and sine transform
respectively as given by each half of the DFT equation. F(u) is a
complex valued function and can be represented either as a cosine
and sine transform (real and imaginary part) or more usually as an
amplitude and phase spectrum, where:

$$amplitudespectrum(u) = \sqrt{costransform(u)^2 + sinetransform(u)^2}$$

and:

$$phasespectrum(u) = \frac{sinetransform(u)}{costransform(u)}$$

Graphically the process can be represented as:

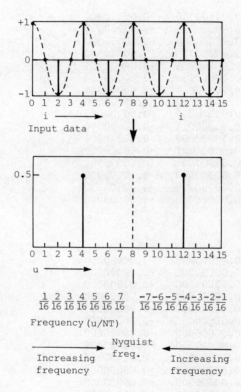

Figure 12.14   Input to, and output from the DFT

From this representation we can relate the important parameters to mathematical reality. Our input data function is the single cosinusoid and is transformed into 2 lines symmetrically disposed about u=8. The input data function is represented by 16 samples numbered i=0 to i=15. The frequency spikes appear at u=4 and u=12, u=N/2 is the so called Nyquist frequency and the discrete transform is symmetrical about this point. If the time interval between sample points is T, then the true frequency for a given value of u is u/NT. (In the above example T=1.) It is conventional to take a value of u>N/2 as representing negative frequency, (u-N)/NT. This is a mathematical convention and we need only remember that the information is the same in both halves of the transform. The true frequency is as shown in Figure 12.14 below the scale for u. It is, however, conventional to plot the DFT results as a function of u so it must be borne in mind that the transform is folded or reflected about N/2 and that the higher the frequency specified by a spike the nearer it is to the u=N/2 line.

The effect of increasing and decreasing the frequency to 0.375 and 0.125 is shown:

```
 0   -0.00000000    0.00000000
 1   -0.00000000   -0.00000000
 2   -0.00000000   -0.00000000
 3   -0.00000000   -0.00000000
 4   -0.00000000   -0.00000000
 5    0.00000000   -0.00000000
 6    0.50000000   -0.00000000
 7    0.00000000   -0.00000000
 8    0.00000000   -0.00000000
 9    0.00000001   -0.00000000
10    0.50000000    0.00000003
11   -0.00000001   -0.00000000
12   -0.00000001   -0.00000000
13   -0.00000000   -0.00000000
14   -0.00000000   -0.00000000
15   -0.00000000   -0.00000000
```

```
 0   -0.00000000    0.00000000
 1   -0.00000000   -0.00000000
 2    0.50000000   -0.00000000
 3   -0.00000000   -0.00000000
 4   -0.00000000   -0.00000000
 5   -0.00000000   -0.00000000
 6   -0.00000000   -0.00000000
 7   -0.00000000   -0.00000000
 8    0.00000000   -0.00000000
 9    0.00000000   -0.00000000
10    0.00000000   -0.00000000
11    0.00000000   -0.00000000
12    0.00000000   -0.00000000
13    0.00000001   -0.00000000
14    0.50000000    0.00000003
15   -0.00000001   -0.00000000
```

Changing the phase angle phi to a non zero value will make the sine transform or imaginary part of the transform non zero. The following is the output from Program 12.4 for a frequency of 0.25 and a phase angle of 2.5:

```
 0     0.00000000      0.00000000
 1     0.00000000      0.00000000
 2     0.00000000      0.00000000
 3     0.00000000      0.00000000
 4    -0.40057181      0.29923607
 5    -0.00000000      0.00000000
 6    -0.00000000      0.00000000
 7    -0.00000000      0.00000000
 8    -0.00000000      0.00000000
 9    -0.00000000      0.00000000
10    -0.00000000     -0.00000000
11    -0.00000001     -0.00000000
12    -0.40057179     -0.29923609
13     0.00000001      0.00000001
14     0.00000000      0.00000001
15     0.00000000      0.00000001
```

12.6.2 The use of the FFT : practical considerations

The FFT (Fast Fourier Transform) is an algorithm that uses a particular technique rediscovered in 1965 by Cooley and Tukey. It has become a very powerful and important tool in many branches of science and engineering. The success of the algorithm is due to the fact that it reduces the multiplication requirements of slow DFT programs (above), and hence the computational requirements by a ratio of N^2 to NlogN. Another benefit that this economy bestows is accuracy - fewer calculations means fewer round-off errors. Nowadays specially designed processors that perform transforms in real time are in wide use.

In this section we examine how to use an FFT algorithm. We are not concerned with the way in which the algorithm works, indeed this would take up a chapter to itself, and refer the reader to the Bibliography. Use of the algorithm does not require a knowledge of its operation, but there are a number of practical points that relate to the DFT that must be understood.

An FFT procedure is listed in Appendix 6 and is referenced by programs in this section. The procedure is based on an algorithm developed by Singleton and is not necessarily the most efficient available. Most of the published algorithms are variations on the theme of Appendix 6.

The input to the procedure comprises two real arrays "xreal" and "ximag", the number of points in the data set N, and, "nu" the power to which 2 must be raised to give N. The transform data consists of a real and imaginary part as for the DFT above, and this is inserted in "xreal" and "ximag" respectively. Input data is normally a time series or a real function of time. This is loaded originally into "xreal", and "ximag" is zeroized. Using an FFT in this way is somewhat wasteful of computer time and techniques exist to overcome this defect (see Brigham or Beauchamp). The original input data in "xreal" is overwritten. Most popular algorithms require that the data length is a power of

307

2 and if the working data does not conform to this constraint extra zeroes can be added during the pre-conditioning of the data (below). Program 12.5 illustrates the use of the FFT procedure. The datalength N is 128 making nu = 7. The data function is simulated by adding together sinusoids of varying amplitude and phase. A varying data function simulated from the sum of sinusoids is chosen to facilitate discussion of leakage (below). The input to the program and the output from it are illustrated in Figure 12.15.

Program 12.5

This program uses an FFT algorithm (see Appendix 6). The input and output are shown in Figure 12.15.

```
PROGRAM FastFourierTransform(input,output);
CONST datalengthminus1 = 127; pi = 3.141592;
TYPE data = ARRAY [0..datalengthminus1] OF real;
VAR xreal, ximag : data; amp, phase : ARRAY [1..3] OF real;
    i, k : integer; sum : real;

  PROCEDURE fft(VAR xreal,ximag : data; n,nu : integer); ...

  PROCEDURE plotdata(x : data); ...

  PROCEDURE plot(x, y : data); ...

BEGIN { main program }
   amp[1] := 0.986; amp[2] := 1.225; amp[3] := 0.707;
   phase[1] := pi/3; phase[2] := pi/5; phase[3] := pi/4;

   FOR i := 0 TO datalengthminus1 DO
   BEGIN
      sum := 0;
      FOR k := 1 TO 3 DO
         sum := sum + amp[k] * cos(2*pi*i*k/32 + phase[k]);
      xreal[i] := sum
   END;

   FOR i := 0 TO datalengthminus1 DO
      ximag[i] := 0;

   plotdata(xreal);
   fft(xreal, ximag, 128, 7);
   plot(xreal, ximag)
END.
```

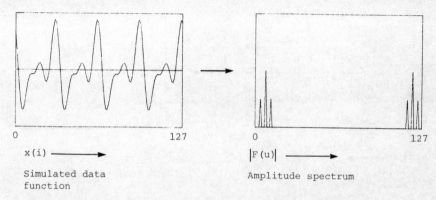

x(i) ──────►

Simulated data
function

|F(u)| ──────►

Amplitude spectrum

Figure 12.15 Input to, and output from Program 12.15

12.6.3 Leakage and pre-conditioning

In this section the important phenomenon of leakage is discussed. We can simulate leakage in our data function by arranging that the data length is no longer an integral multiple of cycles of the component sinusoids. The summing line in Program 12.5 is changed to:

```
sum := sum + amp[k] * cos(2*pi*i*k/29.5 + phase[k])
```

i.e. we are altering the frequency of each component by dividing k by 29.5, where previously it was 32 (a factor of the data length 128). The result is shown in Figure 12.16.

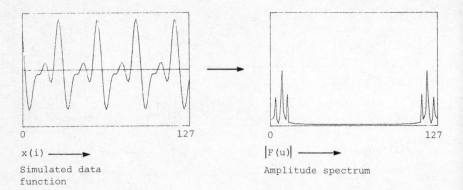

0   127   0   127

$x(i)$ ⟶ $|F(u)|$ ⟶

Simulated data   Amplitude spectrum
function

Figure 12.16   Leakage due to a more realistic data function.
The frequency of each component is no longer
an integral multiple of data length

The spectral lines are seen to broaden, and spectral power leaks
in to frequency components that do not exist in the spectrum shown
in Figure 12.15. Sharp discontinuities have now been introduced at
the end of each sinusoid component and the leakage phenomenon is
due to the presence of these discontinuities. Now, in practice,
when we are dealing with random time series, it is highly unlikely
that all the sine components will be such that their periods
divide exactly into the length of the data window. So we can say
that generally leakage will always occur in practice.

The cause of leakage is the discontinuity at each end of the
square wave 'window function' by which we have effectively
multiplied an infinite data function to obtain samples over a
finite period (See Figure 12.17).

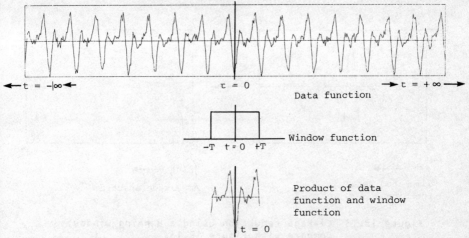

Figure 12.17 Sampling an infinite data function over a finite interval corresponds to multiplying the data function by a square-wave 'window function'.

12.6.4 Tapering data windows

Leakage reduction can be effected by employing a tapering window function. This means that the data function is multiplied by a window function that gradually reduces to zero at both ends of the window.

A commonly used tapering function is the Hanning function which, in its discrete form, is:

$$h(i) = \frac{1}{2} - \frac{1}{2}\cos(2\pi\frac{i}{N})$$

The effect of applying this window to our simulated data function is illustrated in Figure 12.18 which was produced by altering Program 12.5 so that "xreal" is multiplied by the tapering window:

```
for i := 0 to datalengthminus1 do
  xreal[i] := xreal[i] * (1/2 -1/2*cos*pi*i/128);
```

Comparison with Figure 12.16 shows the effect that this operation has on both the data function and the transform. Leakage is reduced but the spectral lines are broadened.

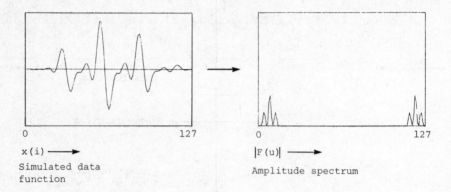

x(i) ⟶
Simulated data
function

|F(u)| ⟶

Amplitude spectrum

Figure 12.18   Leakage reduction using a Hanning window;
Compare with Figure 12.16.

In general we can say that the use of a tapering window instead
of a square wave leads to less leakage at the expense of
broadening the lobes. Thus it is a matter of experience of the
practical context to which the FFT is applied that will determine
whether or not the use of a tapering window is advantageous.

Other operations may be carried out on the data function prior
to Fourier analysis and the general topic of pre-conditioning is
too wide to go into here. A common operation for example is trend
removal: a time series may have a non stationary mean due, say, to
drift in a transducer. This drift can be found by the technique of
moving averages and subtracted from the data.

12.6.5 Noise

Another practical phenomenon that affects the frequency spectrum
is noise. Extraneous noise is usually wide band noise or white
noise and is an unwanted addition to a time series or signal.
There are many practical techniques that are used to combat noise
in information systems. Here we are concerned simply with looking
at the effects of noise on the Fourier transform. We look at the
simple case of corrupting our standard data function with more and
more noise to see the effect that this has on the frequency
spectrum. Figure 12.19 shows the results with 5% and 10% noise
added respectively. You can see from this that the noise
transforms into a platform spread over all frequencies and that as
the noise contribution is increased in the time domain the mean
level of this noise platform in the frequency domain is increased.

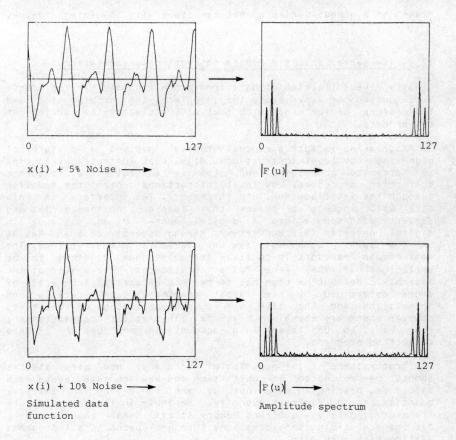

x(i) + 5% Noise ——>

|F(u)| ——>

x(i) + 10% Noise ——>

Simulated data
function

Amplitude spectrum

Figure 12.19   The effect of adding noise to the simulated
data function

The illustrations are output from an altered version of Program
12.5.   The assignment to "xreal" to set up the data function now
becomes:

```
random(x);
xreal[i] := sum + x;
```

The procedure random is as follows and generates a pseudo random
number in the range -0.2 to +0.2 (5% noise) as listed below.

313

```
PROCEDURE random(VAR number:real);
BEGIN
    base := (base*517+129) MOD 1048576;
    number := (base/1048576)*0.4 - 0.2
END;
```

"Base" is a global variable that can start with any integer value.

12.7 Time series analysis - data collection considerations

Clearly the collection of data from a continuously varying source
is unique to the experiment, the interface, the computer used and
the nature of the processing that will ultimately be carried out
on the data.

Programming in such a context usually involves a mixture of
high and low level instructions. High level instructions control
the ultimate processing and globally control the complete
collection procedure. Low level instructions control the transfer
through the interface and into the memory. The interface in this
case will include a device that samples the time series and
converts each sample into a digital number - an analogue to
digital converter (A/D converter). Mixing assembly code and Pascal
in the same program is a feature available in most systems. The
most common framework is to allow assembly code routines to be
called as if they were Pascal procedures. The writer of the
assembly code routine then has to get his parameters from areas of
store determined by the Pascal compiler. Such details on
interfacing and the like are outside the scope of this text,
however there are certain fundamental theoretical considerations
that have to be taken into account in the design of data
collection programs.

Firstly there is the question of accuracy: how many samples
should be collected in unit time and how accurate should each
sample be, bearing in mind that we are converting an analogue
quantity to a digital quantity. Secondly in the case of block
transfer of data via a Direct Memory Access (DMA) channel there
are general timing considerations that are common to all programs
dealing with such data.

12.7.1 Sampling data

Sampling means dividing up a continuously varying signal by
sampling its amplitude at regular intervals in time. All data
collection systems or data logging systems that collect
information from a continuously varying source or time series have
one thing in common - there is always a constraint on the volume
of data that can be collected in unit time. This is because there
is a maximum rate at which data can be converted or sampled, a
maximum rate at which data can be transferred into the memory of a
computer and limited space in the store. Processing may eventually
occur which may be a data reduction process emptying the store as

it is filled from the data source, but again this takes time and constrains the data transfer rate.

To return again to the question – how many samples should be collected in unit time – an obvious answer would be: as few as we can get away with. The sampling theorem tells us that there is a minimum number of samples that we must take in unit time to 'preserve' the information' in the signal or waveform being sampled. Informally we can define the meaning of 'preserve the information' by saying that if we collect the minimum number of samples as specified by the sampling theorem, then we can reconstruct perfectly an analogue copy of the original data from the digitized version. The sampling theorem is enumerated in terms of frequency components and states that:

A continuous signal can be represented completely by, and be reconstructed from, a set of instantaneous measurements or samples of its amplitude which are made at equally spaced times. The frequency of such samples must be greater than twice that of the frequency of the highest frequency component in the signal.

An intuitive grasp of the sense of the sampling theorem can be gained by considering the sampling of sinusoids. In Figure 12.20(a) the sampling frequency is much greater than the frequency of the sampled sine wave; in Figure 12.20(b) the sampling frequency is equal to twice that of the sampled sine wave and in Figure 12.20(c) the sampling frequency is much less than twice that of the sampled sine wave.

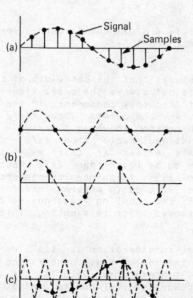

Figure 12.20   Sinusoids sampled at fs > 2f, fs = 2f and
                fs < 2f. In (c) an aliased component emerges.

This shows that if we are sampling sine waves, the sampling frequency must be greater than twice the frequency of the wave being sampled. If it is less than this there is an ambiguity. In Figure 20(c) the samples could have originated from a sine wave (dotted) of much lower frequency. Because of this effect, any frequency greater than half the sampling frequency will be included in the transform as a lower frequency.

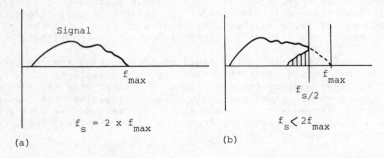

Figure 12.21   If fs < 2fmax the frequency spectrum is folded back about fs/2

This, of course, assumes that the bandwidth of the signal is known a priori which is not always the case. Figure 12.21b shows what happens in terms of frequency components if the sampling frequency is not high enough. Any components above fs/2 are folded back about fs/2 - a phenomenon known as aliasing - where the sinusoid fs/2 + df is indistinguishable from fs/2 - df. An important consequence of this effect is that even if the sampling is deliberately chosen to be lower than 2xfc (because we are not interested in the high frequency components say), the high frequencies must be filtered to prevent interference from aliased components. Thus if the sampling frequency is 2xfc all components above fc must be removed prior to sampling. This is known as anti-aliasing.

Another practical consideration is the transducer bandwidth. The transducer is the device that converts the physical quantity, be it displacement, temperature, velocity or whatever into an electrical signal ready for analogue to digital conversion. If the cut off frequency of the transducer is lower than the highest signal component, then the transducer acts as a filter and there is no point in sampling at more than twice the transducer frequency. The general approach taken is to attempt to match the transducer bandwidth to the signal banwidth to limit noise.

316

12.7.2 Quantization

Quantization is the process of converting the value of an analogue sample to a digital quantity. We have seen that there is a limiting rate at which we can sample a waveform without error. By analogy we can set up a criterion that imposes a limit on the 'coarseness' of quantization (where representing the analogue samples of a signal by 4 bits, say, is coarser than representing the same sample by 6 bits). First of all let us look at the quantization error, which expresses the difference between the waveform whose analogue values are being represented and the digital version of it. This is shown in Figure 12.22 for a simple linear function and shows that the quantization error alternates about 0 and has a maximum value equal to the quantization interval.

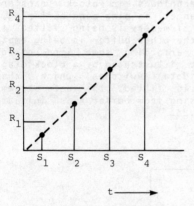

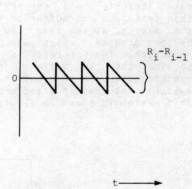

Sampling a linear
function that is
quantized into 4 ranges

Quantization error
is the difference between
the sample value and
original function

Figure 12.22   Quantization error function for a linear function
of unity slope

Again our major constraint is data volume. We want to quantize as coarsely as possible to minimize the data collected in unit time. Now quantization is an extremely non linear process and the criteria used to decide on how fine the quantization should be is based on the statistics of the signal. Quantization must be precise enough to reproduce 'satisfactorily' the statistical properties of the signal. A similar mathematical approach to that taken in the explanation of the sampling theorem leads to a rule of thumb for quantization. This is that the frequency distribution of the signal should be examined and the narrowest peak in it (if it is multi-modal) should be encompassed by at least 8 levels or ranges.

We have seen that to apply the sampling theorem we need a

priori knowledge of the frequency spectrum or bandwidth of the signal. Similarly to apply the quantization rule of thumb we need a priori knowledge of the frequency distribution.

In A/D conversion systems there are many practical considerations - amplification of the signal so that its maximum value fits the range of the A/D converter, anti-aliasing filters etc. but the two most important parameters are sampling rate and quantization accuracy. These are in any practical system interdependent: higher conversion rates invariably means reduced accuracy and higher accuracy needs a longer conversion time. This is a consequence of the electronic design of the A/D converters.

12.8 Real time handling of block transfer data

One of the most frequently used techniques in block transferred data (transfer via the DMA channel) is ping pong buffering. In this technique one buffer or area of memory is being filled from the source, at the same time as the other buffer is being emptied by the program, which may be performing some kind of data reduction. The process is best illustrated by a block diagram showing the two buffer and data switches which change synchronously. After buffer A is filled, the data stream is switched into buffer B and processing from buffer A is initiated. This system is shown in Figure 12.23.

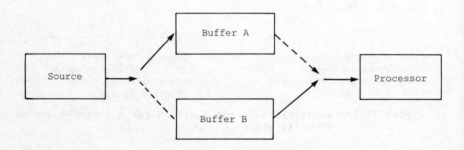

Figure 12.23 Ping-pong buffering

The switches are, of course, software switches that would normally be incorporated in assembly code routines, and would take the form of addresses supplied to the DMA hardware.

Timing is important and an event diagram is shown in Figure 12.24.

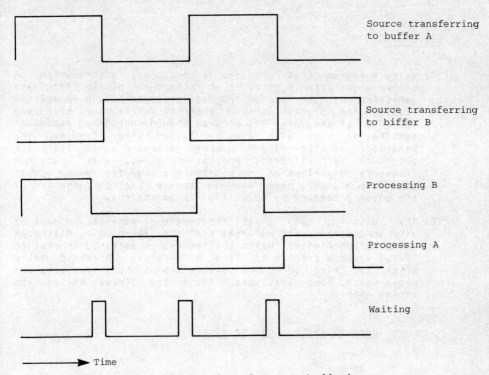

Source transferring
to buffer A

Source transferring
to biffer B

Processing B

Processing A

Waiting

Time

Figure 12.24 Event diagram for ping-pong buffering

In this simple scheme the major constraint is that the processing
time for a buffer is less than or equal to the transfer time T.
These kind of critical time factors become important only when the
practical context is such that the data source has to be sampled
at rates approaching the DMA rate of the computer. A Pascal
controlling program may look something like the following:

```
FOR i := 1 TO nooftranfers DO
  BEGIN
    initransferinto(newbuffer);
    process      (oldbuffer);

    REPEAT
      { do nothing }
    UNTIL bufferfull;

    temp     := newbuffer;
    newbuffer := temp
    oldbuffer := newbuffer
  END;
```

The repeat until loop represents the idle interval in the timing
diagram and is a wait for say an interrupt service routine to set
"bufferfull" to TRUE.

Exercises

(1) Write aprogram that produces a frequency distribution on
either a character plotter or an incremental plotter from data
generated by the random nunber generator given in Section
12.6.5. The program should then calculate the mean and
variance of the data. The program should include an automatic
scaling to cope with any population size. Examine the
behaviour of the random number generator by repeating the
procedure for different population sizes. What shape of
frequency distribution do you think a computer random number
generator ought to have. Can you improve the performance of
the given procedure by adjusting its parameters.

(2) The following data gives the length of survival in days of
mice innoculated with malaria. Plot the (bi-modal) histogram
on a graph plotter. Using the techniques outlined in section
12.1.1 write a program to find a survival threshold below
which the mice could be categorized as short survivors and
above which, long survivors. (Note that **local** maxima and
minima exist)

days to death	no. of mice
0- 3	0
3- 4	0
4- 5	25
5- 6	90
6- 7	75
7- 8	69
8- 9	48
9-10	36
10-11	29
11-12	30
12-13	33
13-14	44
14-15	29
15-16	40
16-17	51
17-18	51
18-19	71
19-20	65
20-21	78
21-22	75
22-23	48
23-24	30
24-25	35
25-26	17
26-27	15
27-28	13
28-29	4
29-30	6
30-31	2
31-32	1
32-33	0

(3) Write a program that overplots, on the histogram of Example 2, a piecewise linear approximation to a continuous distribution line. (Note that there are well known **statistical** techniques for fitting data to probality distributions. They are outside the scope of this text, but the example would be better worked with these techniques if you have knowledge of them).

(4) Using the threshold determined in Example 2, treat the data as two separate histograms, one for short term survivors and one for long term survivors. Now plot two overlapping continuous distributions on the histogram plot, and compare the cross-over point with the threshold obtained in Example 2.

(5) Produce a table for your computer, similar to the one in Section 12.3, that shows the region where random numbers in the range 1-199 cease to have any effect on an accumulating sum. Print out 10 tables, starting each time from:

$$10^7, \ 10^8, \ 10^9, \ \text{etc.}$$

(6) A force applied to a uniform spring produces a displacement that is a linear function of the applied force (Hooke's law).

$$F = kl + s$$

F is the applied force, l is the length produced by F and s the extension with no force applied. Given the following table of length increases for applied weights, use the method of least squares to find the best value for k.

Force (kg)	Length (cms)
0	20
1	23.9
2	27.1
3	36.2
4	38.1
5	43.9

(7) It is suspected that the increase in the height of a plant as a function of time is of the form:

$$h = s \ \exp(at)$$

where h is the height in centimeters, s is the initial height of the shoot when measurements are first made, and t is the time in weeks. By taking logarithms to make the relationship a linear one, evaluate, using the method of least squares, the constants s and a. The data is:

t(days)	h(cms)
1	7.30
2	8.85
3	11.12
4	13.35
5	16.20
6	19.13
7	25.12
8	28.97
9	36.18
10	44.11

(8) Develop Program 12.5 so that it accepts a series of piecewise linear periodic waveforms (such as triangular and square waves). Produce a table of the waveforms and their corresponding Fourier transforms on the graph plotter.

(9) A reverse Fourier transform (going from the frequency domain back to the space domain) can be achieved by:

    (a) changing ths sign of all the elements in "ximag"
    (b) dividing all the elements of "ximag" and "xreal" by "datalength"
    (c) inserting these values into a call of "fft"

Develop a program that takes as input a composite harmonic function, like that in Program 12.5, produces a Fourier transform, and then the original function by taking the reverse transform. Further develop the program such that selected areas of "ximag" and "xreal" are zeroized. A reverse transform will then produce a filtered version of the original function. For example if two out of the three 'spikes' in the transform shown in Figure 12.15 are zeroized, a single sinusoid will be recovered in the reverse transform. This technique is known as digital filtering and is a widely used technique in many branches of science and engineering.

Appendix 1
Pascal reserved words

AND	FUNCTION	PROGRAM
ARRAY	GOTO	RECORD
BEGIN	IF	REPEAT
CASE	IN	SET
CONST	LABEL	THEN
DIV	MOD	TO
DO	NIL	TYPE
DOWNTO	NOT	UNTIL
ELSE	OF	VAR
END	OR	WHILE
FILE	PACKED	WITH
FOR	PROCEDURE	

Appendix 2
Pascal operators

operator	priority	type of operands	type of result	definition
NOT	1	boolean	boolean	changes true to false and false to true
*	2	real/int	real/int	multiplication
/	2	real/int	real	division
DIV	2	integer	integer	division with truncation
MOD	2	integer	integer	remainder after <u>div</u>
AND	2	boolean	boolean	logical "and"
+	3	real/int	real/int	addition
-	3	real/int	real/int	subtraction
OR	3	boolean	boolean	logical "or"
=	4	real/int	boolean	equal to
<>	4	real/int	boolean	not equal to
<	4	real/int	boolean	less than
>	4	real/int	boolean	greater than
>=	4	real/int	boolean	greater than or equal to
<=	4	real/int	boolean	less than or equal to

<u>Note</u>: real/int means that the operands can be both real, both integer or any combination of real and integer. The last six operators can also be used for comparing characters, or indeed for comparing values of any scalar type (Chapter 6).

The operator IN tests for set membership (Chapter 2):

   Priority level: 4; First operand: scalar; Second operand: set

Appendix 3
Pascal standard functions

function	type of argument	type of result	definition
abs	integer real	integer real	absolute value
sqr	integer real	integer real	square
sin	int/real	real	natural sine
cos	int/real	real	natural cosine
exp	int/real	real	exp(a) is e^a
ln	int/real	real	natural log
sqrt	int/real	real	square root
arctan	int/real	real	arctangent
odd	integer	boolean	tests whether an integer is odd or even
trunc	real	integer	truncates a real to its integer part
round	real	integer	rounds a real to the nearest integer
ord	scalar	integer	converts a scalar to its ordinal number
chr	integer	char	converts an ordinal number into the corresponding character
succ	scalar	scalar	gives the succeeding scalar if it exists
pred	scalar	scalar	gives the preceding scalar if it exists
eoln	file OF char	boolean	tests for end-of-line
eof	file	boolean	tests for end-of-file

Note: In the case of sin and cos the argument must be in radians. The result of arctan is in radians.

Appendix 4
Formatted output

It is usually convenient for the programmer to have complete control over the layout of the output produced by a program. We can specify the layout for our output, and also the accuracy to which real numbers are to be printed, by including **formatting** information after an item in a write list.

Integers

Formatting information for an integer consists of a single number after a colon. For example:

        writeln(i:4, 2*i:4, i*i:8)

The number after the colon is the **field width** for the item being printed and tells the computer the total number of characters that should be printed when outputting that value. If necessary, spaces are printed **before** the number to make up the required number of characters. If the field width is not big enough for the value, then the value is printed in full and no extra spaces are printed.

   If no formatting information is supplied, then a default field width is assumed. This default will depend on your system.

Reals

A real format consists of up to two numbers, each preceded by a colon.

   If two numbers are supplied this is called **fixed-point** format. For example:

        writeln(x:8:4, fx:6:2, x*fx:10:2)

The first number in the format is the **overall** field width for the output value (including any minus sign, the decimal point and all digits printed). As was the case with integers. extra spaces are inserted if necessary to make up this field width. The second number indicates the number of digits to be printed after the decimal point, the value being rounded to give this number of digits.

   If only one format value is supplied after a real, then the real value is printed in **exponent** form. The value in the format indicates the field width to be used. For example:

        writeln(136.24359 :9)

would produce output:

   1.36E+02

which is the computers way of saying

$$1.36 * 10^2$$

Note that the output always includes a space or a minus sign at the start of the number and a plus or minus sign before the exponent. The number is rounded so that the output fits into the specified field width. This is a convenient notation for the output of very large or very small numbers which would otherwise include a lot of zeros.

Strings and characters

A single field width can be supplied with a string in a write list. This indicates that spaces are to be inserted before the string, if necessary, to make up the required field width. This is useful when text headings are to be lined up above columns of numbers, for example:

```
n := 5;  x := 7.356;
powerofn := 1;  powerofx := 1;
writeln('Integers':12, 'Reals':15);

FOR i := 1 TO 10 DO
BEGIN
    powerofn := powerofn*n;
    powerofx := powerofx*x;
    writeln(powerofn:12, powerofx:15:2)
END
```

The headings are lined up with the columns of numbers by using field widths for the headings that match the field widths being used for the numbers below.

Appendix 5
Input and output of character files

The string of characters supplied as input to a program is usually
referred to as a **file** of characters. In Chapter 6, we describe the
more general Pascal data structure known as a file, where a file
can contain items of any type. However, it is convenient from a
much earlier stage to be able to write programs that process
realistically large input data files without a large file having
to be typed at the keyboard each time a program is tested or used.
The file of characters to be read by a program can initially be
typed onto a magnetic tape or disc and given a name. The way that
you do this will depend on your computer system. Once a file has
been stored on disc or tape, it can be read by a Pascal program as
often as we like, without it having to be retyped. Programs can
also send their output to tape or disc and have it stored there
permanently in the form of a file.

Character file input

There are two ways in which a program can read its input data from
a file:

(1) Non-standard character file input

The first method is **non-standard** Pascal but is very widespread.
It is very convenient if only one file is to be read at a time.
The program is written in the usual way, as if input was going
to be supplied from the keyboard. Some additional information
is then supplied to the system to indicate from where the input
is actually coming. On some systems, you might supply this
information with the command that tells the computer to run
your program. For example, you might type:

    RUN statsprog, input=datafile

where 'datafile' is the name of the file containing the
characters that would otherwise have to be typed at the
keyboard. On other systems, a Pascal statement is used to
provide this information. For example, on the authors' system,
the Pascal statement:

    reset(input, 'datafile')

causes subsequent read statements to obtain input from a file
called 'datafile'.

(2) Standard character file input

The second method for obtaining input from a character file is
the standard method defined in the Pascal report. This is the
technique that is used for handling files of the other types as
described in Chapter 6. To obtain data from a character file,
we must do four things:

(a) Include the file name in the program heading, for example:

```
PROGRAM statsprog(output, datafile);
```

If input was to be read from the keyboard as well as from 'datafile', the heading would be:

```
PROGRAM statsprog(input, output, datafile);
```

(b) Declare the file at the head of the program along with the other variables used by the program, for example:

```
VAR x, y, average : real;
    i, n : integer;
    datafile : text;
    a : ARRAY [1..100] OF real;
```

"Text" is the standard type name for a file of characters. "Input" and "output" are also of type "text", although it is not necessary to declare them as such.

(c) Reset the file before reading from it by using a reset statement, for example:

```
reset(datafile)
```

Note that "reset" is used **only once** at the start of the reading process.

(d) Include the name of the file at the start of any read statement that is to refer to it, for example:

```
reset(datafile);
read(datafile, n);
FOR i := 1 TO n DO
   read(datafile, a[i])
```

Character file output

It is sometimes convenient to send the output from a program to a file on disc or tape, so that a permanent record of the output is kept for selective examination, for listing on a printer, or so that the file can be supplied later as input to another program. Again, we mention two methods:

(1) Non-standard character file output

We indicate to the system that data sent to "output" by the program is to be directed to a named file. This can be done by, for example, an operating system command such as:

```
RUN analysisprog, output=resultfile
```

or by using a non-standard rewrite statement such as:

```
            rewrite(output, 'resultfile');
```

2) Standard character file output

(a) and (b) as before

(c) A rewrite statement must be obeyed before output is sent to
the file.

(d) The file name is included at the start of any write
statement that is to send output to the file, for example:

```
        rewrite(resultfile);
        FOR i := 1 TO n DO
            writeln(resultfile, frequency[i])
```

Appendix 6
A Fast Fourier Transform (FFT) algorithm

```
PROCEDURE FFT(VAR xreal, ximag : data; n, nu : integer);
CONST twopi = 6.283185;

VAR n2, nu1, i, l, k : integer;
treal, timag, p, arg, c, s : real;

  FUNCTION twopower (n : integer) : integer;
  VAR i, tp : integer;
    BEGIN
      tp := 1;
      FOR i := 1 TO n DO
        tp := tp*2;
        twopower := tp;
    END { of towerpower };

  FUNCTION bitrev(j, nu : integer) : integer;
    VAR i, j1, j2, k : integer;
    BEGIN
      j1 := j;   k := 0;
      FOR i := 1 TO nu DO
        BEGIN
          j2 := j1 DIV 2;   k := k*2 + (j1 - 2*j2);
          j1 := j2;
        END;
        bitrev := k;
    END { of bitrev };
```

```
BEGIN  { FFT }
  n2 := n DIV 2;  nu1 := nu - 1; k := 0;
  FOR l := 1 TO nu DO
  BEGIN
    WHILE k < n DO
      BEGIN
       FOR i := 1 TO n2 DO
        BEGIN
         p := bitrev(k DIV twopower(nu1), nu);
         arg := twopi*p/n; c:= cos(arg); s := sin(arg);
         treal := xreal[k+n2]*c + ximag[k+n2]*s;
         timag := ximag[k+n2]*c - xreal[k+n2]*s;
         xreal[k+n2] := xreal[k] - treal;
         ximag[k+n2] := ximag[k] - timag;
         xreal[k] := xreal[k] + treal;
         ximag[k] := ximag[k] + timag;
         k := k + 1;
        END;
       k := k + n2;
      END;
     k := 0; nu1 := nu1 - 1;
     n2 := n2 DIV 2;
  END;

  k := 0;
  WHILE k < n DO
    BEGIN
      i := bitrev(k,nu);
      IF i > k THEN
        BEGIN
          treal := xreal[k];  timag := ximag[k];
          xreal[k] := xreal[i]; ximag[k] := ximag[i];
          xreal[i] := treal;  ximag[i] := timag;
        END;
      k := k + 1;
    END;
END { FFT };
```

Bibliography

Numerical methods

ATKINSON, L.V. and HARLEY, P.J.,
   An introduction to numerical methods with Pascal, Addison-
   Wesley 1983.

BURDEN, R.L., FAIRES J.D. and REYNOLDS A.C.,
   Numerical analysis, Prindle, Weber and Schmidt, 1981

CONTE, S.D. and DE BOOR, C ,
   Elementary numerical analysis, McGraw-Hill 1980.

Computer graphics

NEWMAN W.M. and SPROULL R.F.,
   Principles of interactive computer graphics, McGraw-Hill 1979.

MYERS R.E.,
   Microcomputer graphics, Addison-Wesley 1982.

Data analysis

STERLING, T.D. and POLLACK, S.V.,
   Introduction to statistical data processing, Prentice-Hall
   1968.

BRIGHAM, O.E.,
   The fast Fourier transform, Prentice-Hall, 1974.

SINGLETON, R.C.,
   Algol procedures for the fast Fourier transform, Commun. ACM.
   vol 10, pp 773-776, Nov 1968.

OTNES, R.K. and ENOCHSON, L.,
   Applied time series analysis, Wiley, 1978.

BEAUCHAMP, K,G.,
   Signal processing, Allen and Unwin, 1973.

Index

335

enumerated types: 132
eof: 141
equations: 159, 168
   linear: 204
errors in large data sets:
   288
errors quantization: 317
Euler's method: 194
executing a program: 6
execution error: 3
experimental errors:
   linear regression: 296
exponentiation: 24
expressions:
   arithmetic: 13, 15
   boolean: 43
   evaluation: 15
extrapolation: 159, 162
false: 44
FFT: 307
   practical considerations:
   307
files: 135, 139, 155
   as parameters: 142
   binary: 138
   character: 138
   external: 138
   internal: 137
   local: 137, 138
   local-external association:
   140
   reading: 141
flatbed plotters: 250
floating point notation: 10
FOR statements: 29, 34
format:
   output: 10
Fourier transform: 299
   discrete Fourier transform:
   302
   effect of noise: 312
   Fast Fourier Transform:
   307
   Hanning window: 311
   leakage: 309
   pre-conditioning: 309
   slow transform program:
   303
   tapering data windows: 311
frequency distributions: 277
   parameters: 284
frequency spectrum: 300
functions: 159
   as parameters: 181
   boolean: 47
   declarations: 123
   standard: 20, 325

   user defined: 123
Gauss-Seidel method: 221
Gaussian elimination:
   213, 215
graphics:
   APPLE: 270
   atomic facilities: 251
   circle generation: 258
   clipping: 272
   difficulties using packages:
   268
   HRMC: 269
   mapping: 252
   object hierarchy: 261
   package: 248
   packages: 249
   paper area: 252
   piecwise linearity: 256
   plotting f(x): 229, 252
   plotting f(x,y): 265
   plotting harmonic functions:
   254
   polar coordinates: 257
   procedure: 251
   shape generation: 257
Hanning window:
   Fourier transform: 311
histograms: 279
HRMC graphics: 269
IF statements:
   nested: 74
   use of compound statements:
   41
IF-THEN statements: 37, 38
IF-THEN-ELSE statements: 40
image processing: 281
IN: 81
incremental plotters: 249
input: 4
input from keyboard: 5
integer: 8
integer operators: 18
integers:
   range of values: 20
integration:
   numerical: 185
interpolation: 159
   in a table: 162
   linear: 159
   polynomial: 166
   quadratic: 165
iteration:
   171, 174, 176, 221, 54
iteration functions: 172, 174
labels: 48
Lagrange interpolation: 167
layout of a program: 30